# Why Am I Here, This Time?

## Memoirs of a yoga teacher

### – CAROLE KERTON –

An environmentally friendly book printed and bound in England by
www.printondemand-worldwide.com

This book is made entirely of chain-of-custody materials

i

www.fast-print.net/store.php

Why Am I Here, This Time? – Memoirs of a yoga teacher
Copyright © Carole Kerton 2013

Disclaimer: The events in this autobiography are described according to my
memory, recognition and understanding at the time.

A catalogue record for this book is available from the British Library

ISBN 978-178035-583-2

First published 2013 by
FASTPRINT PUBLISHING
Peterborough, England.

# Dedication

I offer this book to my family and friends; past, present and future, and to my students; past, present and future. May you always be surrounded by love, light and blessings. Thank you, thank you, thank you.

# *Acknowledgements*

Special thanks go to my book-reading angel, Victoria Lovatt, who has kindly made time for me in her busy life; to my husband Mike, for his practical skills, and to my dog Rudi, who has warmed my feet.

# Introduction

When prompted to write a book describing my journey through life and yoga, I recognized that the yogic philosophies and teachings have moulded my every step. I refer often to the 'Eight Limbs of Yoga', composed by Patanjali, and I do hope that the following article which was published in 2009, will clarify this work for the reader.

## YOGIC APPROACH TO HOLISTIC WELLBEING.

There's more to life than just "getting through" each day. Throughout the ages, man has designed rules, boundaries and guidelines to help him to live a good and fulfilling life. In yoga, we study the 'Eight Limbs' which were set down by an Indian sage known as Patanjali, in about 300yrs B.C. Patanjali (often referred to as the Father of Yoga)did not invent these guidelines, he codified them. Isn't it amazing that they are still so valid today?

The first limb is known as the YAMAS. These are the Don'ts, the abstinences, the things we should avoid doing.

There are five: AHIMSA, non-violence; SATYA, non-lying; ASTEYA, non-stealing; BRAMACHARYA, non-misuse of energy; & APARIGRAHA, non-greed. Mahatma Gandhi devoted his entire life to the first, Ahimsa (non-violence.) Just close your eyes for a moment and imagine that everyone in the world suddenly understood that non-violence was the only way. In a flash of realisation, we would know that wars would achieve nothing. In a flash of realisation, we would understand that aggression and conflict can never work. John Lennon was right: "Give peace a chance"! The second one, Satya, non-lying, is a real challenge. We look at how we are manipulated by the media and by the politicians. How statistics can be read in many different ways and how the spin-doctors 'bend' the truth. Satya encourages us to live with clarity, to come back to honesty and simple truthful values. This involves not lying to others, recognising when others are lying to us, and (most importantly,) not lying to ourselves. Asteya, (non-stealing,) is the third Yama and is not just about stealing someone's possessions, but also stealing another's time or another's peace of mind. We steal someone else's time by being unpunctual, or by being careless with paperwork. We steal another's good name when we gossip about them. Bramacharya (non-misuse of energy,) refers to loyalty and fidelity. In fact, it is not misusing our physical, mental, emotional and sexual energy by being violent, lying, stealing or by being greedy. Aparigraha, (non-greed,) is a lesson that the whole planet is learning right now. Our huge financial institutions are tumbling; even the richest nations are experiencing the 'credit crunch'. Gandhi said: "There is enough for everyman's need, but not enough for everyman's greed." Many, many people are working on our planet to bring food, shelter and comfort to those in need. Every time we donate to charity, either our money or our time, we are adhering to the rule of Aparigraha, non-greed.

If children were brought up to REALLY understand these five Don'ts, the world would change forever. If adults lived by these five Don'ts, the children would really understand them.

Patanjali's second limb is the NIYAMAS. These are the Do's, the observances, the things we should do. We are instructed firstly on cleanliness. This is SAUCHA. In the western world, we are very clean on the outside i.e. showering, washing our clothes etc., but yoga teaches us about inner cleanliness and cleansing the mind and the emotions. The second Niyama is SANTOSHA, contentment. If we are managing to stick to the five Don'ts, we'll be well on our way to contentment. (How wonderful to be given this as a rule for living - contentment isn't a luxury, it's a necessity!). TAPAS is next and is self-discipline. Exercising our bodies, eating nutritious food, meditating, having a healthy daily routine, would all fall under this Niyama. SWADHYAYA is self-study and refers to watching ourselves, watching our own behaviour, caring about our self-development. It also reminds us to read good books, to explore the ancient philosophies and teachings. Last of the Niyamas is ISHWARA PRANIDHANA. This is about leading a good spiritual life. It is about seeing the good or the God in everyone and everything. It is walking in beauty, walking in grace, walking in goodness. Those people who work with angels and spirit guides, those of us who recognise a Higher Being, or Brahman, understand that there are energies beyond our world. This is Ishwara Pranidhana.

Patanjali laid down Eight Limbs as guide-lines for us to find clarity. The first two refer to our behaviour towards ourselves and towards one another. They are totally valid today. If children were brought up to REALLY understand these five Don'ts and five Do's, the world would change forever. If adults lived by these five Don'ts and five Do's, children would REALLY understand them.

The remaining six Limbs or guide-lines are:

*ASANA (the postures or shapes that we practise in hatha yoga. These increase the strength, suppleness & stamina of the physical body, allowing us to sit comfortably still to meditate.)

*PRANAYAMA (the study of gathering, storing and utilising wisely the life-force or life-giving energy.)

*PRATYAHARA (sense-withdrawal, as in gently withdrawing from the external everyday world. We practise this in relaxation.)

*DHARANA (mental concentration.)

*DHYANA (meditation.)

*SAMADHI (bliss or Self-realisation.)

Patanjali's Eight Limbs provide us with a life-time's study, but also guide-lines with which we can check in and test if we're still "on track". Yoga provides us with eight steps to bliss, and proves to us that there is more to life than just getting through each day!

CAROLE KERTON.

© Carole Kerton 2009

# *Chapter 1*

M oon opposes Mars: *No matter how they got on with one another, your parents were certainly united at being at loggerheads with you! (This is an excerpt from my Astrological Report in the year 2000.)*

At three years old, I sat still and quiet with my hands carefully folded in my lap. I was a quaint and oddly thoughtful child, with long brown ringlets and almond shaped eyes. My mother considered my sitting as strange, unusual for a small child, and was astonished one day, when seated in meditation posture, I asked her; "Why am I here this time?" My mother was Welsh and the seventh daughter in her family. She was always inclined to be spiritual, but even so she was taken aback. I have experienced similar interesting behaviour with my grandchildren, though. Lizzie, at three, counted beads and was fascinated by mantra (the repetition of a Sanskrit phrase.) Her favourite mantra was Tibetan: Om Mani Padme Hum, which can be translated as 'The jewel in the heart of the lotus'. Amy, at three, was asking for chants to lull her to sleep and Ben, at three, could make a Tibetan Singing bowl sing and knew how to stop the sound instinctively. However, it might be argued that our grandchildren have grown up in a yoga family, which I did not.

I am convinced that, at three years of age, I had total clarity. I knew that I was here on a mission and obviously felt that it was time to begin. There is power in beginning. I can remember before that feeling frustrated with my slowly growing and developing body. I was in a hurry to get on about the business of this life-time!

I had chosen an interesting family in which to be born. My two grandmothers were particularly fascinating. My paternal grandmother, Clara, was a vegetarian long before it became fashionable! She was very concerned with the environment and always used soap flakes. I remember staying with her and being fed the most delicious macaroni cheese, which she had put into a pudding bowl and turned out on the plate. It made a most pleasing sandcastle shape! My maternal grandmother, Elizabeth, was a very busy little Welsh lady. She had eight daughters, seven of whom survived, and my mother was the seventh. She claimed that this made her a white witch. (On one occasion, my mother arrived for a visit and woke in the morning to the sound of children's voices outside her bedroom door. Tim, our son who was then aged seven, had a neat line of his friends, all eager to pay for the privilege of seeing his Nana, the witch!) My Welsh Grandmother adored my brother as Mum and Dad lived with her after the war and Leigh was there as a baby. To have a baby boy in the house, after all those girls, must have been a delight! She had a lot of grandchildren and never did remember my name. When we reached her door, she would throw it open and say: "Leigh, my boy, how are you?" and wrap him in a huge embrace. Then she would look at me and say: "Hello, um, um..." and give me a quick pat on the head. She once gave me a huge plaster-caste Alsatian, which someone had won at a fair. I lugged it home with me on the train, jubilant! It stood for years in the corner of my bedroom.

My paternal grandfather, Frank, was the Chairman of a Hide and Skin firm, and my father followed in his footsteps. Extraordinary that Clara, a staunch vegetarian and a member of the Iron Cross, should marry a man in the Hide and Skin trade. My maternal Grandfather, Griff, sadly died when my mother was eleven years old. I don't think she ever completely got over it. She remembers blowing a large bubble with chewing gum, the day of the funeral, and when the front door opened, the bubble burst all over her face. She was in big trouble. In those days, traumas were not discussed. Her father had been a pivotal character in the story of her life, and suddenly he was gone, and not mentioned again. They were very close, perhaps because she was the youngest. (The other sisters always said that she was thoroughly spoilt!) Mum's father was a craftsman and could turn his hand to anything. Mum was astonished to discover that my Dad didn't know one end of a hammer from the other, as she had believed that all men were like her father. She used to tell me stories about their dog, Carlo. Grandad Griffith had a butcher's shop in Newport and Carlo would board a bus to go and see him. At the end of the month, they would receive a bill for Carlo's journeys from the bus company. Grandad Frank and Nana Clara always had two Scotties, one white one and one black one. I remember sitting beside Grandad Frank's bed at the age of three and holding his hand. I remember his pyjamas. He died soon afterwards. My mother told me that when she was taken home for the first time to meet the family (as my father's girlfriend,) she was terrified of him. He played a tune on a violin with only one string and demanded that she named it. Luckily she chose the right song and she was in. (He was later to comment that she was a trim little craft!) He embarrassed everyone regularly and my mother vividly remembered having to accompany him on a bus where he proceeded to give all the passengers a packet of cigarettes each for Christmas.

So, my mother was born in the valleys and was very proud of being Welsh. Her mother managed incredibly well on very little money, and was very proud. She "took in theatricals", providing bed and breakfast for actors from touring troops. Her neighbours referred to her as Mrs.Davies, she was only Liz to her husband. (Our oldest grand-daughter was named for my maternal and my paternal grandmothers – Elizabeth Clare, Clare being a shortened version of Clara.) My brother, too, considered himself to be Welsh as he was born in Wales. He always wore a daffodil or leek on St.David's Day, and it was a lively occasion, in our house, when the Welsh were playing

15

rugby against the English. Mum and Leigh shouted for Wales, and Dad and I for England. (I didn't acknowledge that I was half-welsh until well into adulthood.) I have never been able to understand the attraction of playing rugby; actually, I came ingrained with a belief in non-violence, AHIMSA. (Please refer back to the introduction for clarification of the Eight Limbs of Yoga.) My father, though, was very keen and was the captain of the Old Boys Team, from his public school. The team always went to the Isle-of –Wight each year for a holiday together. I LOVED this. I sat in the back of the car, on top of the suitcases and the dogs came, too. The 30 minute crossing was pure joy for me. I loved to stand alone on the ferry and look over the edge to watch the sea.

Standing, or sitting, alone was a feature of my childhood. I didn't seem to fit. Both my parents and my brother were very volatile. My father was a stocky guy, useful on the rugby pitch! He was handsome and charismatic, but he had a temper. He had a loud, bellowing voice, (also useful for supporting the rugby team.) He smacked me only once. I was three at the time, and I was horrified. I have no idea what I did wrong, but I do know that I sat on a chair for three hours afterwards, in case he did it again. He did shout at me regularly, but after his temper had abated, always gave me a big hug. I always felt that when my Dad put his arms around me that everything was all right in the world. That was very special, and I now feel the same when my son gives me a hug.

My mother, on the other hand, was a sulker. She could sulk for Britain. I remember once that she did not speak to me for three weeks. She would cook my meal and slap it down in front of me, without a word. At the end of the three weeks I would have done anything to break the cold, angry silence, and I blurted out: 'I am SO sorry, Mum, I have no idea what I have done, but please speak to me again.' She then admitted that she could not remember what I had done, either! Normal service then resumed, until the next time.

My brother had both characteristics. He had the temper and the sulking. When I was small I adored him. And the stories that my mother always told indicated that he was very kind to me. He once protected me from our father. I had fallen in love with a beautiful, black doll in the window of the toy-store. I was told that I had enough toys, and could not have it, so I saved up my pocket-money. It took weeks, and I was very concerned that Topsy, for I had already named her, would be sold. But the day came when I had enough money and I bought her. Leigh and I went home, jubilant, to find Dad waiting on the doorstep, with his arms folded. Leigh, resplendent in his cow-boy outfit, drew his toy gun and said: "Let her keep the doll". Dad was highly amused and we got away with it. I still have Topsy, to this day, neatly dressed in a beautiful lemon outfit, which my mother knitted.

Mum was a great story-teller, and even her everyday chat was peppered with interesting sayings, and colourful detail. Leigh was her favourite. She had waited for six years to conceive, pretending all the while that they were waiting for the end of the war. An intelligent suggestion from the family doctor led them to buy a dog, which they called Carlo, in remembrance of Mum's childhood companion. The distraction was all that was needed and Leigh was born in 1946. My father was safely returned from the war, where he played a heroic part as a R.A.F. Flight Engineer. Indeed, he was training to be a pilot but when his brother, Uncle Ron, was captured and incarcerated in a Japanese Prisoner-of-War camp, he said 'just get me out there' and took the engineer's job. He had huge respect for his pilot, a wonderful man from New Zealand.

Maybe because Leigh was so obviously my mother's favourite, my father was occasionally very hard on him. I believe that Leigh was ambivalent in his feelings towards Dad. He was afraid of him, but he was also desperate for his approval. Leigh was sent away to boarding school when he was ten years old. My mother was hugely opposed to this decision. Dad pushed it through, partly, I believe, to remove Leigh from his mother's apron-strings, and partly because this was the family tradition. It would make a man of him! Wouldn't it? Well, it was certainly the first nail in the coffin of my parents' marriage. Its repercussions are still being experienced now – 56 years on.

I never remember decisions being discussed in our house. The decision was made and then you were informed. I had such a strong reaction to this way of operating, that my husband and I pledged to have a complete democracy with our children. Everything was discussed, and we always acknowledged their views and feelings. Even if, sometimes, they had to be overruled.

The day we took Leigh to his Prep school is indelibly printed in my memory. I sat on the back seat of the car as we drove away, waving at the brave little figure, as he became smaller and smaller. My mother sat in frozen silence. Shock, I think. The next day, I came out in a rash from head to foot. Mum rushed me to the doctor, who said that it was stress. I was missing my brother. Did I, on some level, realise that we would be estranged from that day forward? I lost my brother at the age of seven, and a piece of my mother died, too.

But I am moving on too quickly. Let's return to the beginning.

I was a pretty baby, apparently, and once won a Beautiful Baby competition. My mother loved to tell the story, and always said that I won because I was the only baby who slept the entire time and didn't yell! Looking back, I believe that I 'slept' a lot through my childhood. Retreating into myself, standing and sitting alone, being quiet, these were means of self-survival.

Why was I here this time? I was here to heal a volatile family. A task at which I was only partially successful. I was here as the Peace-maker. I was definitely here to master ways of surviving. My choice of family was crucial to this incarnation, and to my life's purpose. I was here to understand love and its many complexities. I learnt all about unconditional love from our beautiful pets. My relationship with our animals has always been a great source of comfort to me, and helped me through many painful times as a child.

I loved my parents and I loved my brother, but I learnt unconditional love from our animals.

I do know that I was wanted. Apparently, Mum wrote to her sister to say that Leigh was now such a good little boy that they were considering having another child. By the time the reply arrived, Mum was pregnant. I was to be the easy baby, no crying all night with colic, no volatile temper, gentle and quiet. Both Leigh and I were caesarean births. The doctor asked my mother: "When would you like to have the baby?" and she replied: "Five o' clock, tea-time."

I always felt that Dad was delighted to have a little girl. He was over the moon when our daughter was born, having been relatively indifferent to the births of the four grandsons. Mum used to go to the cinema, once a week on a Thursday, when I was little. One night, the film was cancelled and she came home early. She was appalled to find me out of bed – Dad had got me up 'to play.'

I was here to learn about discipline from my mother, which would stand me in good stead for my future yoga career. Sitting in silence was not just an ability; it was an urge, a motivation. I believe that I was continuing on from a previous incarnation as a yogi. My childhood years, experiences and relationships were to set the scene for my life's purpose. I read recently that we are never too old to have a happy childhood. One of the greatest joys of growing older, and having a family of my own, is that I have relished revisiting childish pleasures with my children, and again with my grandchildren.

# Chapter 2

Sun in Pisces: *Your life is spent in an ivory tower, wearing rose-tinted spectacles and counting unhatched chickens. Fortunately for you, the tower is ivory, the sky is pink and the eggs will hatch... as long as you keep believing it all. (An excerpt from my Astrological Report.)*

So my little life was turned upside down at the age of seven. My brother was sent to school, and then my father announced that we were to move. Our house in Bristol was modest, but I liked it. Out the front was a small garden, and in the middle was a round bed full of rose-bushes. I have always loved roses, and used to skip happily around this bed for hours. The house on our left was the home of a retired police dog – a German Shepherd, or Alsatian, as they were called then. I was once playing with a whistle, and blew it on our side-way. The Alsatian came flying over the fence, rushing to my defence! Quite a sight. Fortunately, I have never been afraid of dogs and was delighted to see him.

We lived in a long residential road, so had lots of play-mates. My mother walked us up the hill each day to school. (My brother's method for teaching me to roller-skate, was to strap my skates on firmly, pull me to the top of the hill, and then to leave me there. It worked!) Mum liked to tell a story which illustrated how animals communicate, one to the other. When I was little, and still in the push-chair, we had two dogs. Bob was a most attractive collie-cross. We inherited him from a farmer, because he was gun-shy. (He was into non-violence, like me.) He was petrified of thunder, and his only comfort was to be shut in the  cupboard under the stairs until the storm passed. He taught all our successive dogs to be afraid of bangs, too. Our second dog was a bearded collie, called Kim, who was a real character. Anyway, Mum took it in turns to take the dogs to school, with me in the push-chair and Leigh walking beside. She never had them on lead, they were beautifully trained, and in those days traffic was not a problem. One day, a big bully dog charged Bob and bit him quite badly. The very next day, Kim eye-balled this dog, strolled over and gave him a good hiding!

Kim was a wanderer. No fence could keep him in. We had high chicken-wire at the end of the back-garden. He would jump it, turn round, stretch up and hold the fence for Bob to get out, too. Bob was a lady's man; there were an awful lot of pups looking just like Bob, around our house. Usually, Kim would return after a day or two, having satisfied his adventurous itch. But one day he left and never came back. I was totally heart-broken. Strange

23

to tell, years afterwards, and two moves later, our paths crossed again. It was twenty miles from our original house, and I was walking in the lane one day when I saw an old bearded collie. It was Kim and he recognised me immediately! What a reunion! He looked pretty rough and was stiff in all his joints. He was a free spirit. I wanted to take him in and never lose sight of him again, but my Dad followed him home. He discovered that he lived on a farm and was now called Jack. The old farmer loved him, and gave him what he needed – freedom to come and go as he pleased. Kim loved people, and I believe that he loved me, but he was his own man and needed to live his life in his own way.

We also had two cats in my first house. They were called Whiskey and Ginger. Whiskey belonged to Leigh, and he would walk the length of our road, on the garden walls, to meet him from school each day. Ginger was mine and came to be known as Ginny. He lived to a very ripe old age; in fact he died just before I left home. Ginny was half Persian and stunningly beautiful.

So, I remember my first seven years as being reasonably happy. I remember my Dad bringing home his 'new' car and insisting on taking us all for a spin immediately. Mum in her apron! I remember the night we were struck by lightning. Mum was authoritarian and when she said 'jump', we did. It saved our lives on this occasion. Leigh and I were playing pirate ships on the big chair in the dining-room, when Mum shouted: "Leigh, Carole, come here now". A moment later, there were great shards of glass plunged into the back of the chair, where we had been playing. We would have been killed for sure, if we had debated the instruction. We all had to sit out in Dad's car, while the firemen put out the flames. Leigh and Bob cried; Kim and I were too young to realise what had happened. Our kind neighbours took us in for the night, and Dad kept the newspaper report of our ordeal with the photograph albums. It was a good area to live, we looked out for one another and I felt secure.

After Leigh was sent to school, Mum mourned. We moved to Weston-super-Mare. We were just yards from the front and the sea. In fact, I could sit up in bed, first thing in the morning, and see the boats. Our house was right on the road, so no front-garden and no beloved roses. People would eat their fish and chips outside, and leave their papers on our window–sill. It was a strange house, with a basement, which once got badly flooded. Mum had her utility room in the basement, and was meticulously fussy about laundry. She recounted tales of her mother doing the wash on a Monday. Imagine how much there was with seven girls! Mum was sat on the table and watched the whole procedure from this vantage point. Great baths of soap-suds, and a blue rinse to make the whites look really white, and, of course, an old mangle decorated gran's kitchen. Mum's system was only slightly more modern. She had a huge churning washing-machine which had a mangle attached to the top. She would fold her sheets and pass them through the mangle and I would watch. One day, the phone rang upstairs and I decided to continue while she answered it. I put a sheet through the mangle,

25

but failed to let go, so my arm went through the rollers. My mother returned in response to my yells, and released the mangle, but by that time my arm was completely flat. It was an extra-ordinary occasion, but somewhat demonstrates my nature. I was a born volunteer, always ready to help, even when my interference was inappropriate.

Dad bought an electric railway to surprise Leigh, one Christmas. He had it built into one of the rooms in the basement. It was excellent. Of course, girls were not allowed to play with it, and, I have to say that I think Dad, Uncle Joe and Uncle Wally had more fun with it that Christmas than Leigh did. Especially after a couple of beers!

So here we were in Weston-super-Mare. Leigh was away at school and Dad was away a lot on business. Mum and I rattled around together in the house, but never really together. I did not fit at home and Leigh did not fit at school. He was desperately unhappy. A strange syndrome set up in our family. As Leigh's school holidays drew close, my mother would begin to make all sorts of plans. She would make his favourite cakes, and prepare his bedroom lovingly. When he arrived home, it was a major celebration. Mum would spend ages creaming his feet, and removing the ingrained dirt from them. I guess bathing was not a high priority in a boys' school! We would have lots of fun day-trips, and the whole atmosphere of the house would lift. But the last few days before he went back to school, the black clouds would descend again.

Mum would fill his tuck-box with his most favourite goodies, and we would have horrible tearful good-byes. After he left, Mum would thoroughly clean his bedroom, and then it would be closed up. No-one went in there. It was treated as a shrine. Our life would go back to normal – Mum and I rattling around in the house together, but not really together. So many years later, it came into my awareness that Leigh felt enormous resentment towards me. He thought that my life was always like that – daytrips, picnics, favourite cakes etc. I knew better. I knew that celebrations and fun only happened when Leigh was home. I don't remember feeling resentful; it was just the way it was. But it was because of this misunderstanding that Leigh and I were estranged so young. I believe he hated me with a passion, and neither of us had the words to articulate our perceptions.

I would have loved to have escaped and to have gone to boarding school. But by this time I had developed asthma, and it was decided that I was not well enough to be sent away. More fuel for Leigh's hatred!

I had had what the doctors called 'nettle rash' for some years. When we went on the holiday to the Isle-of –Wight, I would be covered in a very itchy rash, from head to toe. I would have to stay in the beach hut and away from the sun. Then, when I got to the age of seven, the nettle rash disappeared and I developed hay fever and asthma. Nowadays, hay fever is quite common, but in those days it was unheard of. It transpired that I was allergic to forty three different grasses and trees. I was also allergic to dust

27

and to animals' fur. For six weeks every year I would be in bed. I couldn't even go to the toilet without having a major asthma attack. I was a very poorly little girl.

I must say that my mother was a very good nurse. In fact, I think she missed her calling – she would have made a superb matron in a hospital! She was an immaculate house-keeper, so the wards would have been spotless. She was strict, and stood no nonsense, so the staff would have been respectful and disciplined. She had a wealth of knowledge about health, both of the conventional variety and the alternative. This she had inherited from her welsh mother, and also picked up from her mother-in-law. She took care of me very well, but it was my Dad who would sit beside me at four in the morning, whilst I fought for breath. Dad developed hay fever as a young man of twenty-two. He was in the R.A.F. and was on an air-field which was surrounded by fields full of tall grasses. I've got a feeling that it was in Lincolnshire, but that could be incorrect. He had the most dreadful asthma attacks. Mum said that he would hang out of the window, gasping for air, and that the doctor would arrive and give him a shot of adrenaline. Perhaps he felt guilty that I had inherited allergic asthma from him. He would go to St. Mary's Hospital, Paddington, each year and receive a course of injections. He would then inject himself, every day, throughout the hay fever season.

My mother, of course, was on a mission to cure me. She had succeeded where the doctor had failed, when I was eighteen months old. I had contracted gastric enteritis, and, after three days, the doctor was shaking his head and preparing her for the worst. Mum began to administer the good old-fashioned remedy of brandy. After twenty-four hours I was sitting up and requesting:'Marmite n mato sandwiches'. Still a favourite, to this day! Mum left no stone unturned to cure my asthma. I went to school with garlic leaves in my shoes! And she would rub my back with goose grease, and then pound me. Not a very pleasant experience! I took anti-histamines, which helped a little, and had a most curious 'spray'. It was filled with rat poison. It had a rubber ball at the bottom and an amber coloured tube. It was my life-line. The doctor also tried all the injections, but my mother was adamant that she would not allow me to have cortisone ones. A friend's daughter had been on them for years, and had developed a 'moon-face'.

When I was taking my G.C.E's, my mother would drop me as close as possible to the school door. Then someone would help me into the hall, for the exam. I had my own 'runner' to fetch me water, or whatever I needed, during the exam. Then I would be assisted back to the car, and would go home to bed.

It was a curious illness which incapacitated me every single year, and then was gone. I was constantly told that I would outgrow it. My Dad used to tease me that I would be fine by the time I got to fifty-five, as this was when his stopped being a problem. I now realise that the asthma attacks gave me an incredible understanding of the breath. When I came across a yoga book on Pranayama and breathing exercises, at the age of fifteen, I had a real 'light-bulb' moment.

So, why was I here at this stage of my life? Certainly, I was here to learn that your body manifests what is happening in your mind and your emotions. (Hence the rash, when my brother went away to school.) I was here to learn about being alone. Yet I was here to discover, from my quiet time, that we are never completely alone. I learnt to trust my Inner Self, my Inner Guru or teacher. I learned patience. I learned how it is for people to be really ill and unable to function normally. In my case, this was temporary, but it gave me a good insight for my future career. I was to gain an insight into family dynamics, and to experience the feeling of being powerless.

# *Chapter 3*

Moon opposes Sun: *You were born under a Full Moon. This suggests that your childhood was eventful and somewhat tense at times. When you were little, you were aware of a lot of drama in your world. Perhaps your parents were at loggerheads, or other factors in your family life led you to feel a little insecure. At a comparatively early age, you learned to assert yourself and to draw strength from your own sense of identity. (An excerpt from my Astrological Report.)*

Whenever my mother's family got together, it was a very noisy occasion. The voices of the sisters would rise and become evermore shrill. I found it daunting, in the extreme. I sought out Uncle Joe; he was my refuge, my safe harbour. Uncle Joe was 'married' to Auntie Lo, who was always known as Auntie Pobs, when I was little. (I think it was because Mum's name, Barbara, was shortened to Babs and so it became Babs and Pobs.) Uncle Joe was gentle and quiet. He demonstrated 'detachment' very well. He was in the world, but not of the world. He was a staunch Roman Catholic, and a socialist. He did not believe in owning property, everything should be shared. He and Auntie Lo did not have children. (She became Lo when one day she confided to me how much she hated 'Pobs'. She said that she had a beautiful name – Lorraine Alexandra - and she would very much like to be called by it. I converted immediately to Auntie Lo, and the whole family followed suit.) The rumour was that Joe had had a daughter by his first wife. She was apparently an actress. He was a bit of a lad in his youth. He came from a 'good' family, but it seems his parents died young. He was brought up by a very strict guardian. His sister, Mary, was a diplomat and a strikingly intelligent woman. She spent a long time in Japan. So Joe, as a young man, was into motor-bikes, sports cars, and hanging around the stage-doors of the theatres. Of course, most of this is conjecture, but he did love to show me his photograph album of his cars, and I did notice that some photos had been removed. It was said that he and Auntie Lo went away for the week-end, and when they came back she was wearing a wedding-ring. It was generally believed that, since he was a Roman Catholic, he could not divorce his 'first' wife.

I knew nothing of all this, when I was young, and now it is such a small scandal! I just knew that Uncle Joe's lap was my safe harbour. He talked quietly, he sat still and he could be relied upon to protect me from the loud sisters. I have a huge number of cousins, twenty-six in fact.

My father introduced Lo to Joe. They were both in the R.A.F. and one week-end Dad took him home. I believe that Joe worked on the maintenance of the Aircraft. They were unlikely friends, so very different in nature, but I felt the enormous respect that they had for one another. Certainly Auntie Lo adored my father, and was always grateful that Dad secured a job for Joe in his firm. He was the Transport Manager. He was slow and thorough. There were times when my Dad thought he was a bit of 'an old woman', but they rubbed along well for the most part.

Every year, when Uncle Joe received his bonus from George Webster and Co. he would book a table at a smart restaurant, and take my parents out for a meal. It was his way of saying 'thank you' for the job, and for the many week-ends that they enjoyed at my parents' house. When I was twelve, he invited me too. I received a hand-written invitation, and felt terribly grown-up. We were to be taken to Wells, which is a very pretty place in Somerset. I wore a lilac striped dress, it was sleeveless and I was very pleased with it. Mum put my long, dark brown hair up on top. I can remember seeing the swans, and I remember the restaurant most clearly. The waiter made a big fuss of me. I guess it was a novelty to have a shy young one to smile at. On the way home, my mother was somewhat 'huffy'. She was used to being the centre of attention, and said: 'Well, that's the last time we're taking Carole!'

Mum was a very attractive woman. She worked at it. Her hair took a long time to look as she wished, and she was happy to give it that long time. Her nails were always painted, and she was adept at making an outfit stylish. She certainly stood out in a crowd, but she was not naturally beautiful. She grew up in a house-hold of girls. They all followed fashion and had their favourite film stars. Auntie Dode and Auntie Una shared a bedroom. Mum told the story that one night, when Una went up to bed, she found Dode asleep with her hair half-curled. She propped her up, holding her in place by putting her knee in her back, and finished curling her hair!

There were also the stories of the rows, and one of them putting an iron, really hot, in the middle of her sister's back!

Apparently, when they were young, Lo was beautiful. When they went into town with their father, if they met a friend of his, they would invariably say: "Isn't she beautiful?" about Lorraine. And then they would pinch Mum's cheek, and remark upon her chubby face. My mother was about three when she was caught brandishing a piece of wood, with nails sticking out of it, at Lorraine and saying: "I'll spoil your pretty face, I'll spoil your pretty face."

I realise now that Mum was always insecure about the way she looked. She came over as being very confident – a typical Leo – but she had severe misgivings about how attractive she was and about her intelligence. When they were first together, Mum showed an interest in the car and asked what a shock-absorber did. Dad replied, with heavy sarcasm and an aloof arch of the eye-brows, "As the name implies." I suspect that he had no idea what it did, but Mum never asked questions about the car again.

My mother married a young man with 'potential'. Out of all the sisters, it was considered that she achieved the best standard of living. She was ambitious and so was Dad. She liked the finer things in life, and despite lacking confidence in some areas, she had a keen belief in her own worth. She felt that she was due some luxury at the end of the day. My parents were stereo-typical. He was the charismatic and successful business man, and she was his very attractive wife, who kept an immaculate home and a good table. Dad would bring home work colleagues to stay, and from the age of three, I was expected to shake hands politely and respond to questions. We had a Dutch friend who was a frequent visitor, and was a favourite of mine. He brought me a Dutch doll, and I began to collect dolls of all nationalities. Many of my friends now are from other countries, and I'm always fascinated by different cultures.

Periodically, Mum and I would take the train to Newport to visit her mother. Now this placed me in a terrible dilemma! You see, Mum could sleep on anything that moved – she even used to sleep on the back of Dad's motorbike, when they were young! As soon as ever the train pulled out of Temple Meads, Mum would go to sleep. If I woke her up to tell her that we were approaching Newport, I was in trouble, and if I let her sleep on and pass the station, I was also in trouble! I never did work out what was the best course of action.

In fact, dealing with my mother was a permanent conundrum. Once I had a new school dress, and, on the very first day of wearing it, I managed to spill ink all down the skirt. I was mortified, and dreaded seeing my mother's face when she met me at the school-gate. To my utter astonishment, she was fine about it! She said that it was obviously an accident, and that since I had clearly worried myself sick about it all day, I had been punished enough.

I felt as though I was in a permanent state of confusion, as far as grown-ups were concerned. Our family dynamics were extra-ordinary. I think we put the funk in dysfunctional! Mum operated a sort of see-saw programme with Leigh and with me. If one of us was in favour, then the other one was not. I never could work out what tipped the see-saw. I would be enjoying a little plateau and would seem to be in favour, and then, for no apparent reason, I would be in trouble again. It didn't seem to be to do with what I had done, necessarily. It was far more random. Sometimes, Leigh would have done something wonderful, and then he would swing to the top. But it wasn't always the reason. I seemed to spend more time at the ground level than Leigh did, regardless of how good I was. An enigma for my small brain! Leigh and I both grew up with a strong sense of injustice.

Talking about see-saws, there was a day when Leigh and I were on a real see-saw at the park. Leigh is three years, two months and nine days older than me, (I know this fact because he told me so often!) Naturally, he was heavier and Dad was lending weight to my end. When Leigh went down and I went up, as Dad put pressure on to bring me down, Leigh grabbed a tuft of grass. This caused me to have a sudden bump at the top, and I bit off the tip of my tongue. Mum, in her very practical way, put it back into place and it knitted. There's still a scar there. Even though Leigh was older, it never seemed to be his fault when he harmed me. I wore glasses from the age of three, national health ones. One day, Leigh was playing soldiers and he had a large stick over his shoulder. He wheeled suddenly, and the stick took out one of the lenses from my specs. Mum shouted at him at the time, and checked that my eye was OK but within half an hour the story had changed. I had walked into his stick.

It is no wonder that Leigh and I had a complicated relationship. In fact, when I became interested in astrology, I realised that our family of four comprised a fire sign, an air sign, an earth sign and a water sign. It should have been perfect, but in reality I can never remember a time when all four of us were talking to one another!

Why am I here this time? It seems to me that we must play out the hand that we have been given. When I sat in Spirit World and planned this incarnation, I must have had to learn about human dynamics. I must have had to learn about confusion, and about living the questions. I never felt that I was on a level playing field, but I learned to live alongside that. I developed a little private world of my own.

Most importantly, at this time, I learned to grow quiet and to predict. If Mum told me that we were going to one of the dreaded, loud parties with her sisters, I would take myself off somewhere quiet. I would then 'go inside' and see whether I could imagine being there or not. If I could, then I would know that it was going to happen, and I would have to brace myself. But if I could not imagine being there, then we would not go, and I could relax. I discovered that this was amazingly accurate. Having quiet time and being around quiet people was a great solace to me, and escaping to my inner world gave me some control over my life.

# Chapter 4

M oon in Virgo: *This makes you yearn for a world that "makes sense", but the sad fact is that few things in life ever do. Your over-whelming sense of duty makes you yearn to do your best at every juncture."*

Our house in Weston was opposite a Jeweller. The owner was called Mr.Prince, and our ginger cat, Ginny, loved to visit him. Dad bought Mum a beautiful bracelet from him for her birthday. She was so thrilled with this bracelet, that he bought her the exact same one again for Christmas!

Next to the Jewellers was an ice-cream parlour. One of the owners loved children, and if I went to the back-door with a jug, he would fill it up with ice-cream for me. I took care not to abuse this privilege. Right now, as a vegan, I can still remember that delicious taste. Dad's sister, Auntie Mel, lived up the same road. She had a small hotel. Auntie Mel played the cello, as a girl, and worked for the Bournemouth Symphony Orchestra. There she met Uncle

Lew. He played the xylophone. He was a very colourful character, and I had a real soft spot for him. But when Melba announced to her family that she intended to marry him, it caused a major uproar. Frank said that, if she went ahead with the wedding, she would never darken his door again. She did go ahead, and from there on had to contact her mother through a post office box.

Apparently, Lew did not want children. Mel, on the other hand, wanted a large family and she got her way, birthing four girls. Lew was always threatening to leave. One day my mother was there when he threatened Mel with his departure. Mum said: "Go and pack him a bag". Mel was tearful and not quite sure, but she did and placed the bag by the front door. Lew never threatened again, and never left. He used to say to my mum: "When I drop dead, you get to my body first. There will be a wad of notes in my back-pocket; use these for a good 'knees-up'. If Melba gets there first, she'll find something practical to spend the money on." It is certain that Auntie Mel had to be practical, with four girls to raise and a cigarette habit. The family would sleep downstairs, in the summer season, so that all the bedrooms could be used for guests.

I was a little afraid of Auntie Mel, but I liked her better than her sister, Auntie Ray. My father adored his younger sister, who was a dizzy blond. She once looked after us, when Mum and Dad were away. I believe I ran away from her, when we were out, and she threatened me with discipline when we got home. When we arrived, she sat me on the kitchen table, rolled down my socks and resoundingly slapped my legs. It was the pre-meditated nature of this attack which astounded my sense of justice.

Auntie Ray married a pilot called Bruce. He was very dashing and handsome, and they had a glamorous life of globe-trekking. They lived in Australia, Trinidad, and the Bahamas. Their son, Ricky, would come home to us for his school holidays. He was at a public school in Ireland. He once threw a milk bottle at me, when I was riding my scooter behind our house. I had to go to hospital, my shoe was full of blood and my foot was badly cut. I've had lots of injuries to my feet over the years. I always say that it is because I'm a Pisces – more used to having a tail than feet!

My father's older brother was called Ron. He was the hero. My mother thought he was amazing as he was passionate about fighting for causes. There was something romantic in his nature. His five and a half years in the Japanese prison-of-war camp was never referred to, but he did not ever eat rice pudding. He had married Auntie Margaret, before the war. She was from north Wales. She had red hair, and was very kind. She spoke quietly. They had a son, Barry, who had not seen his father until he was five. It must have been a most difficult adjustment for the little chap when Ron returned, after his horrendous experiences. Auntie Margaret and Uncle Ron, who became a school-teacher after the war, had two more sons. I always felt that she would have liked a daughter. I can remember her, very carefully, putting on my coat. She treated me like a precious doll. My mother was into co-ordination so my hair ribbon always matched the stripe around my socks, and the trim around my knickers. Still now, I always have a clean hankie on me which matches my outfit! Auntie Margaret did have a little girl, late in life. She was called Jane and she had Downs' Syndrome. They all adored her. She was very affectionate, a special spirit, but she was not to make old bones. Jane died at age three, and Uncle Ron and Auntie Margaret took on a Children's Home, in her memory. They were wonderful carers.

At this time, I discovered formal religion. I would knock for Cousin Anita, and we would go to the church in Lower Church Road. It is a beautiful building, and I really enjoyed the singing with a community. I didn't feel quite at home, though, and had a 'nearly right' reaction. I still feel like this, if I go to a church wedding or funeral. I love the buildings and the feeling of the many people who have been here before, and I love the singing, but there is a reservation in me. It's too formal and stiff, regimented. My mother did not have us christened. She said that she would rather we chose our faith when we were grown. I admire that decision. She had been a Sunday School teacher, and in South Wales there seemed to be some rivalry between the Methodists and the Baptists. We did not have our children christened, either, and nor has our daughter christened hers. It was not until we went to an Ashram in India, that I understood what it was to 'come home' and to feel comfortable and entirely 'at one' with a community.

Living right beside the sea meant that we could take a dip and run home. I loved the water; always felt that this was a connection on a deep level. Another facet of being a Pisces! Mum would wait with a warm towel for me, wrap me up tightly, and then send me for a run to get my circulation going. Mum did not swim. She was afraid of the water. (Years later, when we were living in Kentucky, she came to visit and was horrified by the humidity. The temperatures would range from -20degrees in the winter to 100degrees in the summer. When it was 100degrees, it was often 100% humidity, too. I placed a deck-chair in our swimming-pool for Mum, to cool off, and there she would sit sipping her gin and tonic!) Dad was the swimmer. Every summer, before we went to the Isle-of-Wight on holiday, he would give up alcohol for a month. He would lose some weight, and feel presentable in his swim-trunks. Each year he would swim out to a large rock off the St.Helen's beach. It was a mile there and back, and I longed for the year when I would be able to do it with him. He would not let me. He said that it was too risky, because I was an asthmatic. But I was always fine in the water – never felt breathless, always confident. One year, Cousin Anita came to the Island with us. She also loved to swim, indeed her older sister, Lesley, was the breast-stroke champion for England. Dad took Anita on the swim to the rock. I felt the betrayal keenly. That's the first experience I had of being over-looked by him, and I was very hurt.

I was a quiet, quaint child, who was painfully shy. A lot went on in my head, and in my heart, that no-one knew. I discovered that I liked to write. I wrote a series of short-stories, mostly about our animals, and about living by the sea. I came into the lounge one day to see my mother showing my short-stories to her friend. I retrieved them, later, and destroyed them. I felt that a piece of me had been exposed, a piece that I was not ready to share with the public. I don't remember dwelling on this experience, I certainly felt betrayed, but I wasn't damaged by it. Just learnt to be more careful about where I hid my work. But my mother never forgot this occasion.

I was shy at school. I wore glasses, again unusual in those days. The school photographs show a somewhat serious little girl, with a high curly pony-tail, and spectacles. I was pretty, but never felt it. The whole 'four-eyes' thing was rife at that time.

It was at this moment that I received a message from Spirit World. It was not my first, and it certainly was not going to be my last. But it was very important. I was told that I must develop my personality. That if I was to be successful with my mission for this life-time, I would have to learn to speak up, and to put out a friendly vibe. From there on, whenever anyone asked for a volunteer at school, my hand would go up – of its own volition. I can remember volunteering to read in Assembly. It was my last year in Junior School, and I was so nervous that you could hear my knees knocking, as I walked out to the front of the hall. I had learnt the reading off by heart, in case my eyes went out of focus. This was something that would occur, if I was very anxious.

I continue to be a volunteer to this day, and have learnt a great deal about myself in the process. In yoga, we call this Swadhyaya – self-study. (Please see the introduction.)

And now we moved again. We were not long in our house by the sea, where my mother walked the dogs along the beach to take me to school. But Mum, whose great joy was to go to Barry Island with the Sunday School as a small child, remained a 'tripper' all her life. She would beg my husband, Mike, to take her to Hayling Island, when she lived near us in Hampshire. She loved the cockles, the fish and chips, the ice-cream, the tacky fruit machines. Indeed, everything except the sea!

Dad was doing very well at work and could afford a larger house for us. He took me around to view some properties. I was very flattered by this (I enjoyed his company enormously) and I felt that he might even listen to my views. We went to see 'Yeolands'. It was a lovely, large, black-and-white house set in the beautiful countryside of Somerset. I told Dad that Mum would not like to be that far out in the country, with only cows for neighbours. My mother had always struck me as a townie. Anyway, I was wrong. She loved the house, and we duly moved. The address was 'Yeolands', Totterdown lane, Bleadon Hill. Mum was brilliant at moving, she had Auntie Lo hemming the curtains, everyone carting around boxes, and she had the kitchen spick and span. Within twenty four hours, you would have thought that we had always lived there. The house was spotless. The Britons owned the house previously, and had built a smaller property beside, to which they then moved. The lady of the house, Esme Briton, left everything pristine, which was just the way Mum continued to keep it.

It was an area favoured by retired folk, and I set about on my new mission: to put out a friendly vibe. Each time I walked the dogs in the lane, I smiled at all the old folk that I met. I became known as 'Smiler', but it took me a while to break down some folks' barriers. I learnt the power of the smile! And something else – that when you meet and greet, from the heart, you will connect on a deeper level. I learnt that I genuinely like people, I'm interested in them, and if I'm interested in them, they open up to me.

Shortly after moving to our five bedroom, beautifully proportioned house, I passed my Eleven Plus and went to Grammar School. Now, I caught the bus to school and Dad still exercised the dogs on the beach, but now he had to drive there. Mum and Dad had taken on a puppy as a surprise for Leigh, when he came home from school for the holidays. Mum was adamant that we were not to name her, as that would be Leigh's privilege. So she became known as Puppy. By the time Leigh came home, he had to come up with a similar name, as she responded to Puppy so well. He called her Lucky, and, bless her heart, she was the most unlucky of dogs. She had endless operations, and Dad once ran her over and damaged her hind leg badly. He was tired, took the dogs to the beach, but stayed in the car and cruised along slowly, while they ran. He was mortified to have hurt our dear little girl, but Mum never forgave him. This was another nail in the coffin that was my parents' marriage.

So what was I learning about why I was here this time? I learnt that conventional religion was not a fit for me. I learnt how painful it was to be betrayed and overlooked. I learnt that I was sensitive.

I learnt, most importantly, that a smile is a powerful connecter. And that, if you approach someone with your heart open, you will break down barriers. I learnt how much I like people, and how much I love animals. I learnt how much I enjoy a project. Once I received a message from Spirit World I acted upon it with commitment and enthusiasm. I seemed to recognise that there were forces at play who would guide me and I never doubted that these forces had my best interests at heart. I was here to serve, of that I was sure, and I was prepared to grow and develop to accomplish that task.

# Chapter 5

**M**idheaven Ruler Mercury in the Sixth House: *In general, you are at your best when you are doing things for other people. Anything from waiter to Prime Minister, as long as it involves serving others.*

Grammar School was a revelation to me. It was huge, split down the middle both inside and out, with girls on one side and boys on the other. My best friend and I volunteered for the school play in the first year. Yes, my hand was still going up, of its own volition! We were page-boys. I loved school. I am one of the few people who cried at leaving school, at age eighteen. I loved learning. My two favourite subjects were English and History. Our History teacher was known as 'Gypsy Jones'. She was wonderful, a really inspiring teacher. She was only tiny, but crowds naturally parted as she walked by. She told us that eating was a social occasion. Actually, she treated everything as a social occasion. She had a regal bearing and genuinely loved us girls. I loved her eccentricities, her spirit and her energy. I believe that, observing Miss Jones, was the first time that I picked up on people having different energies. There was something about her 'aura' which drew you in. Of course, I had never heard the word 'aura' at that stage, but I did know that I found her magnetic, and that learning with her was fun.

I was not the most brilliant student, but I was certainly a willing one. The Deputy Head, Miss Moss, was to remark the day that I left the school that I had contributed in many ways, and that I was well-rounded. She loved that I put on a production of 'Midsummer Night's Dream', on the Quadrangle, after completing my 'A' levels. I played Puck. Extraordinarily, a few years back, I found myself on a yoga holiday with the Head Girl from my first year at Senior School.

Our school uniform was maroon. We had to wear berets, and would fasten them, precariously, on the back of our heads with grips. I was actually proud of my uniform. In those days, it was an achievement to get to the Grammar School, and not to be sent to the Secondary Modern.

My brother was, of course, still at Public School. My memory is that he did not like academic subjects, and found few, if any, inspiring teachers. He always had a brilliance for mental arithmetic, and can still remember phone numbers and license plates from forty years ago. He took up the trumpet. I can understand why – when he played the trumpet, he was heard. He played in a parade on one occasion, and we went to watch. My mother was smart, and loved to dress up. She always stood out at

49

Leigh's School, where most of the mothers were more conventional. You could see the disapproval, when my mother appeared. She also stood out at my school, and would be the only mother to wear a hat on Speech Day. I would slide down in my chair, as she walked in, mortified. All my friends would be saying: "What is Carole's mother wearing on her head, this year?"

My Dad was brilliant at Geography, and at quizzes. He adopted the habit of giving Leigh and me Maths problems to work out. Now, Leigh was three years, two months and nine days older than me, and I (innocently) always got the answer first. This did nothing for sibling rivalry, and added fuel to the dislike my brother already felt for me. My mother was very critical of me. I believe that this was her way of being on Leigh's side. It began to dawn on me that you can love more than one person, that love is not rationed and that withdrawal of love was a most unkind manipulation. It leaves you powerless, and at the mercy of others. I became fiercely fair. If I shared my biscuit with the dogs, I was scrupulous about giving them even portions. I had adopted the practice, as a small child, of taking it in turns with my teddy-bears to share my pillow. Even taking it in turns as to which side my head was turned, so that none of them felt 'left out'.

About this time, two boys at Leigh's School were looking for a home for the holidays. Their father, Alan, worked for the Shah of Persia, and so their parents were away. Mum felt that it was an ingenious plan to take the boys, her strategy being to ease the return to school for

Leigh. He would have company. I realise now, as an adult, that the only way it would have been easier on Leigh was if Mum had treated it as normal. While she went on bearing a grudge, and hating that he was away, he went on hating it, too.

So, Keith and Chris became known as 'the foster boys'. One important aspect of this new situation was that I acquired the perfect big brother. I adored Keith. He was a year older than Leigh, and was such fun. He was very good-looking and very protective towards me. He cared about my mother and called her 'Auntie'. He was naturally sunny-natured, and he took a special place in the family.

On one occasion, when my parents were out, Leigh shot a bird with his air-rifle. I was distraught. The poor bird was not dead, and was in dreadful pain. Keith took absolute control of the situation and looked after us all. He was my hero. No wonder that he became a Naval Officer on submarines. I do regret that we lost touch with Keith, and quite recently I tried to find him, through a yoga student whose husband knew him in the Navy.

The four of us did have a lot of fun, though, and Keith's kindness and acceptance towards me was a protection. We used to work out gymnastic displays on the front lawn. Chris would hold my feet, Leigh would hold my hands, and they would swing me, and then throw me, and Keith would catch me. I had utter faith in him. He would not allow the soles of my sandals (with my feet inside!) to be used as target practice for Leigh and his air-rifle. This desire to use your sister for target practice seemed to run

51

in the family. Auntie Ray carried a pellet in her thigh all her life, from Dad!

We also worked up a pretty neat band act. Keith played the Euphonium, Chris the Trombone and the violin, and Leigh the trumpet. I played the Recorder. They would put an old hat on my head, and every time I tried to join in, they would give me a toffee and pat me on the head. It became a hilarious party act and my parents laughed so much. I found that I rather enjoyed being a clown and making others laugh. I discovered that humour can soften a tense situation and put people at their ease. I use that a great deal now, as a yoga teacher. One of my student teachers once remarked that I am full of 'unexpected laughter'.

Being the youngest, I was only allowed to join in the games if I could adhere to the correct criteria. I had to be good enough to play against, but not ever beat the boys. My brother taught me to play chess, but once I had beaten him, he never played me again. I was rather good at Table Tennis. I still love that game! I learnt to get close to winning, and then to make a few 'careless shots'. Actually, it was really good practice. It is quite hard to miss on purpose. This was all a lesson in egos, particularly of the male variety.

We began to go to a rather lovely hotel on the Isle-of-Wight each year, taking all the boys. Mum would sit, or sleep, on the balcony all afternoon, with her hair in rollers, and we would be round and about enjoying ourselves. We would meet up at our table in the restaurant, and Mum would always 'make an entrance'. She would look stunning, in a cocktail dress, and loved that all the boys stood up, smartly, as she reached the table.

I was still somewhat quaint, quiet and bookish. I always loved to read, and still do. I went pony-riding and loved it when the calves were born, at the local farm, and I could feed them with baby bottles.

Leigh and I joined the Pony Club. I was riding an old plodder called Dolly. She was totally bomb-proof, short and plump, and a little boring. Leigh was riding a chestnut, called Ruby. We went to an all-day event. Leigh was competing in an older class to me, and my parents went to see him jump. Just before I was to go around my circuit, the daughter of the local publican, Bridget, asked to swap ponies with me. She had been riding a very young grey, and wanted to do well and to feel safe on old Dolly. The Lass who owned the Riding Stables was very thick with Bridget's family, and she insisted on the swap. So round the course I went on this young and eager grey, called Thunder. I won! My parents were still in a different field, supporting Leigh, and they missed it. To this day, I cannot work out why they did not split – one supporting Leigh and one supporting me. Our daughter, Gemma, is the most wonderful mother of three. She would never make that mistake. But I do understand the difficulties of parenting. I realise that my parents were doing their best. They, too, were playing out the hands that they had been dealt. Their relationship never did run smooth. It was not Leigh's fault that our life was so stormy, and it was a great shame that we never enjoyed the loving relationship that a brother and sister should share.

About this time, I discovered boyfriends! I discovered that personality mattered, and I began to attract the lads. I started to go to the 'Teen and Twenty' with my friends. I was coming out of my shell, and I was beginning to develop a figure, and to find ways of enhancing my assets. Despite the fact that my brother continued to taunt me, I began to turn heads.

But, oh, the very best thing about boyfriends was the ability to shock my parents. I had never realised what snobs they were! What fun I had! Going out with boys who were from the Council Estate, and who went to the Secondary Modern, was sure to cause a stir. I rather veered from being always the 'good girl', and became a bit of a rebel. I learnt to lie to my mother. I was not keen on lying, but I was keen on having some freedom, and some fun. I also had occasion to get my own back on my brother, and to feel rather smug!

Leigh had his own car at this time, and being a very good-looking boy, (a sort of Elvis look-alike,) he would drive around town looking for 'talent'. I was walking over Devil's bridge, on one occasion, off to meet my boyfriend. I was wearing a black trench-coat, pulled in tightly at the waist. Leigh came up behind me, obviously thought that I was 'talent', beeped the horn and wolf-whistled out of the window. You should just have seen his face when he passed and realised that this pretty, trendy girl was indeed his little sister! His taunts never did have the same sting after that.

Poor Leigh had never received what he most needed – a secure, loving home; the approval of his father; a worthwhile education. Seven years at Boarding-School did not equip him for the next stage in his life. Having said that, we must look at Keith (the oldest of the foster boys, and the perfect brother.) He got excellent grades in his 'A' levels and went on to have a brilliant naval career. He came out of the same school, well-adjusted, loving and ambitious. I suppose this is an example of 'horses for courses'.

Dad set about finding a niche for Leigh in the Hide and Skin business. One talent that Leigh had in spades was finding girl-friends. He was, as I have said, a very good-looking young man. And he could be charming. Certainly, all my friends fell in love with him. He had a series of beautiful girl-friends.

I must confess that neither of us seemed to have a well-developed conscience in our romantic dealings! I remember, on one occasion mischievously arranging to meet three different boys at the Town hall on a Saturday at seven o'clock. Leigh drove me round the block several times until there was only one lad left, patiently waiting. I went out with him. Clearly I valued patience in a boyfriend!

When I arrived back from a school-trip to Switzerland, at the age of fifteen, I was surprised to be met by Leigh. All I wanted to do was to go home for a bath, and to unpack, but nothing must do, I must be introduced to his new love. He drove me to Worlebury, and I met Meg, for the first time. She was very glamorous and friendly, and clearly Leigh was smitten.

Meg had, and still has, lovely parents. Sylvia and Ivan are warm, caring, supportive family people. They had a Shetland Collie and a house-rabbit, and were always very kind to me. Meg ticked a lot of Leigh's boxes. She was very attractive, very made-up, and she seemed happy to put up with his dirty jokes and constant innuendoes. Leigh had always said that he wanted a girl who looked as good in an evening gown as she did on the back of a horse. Meg did. Appearance really mattered to him. I always liked Meg, and clearly she doted on Leigh. My mother, always the prude, was horrified by some of their conversation, and the very public displays of amorous inter-action. She said that they "did not bring out the best in one another", which was true. Meg, bless her, was to admit as much, forty-one years later. Meg and I are now very close, and she always refers to me as her 'little sister'.

Leigh, meanwhile, was working for Dad's firm. No doubt Dad imagined that Leigh would eventually become Managing Director, following in the footsteps of his father and grandfather. I am guessing that Dad could readily see what it was that attracted Leigh to Meg. The two of them certainly turned heads, they were such a handsome couple. But he did agree with Mum that they may not make an ideal partnership, if Leigh was to rise through the ranks to the dizzy heights of Chairman. They set about driving a wedge between the young people, first by manipulation and then by bribery. They offered Leigh a shiny, new sports car, if he would give Meg up. He did finish with her, briefly, but Mum's obvious delight at her victory, and her snide comments, caused Leigh's eyes to flash. And when Meg arrived, all upset and tear-stained, the cause was lost. They were re-united and were determined to have one another. They planned their wedding for a month after Leigh's twenty-first birthday. In this way, history repeated itself. My father married my mother three days after his twenty-first birthday, as in those days you had to have your parents' permission to marry before that age. He was not going to ask anyone's permission, and nor was Leigh. History repeated itself again later. My mother left my father after forty years of marriage, and Meg left Leigh after forty-one. I draw a veil over their life together, as it is their story to tell and not mine, but they did have three beautiful boys, and a host of enchanting pets.

I had settled into a steady relationship with a really nice lad. He had enough in his back-ground to shock my parents, but he was a good-looking young man and very willing to please. As time went by, my mother was to find enough problems with our liaison, to endeavour to part us, also, by fair means or foul.

So what was I learning in my teenage years, to equip me to become a yoga teacher, and finally the Chairman of a yoga society? I was learning about the complicated games that people play. That people may be beautiful on the outside, but may not necessarily be beautiful on the inside. I learnt to use, and to appreciate humour. And I found out about the images that folk put out into the world. Anyone meeting my family, for the first time, may well have thought of us as successful and harmonious. We were all good actors, in our own way. I look back and count my blessings that we always had animals. I believe they kept us grounded and constantly in touch with unconditional love. We all loved animals. This was perhaps the only constant that we four shared. I would come to realise that the complicated issues lying deep in the sub-conscious, were played out even in our relationships with our pets. With them I did not feel different, and did not experience that 'aloneness', which was a feature of my early life. As a teenager, I wanted to be accepted, so I developed the external life, and experimented with a more noisy version of myself. I could more readily choose the people with whom I wanted to spend my time.

On my trip to Switzerland, we had visited Chateau Chillon. I was climbing the steps, rough-hewn in stone, when I had a powerful experience of deja-vu. Then, in my head, there was the sound of battle. I was a young lad of about twelve, dirty and skinny but alive with a mission. I was running up the steps to do my master's bidding... The past-life flash was fleeting and vivid, but I knew it to be real. Along with this noisy, teenage version of myself, my inner spirit was growing and developing, too.

# Chapter 6

**M**oon trines Jupiter: *You really are a loving, giving, caring and sharing soul. When you laugh, you roll in the aisles, slap your thighs and guffaw wildly. When you cry, you shed bucket loads of tears, writhe in agony and moan in misery.*

I am hopping forward to the present time. I have been having Bowen Technique to see if it will cure my Restless leg Syndrome. Roessa, who trained with me to become a Yoga teacher, is the Practitioner. I have suffered with this annoying affliction for fifty years! It is not life-threatening or serious in any way, but it does impinge on my rest time and my sleep.

I am convinced that the problem lies in my lower back and hip region. It is associated with the Root Chakra – the wheel of energy which governs our survival, fight or flight. Yoga teaches us that there are seven main wheels of energy which run from the base of the spine to just above the crown of the head. The root chakra, or wheel, is situated at the base of the spine. I attribute the beginning of the Restless leg Syndrome to two injuries, one at the age of twelve and one at the age of thirteen. One was a horse-riding incident. I was riding the young grey, when he spooked and took off at full gallop. He suddenly put down his head and I went over the top. He galloped over me, placing his hoof on my lower back, very briefly. In those days, you got right back on the horse! He was caught, and I re-mounted. The injury was never checked out. Then the second injury was on holiday on the Isle-of-Wight. Dad, Leigh and I were fooling about with a Catamaran. It flipped and cracked me on the lower back. Apparently, I became unconscious, and Dad dragged me to the shore. I seemed to be okay, could walk and so on, so the injury was again never checked out. I believe that the fidgety legs were somehow connected, as they commenced at the age of thirteen.

I remember the very day. We were doing a day-trip from school to Stratford-upon-Avon to see the Royal Shakespeare Company, and I was extremely excited. I was a big fan, and remain so to this day. Indeed, some of my happiest moments are sitting and watching Shakespeare videos with our oldest granddaughter, Lizzie. She is so like me, loves historical dramas, loves the theatre, and loves Audrey Hepburn! It was a fair old journey to Stratford from Weston, so we had to leave at six a.m. and were not back until late. On the way back in the coach, my legs were really uncomfortable and fidgety. The sensation is almost like a spasm – you MUST move them. It is always worse in confined spaces such as theatres, airplanes, coaches and so on. And it is always worse when I am overtired. Unfortunately, I have passed on this nuisance problem to both our children and to Lizzie, our granddaughter. Gemma's is exactly like mine, and you would laugh to see us, both together, with our legs waving in the air! We would do anything to try to relieve it.

Indeed, I have tried everything: cranial osteopathy, reflexology, reiki, shiatsu, acupuncture, aromatherapy, healing, magnesium citrate, extra iron in my diet etc. Of course, being me, I have not gone to the doctor about it! I am convinced that one day I will find a permanent cure. The most relief I ever experienced was when I was doing a head-stand every morning, first thing. I did this for five years, and it really helped. Unfortunately, I then had an eye trauma, 'acute angle glaucoma', so inverting each morning was off the menu.

So, I'm having an interesting time. I'm writing my 'memoirs', which is bringing up all sorts of fascinating stuff, both painful and enlightening, I'm having Bowen Technique, and we have been re-modelling the house. Having the bathrooms replaced was a process on all levels! Definitely it is connected with the first of the Niyamas; SAUCHA. (Please see the introduction for an explanation.)The Niyamas are the second of the Eight Limbs of Yoga. They are known as the 'Do's', or Observances. Saucha means cleansing or purification. Cleansing is taking place through my writing and recall. Renewing the bathrooms is cleansing and is about letting-go. Yoga's message is to let-go, to release. This connects us to the Sacral Chakra, which is represented by the colour orange, according to New Age texts. Orange is said to be the colour of yoga. The seven main wheels of energy, or chakras, run from the base of the spine to just above the crown of the head, as I mentioned before, and the sacral chakra is situated two inches above the base of the spine. It is concerned with creativity and procreation. It is about enjoying living in a physical body, and letting-go. I'm a great believer in laughter, and when you experience a real belly-laugh, that is a terrific release for the sacral chakra.

I have faith in instant healing. I have seen this occur with my yoga students. I stand in awe of what yoga can achieve, and am humbled to be present when healing takes place. I feel that a yoga teacher is like an Indian guide, pointing the way. You offer a buffet, a colourful collection of tools, techniques and philosophies, in the hope that the students will absorb the ones necessary for them. As a yoga teacher, I am eclectic. My explanation is that it is like going into the garden to gather a bouquet of flowers, you take a little of this, and a little of that, until you create your very own offering. Having said that, I do stick firmly to the original teachings of yoga. I believe that all classical yoga practice is based on Patanjali's Eight Limbs and the Bhagavad Gita. I enjoyed being a FRYOG, (FRIENDS OF YOGA SOCIETY), tutor. I trained eighty teachers in Hampshire and am still in touch with a large number of them. Some of the connections made have been very deep.

So, my journey continues and now I am endeavouring to heal my Restless Legs. Wouldn't it be amazing if, having healed my syndrome, the rest of the family were cured too! Yoga is a journey of self-discovery, and I feel like a detective. I am not just fascinated with my students' journeys, but also my own. I always told my student teachers that, when they are teaching, the class time is for the students' growth not their own. We are professionals. Yet there is a definite overlap. Often, if I walk into the hall from the car-park with a student, they will say something which connects with an aspect of my life at that time. I always have a lesson-plan for the week; I always have a theme, but it is a joy to be able to 'fly by the seat of my pants' sometimes! I have an invitation to expand and grow that theme, so that it encompasses the very aspect that we are all facing in our lives right now.

An interesting occurrence is that I plan my class on a Monday morning, and then I might be chatting to another teacher, later in the week, or indeed our daughter, Gemma, (also a yoga teacher,) and we discover that we have been teaching a very similar practice containing the same theme! It is as though the Universe says: "We have a message to get through... give it to the Yoga Teachers. They'll spread the word". I currently see about one hundred people per week. At one time it was closer to three hundred. If all of your students take on board an idea or practise, and then share it with their little gang, lots of people can benefit. Each one goes back into their life, and even if they simply feel better about themselves, that will benefit the planet. I do believe that Yoga Teachers can and do change the world. Gandhi said: "You must be the change that you wish to see in the world." The longer that you practise yoga, the more it makes sense. It is endlessly fascinating. You continue to move down through deeper and deeper layers, shrugging off the illusions and connecting with your inner truth.

I was given the tools that I need for this incarnation. I have two major, and often conflicting, characteristics or motivations. Firstly, I am a People-Pleaser. I like to be liked, I love to be loved, I need to be needed. Secondly, I have a will of iron, and a huge drive to speak the truth – no matter how outrageous, or how provocative that truth may be. It has been, and continues to be, a challenge to keep these two characteristics in balance.

I see why I am here now. Mine has been a long yoga journey. I have been teaching for thirty seven years, and I still love each and every class. The best of what I am sits on the yoga mat. I am still so excited and motivated by progress that new students make. I say to our dog, Rudi, when I leave for work, "I am going to help all those lovely people", and that is, sincerely, what I wish to do. I believe that yoga is a way of life and I have always had enormous enthusiasm for living that life – authentically and totally. I believe that yoga is about service. I have been content to move out into the communities, to teach in different areas and different buildings. My own little yoga room at home, our conservatory, has only been used for teaching the FRYOG Diploma and the Post-Graduate courses.

Stepping down from the Chairmanship, consolidating my classes, moving away from being a Tutor, has freed me up to write. At the age of sixty three, with a retired husband, my life is changing. I must 'let-go' again. I must continue my journey of self-discovery and trust in my process and in my guides.

I recently had an extraordinary and very vivid dream. I was standing at the bottom of the stairs and I was shouting upstairs to someone on the landing. We were having a long and detailed conversation. I realised, after a while, that the person at the top of the stairs was me, too. Writing this book involves living two time-lines concurrently, and can be most disorienting. The dream represents that scenario; the younger Carole is informing and reminding the older Carole. Or is it the other way around?

# Chapter 7

**M**idheaven in Gemini: *Your insatiable curiosity is going to take you to the ends of the earth.*

I return to the age of sixteen or so and the continuing saga of what made me who I am today.

I had settled into a long-term relationship with my boyfriend. He was good-looking, fun and affectionate. He was also intense and passionate about many of his beliefs. He came to my fifteenth birthday party as a swash-buckling pirate! It suited his personality in many ways. I was the Fry's Turkish Delight girl. My mother made me harem trousers out of net curtains! My best friend, Maggie, was Cleopatra. One lad managed to put his hand through a leaded-light window-pane and cut his artery. Fortunately, I had a friend who was excellent at First Aid. She applied pressure and organised for him to get to hospital. It was all rather dramatic, especially since my parents had trusted me, and had gone out. I remember being terribly concerned about cleaning the blood of the floor-tiles in the hall, before my mother returned.

At about the time that I was doing my 'A' levels, we moved again. This time from the oldest house on the hill to the newest. 'The Dell' was very modern, almost Swiss-looking, with a lovely drive and front garden, and a paddock behind. The sitting-room was particularly attractive, as it was a split-level house, and the ceiling was very high. The builder had wanted to paint the ceiling pale pink, and Mum said "No, it should be a deep turquoise." It looked stunning – all wooden floors and rugs.

We took on a goat to eat the grass in the paddock. He was called Sam, and was a real character. He loved Dad, indeed he loved men. He would chase Mum around the garden and bowl her over. She couldn't even hang out her washing! Years later, when our children were young, Tim would delight in shutting Gemma in the paddock, and watch as Sam bore down on her. Her screams would soon bring us all running, and no damage was done.

Dad would feed Sam dog biscuits, and he would stand on his hind-legs to reach them. But if one fell on the ground he wouldn't eat it. He was a very fussy goat. My mother decided after a while that he was lonely, so they borrowed a ewe from the local farmer. He kept his flock in the field next to our paddock. She was called Emma, and Sam was delighted with her. After a while she birthed a lamb, and Mum named her Penny. Each morning Dad would open the gate and let our little group out into the field with all the others. Then, in the evening, he would send our collie, Minty, out into the field to collect them and to bring them home for the night. It was adorable to watch.

At some point, in our new home, my boyfriend and I fell out of favour. Mum, still very much the authoritarian, banned him from the house. Now, I was studying hard at the time, but what we would do was to meet outside the house, where a convenient bench had been placed. 'The Dell' was on a steep hill, Celtic Way, and the bench was to give walkers a break. It became our home. There we would sit, rain or shine; sometimes I would knit or sometimes read. Our neighbours were highly tickled. Pat and Peter would bring us out a tray of tea and biscuits. We became a bit of a local attraction! Anyway, long story short, it became so embarrassing for Mum, (although this had never been our intention,) that she begged us to come back in.

My relationship with this young man lasted for five years, and we did become engaged. It was to have a resounding effect on my life, as it took place at the time when I was considering a career. My parents showed little or no interest in what I planned to do after my 'A' levels. They were viewing it stereo-typically. Their son should, of course, forge a brilliant career; their daughter should, of course, make a brilliant marriage. My mother was of the opinion that it was just as easy to fall in love with a rich boy, as a poor boy! One of my teachers mentioned that I should think of going to Teacher Training College, and I did have a hair-brained idea of going to Newcastle

University to study Psychology. Funnily enough, my career has been teaching, and I use psychology constantly. Said boyfriend was opposed to me going away to University for years, and there was a distinct lack of support or encouragement on the parental front. Finally, I made an extra-ordinary decision, based on a newspaper article. I applied for a beauty therapy course in London. It was a six-month course, and, actually it did me no harm at all. I learned massage, I learned anatomy and physiology, and I developed a great love for London. My boyfriend and I managed a long distance relationship, and my mother was highly tickled by her 'dolly-bird' daughter. The first time I came home, after six weeks away, I was resplendent in a long black wig, the shortest of mini-skirts, and an abundance of false eye-lashes!

The week-ends when I stayed in London, I would walk in to the centre, from the Hostel in Baron's Court, and do the tourist bit. I loved it. I still have a wonderful rush of energy when I approach London. Our son has lived there for nineteen years, and I can fully appreciate why. There is such a buzz, a feeling that you are where it is all happening. When I went back to Weston-super-Mare, I would feel as though I was missing out. It felt such a back-water.

But back I did go, at the end of the six-months. Boyfriend happy, parents happy, me not so sure. Indecisive Piscean? Or dyed in the wool People-Pleaser?

Now, when I look back, I feel that it panned out just the way it was supposed to. I took a job in a Health Clinic as

Manager. I worked for a wonderful osteopath and his Swiss wife. I adored them both. The osteopath would call me in to watch, when he had a particularly interesting case. Many times I saw folk arrive in a wheel-chair, and leave walking. He was a real healer, so experienced and so knowledgeable. He instilled a huge enthusiasm for alternative medicine in me. And his wife was the most amazing masseuse, and such a character. We had a lot of fun working together.

I massaged Jane Russell, while I worked at this clinic. She was such a beautiful and famous actress, and was delightful to be around. She was there with her husband, who clearly adored her. I also met Dave Berry, who was a very popular singer at the time, and who was charming. I was later to encounter another famous actress, Stephanie Powers, who proved to be beautiful inside and out.

My boss and I set about promoting the Clinic, and introducing new treatments. The sauna and massage was very popular, but we wished to add facials, hair-removal, manicures and pedicures. There was a newspaper in Weston known as 'What When and Where in Weston-Super-Mare'! We contacted the paper about doing an article about us, and a journalist duly appeared. Little did he know that he was about to change the course of my life! I showed him around the Clinic and he made lots of notes. He then asked me if I would mind posing for some photographs. He offered that if I would be 'Miss What When and Where', on the front-page of the newspaper, he would do our advertising for free. This deal really appealed to my boss.

So, the reporter sent along a photographer, who was called Cliff. He was one of the nicest guys I ever met. We clicked immediately – he must have been twenty years older than me, had a lovely wife and kids –he was serious about his photography, but had a real sense of humour and a twinkle in his eye. My boss was present throughout the photo shoot, and she loved it. Cliff took a number of photographs around the Clinic, and then said: "How about a picture in the sauna, with a towel wrapped around you, Carole?" I kept my underwear on, under the towel, and the photo was duly taken.

Now, my grand-children would find it hard to believe, in this day of digital cameras, but back then, it took a while for photographs to be developed. At the end of the photo shoot, I had asked Cliff if he would take our wedding photographs, and he had readily agreed. When he brought the results of his work into the Clinic, I was thrilled. I asked if I could hang on to the photographs, as my fiancé was meeting me for lunch and I was excited to show them to him. I was ill-prepared for his response. He was horrified and incredibly jealous! He went maroon in the face. I had always known that he was passionate, but had no idea that he would miss-read this very innocent photography so badly. Well, suffice it to say that I realised, in a flash, that if he could not trust me and could not accept these very chaste images in their correct context, we were ill-suited. I did the whole Jane Austen thing, and threw his engagement ring back at him. It landed in our gravel drive, and I remember him having to stoop down to find it.

I cried a lot that night. My mother said: "Do all your crying tonight, and get up with a smile on your face in the morning."

Now little did I know, at this point, that Cliff the photographer worked with my future husband. He took the photographs in to work, as he was planning to enter some in a competition. He spread them out on the desk and asked Mike which ones he liked. Mike chose two, and asked if he could have a print of one of them. Cliff told him that he was wasting his time, since I was engaged and planning my wedding, but Mike was not daunted. He took the photograph home and put it up on his wall. And so it was that, a couple of months later, we passed one another in a doorway at the local discotheque, and he uttered the best chat-up line ever: "I've got a photograph of you on my bedroom wall".

Having been engaged and having decided that it was not much fun, I was busy 'playing the field'. I believe this was the happiest time of my mother's life! She loved all these young men dancing attendance on her daughter, and the fact that I was getting dressed-up and going out and having a good time. Mike became one of my four or five regular escorts. This was a very happy time of my life, too. Mike was not, and is not, a jealous type. He was perfectly happy to date me when I was free. It was quite a novelty for me, after my family and previous boy-friend, to find someone who did not want to change me or to control me.

I had a vividly clear idea of what I did not want in a husband. I did not want someone like my father, and I did not want someone like my brother. And now I did not want someone like my previous fiancé. I wanted an easy-going person with a keen sense of humour. I wanted a guy who would listen to me. I wanted a husband who had the same values and the same outlook on life as me. Yes, I was looking for Mr. Perfect! Mike looked nice and was nice. I believe now that putting my photograph up on his wall was Cosmic Ordering.

We began to date just after New Year, and I remember our first date clearly. I was in my bedroom, getting ready, when I saw a red sports car whizz by in the distance. (I could see Roman Road from my window.) A few minutes later, it whizzed by again and then again. I was witnessing one of Mike's eternal characteristics! He is early for everything... I always tell him that he will be early for his own funeral! I had been brought up to be punctual, he is obsessively early.

By Valentine's Day, I would be out with someone else and would find myself thinking about Mike. He plucked up the courage to go into a florist, (having driven around the block three times), and sent me a massive bouquet of flowers on February 14th. My mother phoned me at work to tell me it had arrived, and I asked her to read the card and to tell me who it was from. The words on the card were very sweet, and it dawned on me that we were heading for a more serious relationship.

Mike listened to me. He could remember what perfume I had been wearing on which occasion, he could remember all my anecdotes from the Clinic, he laughed at all my jokes. We had a lot of fun together. (It is our sense of humour which has held us together for forty-three years.)

By Easter, he was staying over with us, and by May we were making plans to move to London.

It was all moving a bit fast for Mike's parents. They wanted him to marry a quiet little girl, who would join the W.I. and make her own marmalade. I was not that girl. In all fairness, it must be a bit of shock to hear your son talk of spending the rest of his life with his pin-up! His father, after meeting me for the first time said: "I suppose she can only prepare prawn cocktails?" Mike replied: "I seriously doubt that she can even do that!"

To my utter amazement, my mother became our champion. She really liked Mike. They got on like a house on fire. Maybe it was because they were both Leos... I don't know, but they certainly gelled. She stood up for us, against the other three parents, and, despite the fact that I was not going to marry the rich, young man she had planned for me, she was very supportive of my choice.

Indeed, it is down to Mum that we did in fact get married. I was all for 'living in sin', as it was known in those days. Mum took me quietly to one side and said: "Think of your family present and your family future, and do get married". Mike managed to get down on one knee, in his Austin Healey Sprite, (no mean feat!) and, when I said 'yes', he drove through the town jubilant. He had the top down, and cruised along the sea-front, pounding on the door of the car and announcing loudly to anyone who cared to listen that we were getting married!

We set the date for August 30th, mainly because Mike's mother said we should wait for September! Mike was an only child, and I very soon realised that, if we were to have any life at all, we would have to move away. I loved London, and he had always wanted to live there. By the end of May I had found a job in Baker Street, and moved back to the city. I left Mike and Mum planning an unusual wedding in Somerset. She was an absolute star. She recognised that we were good for one another.

Our wedding was delightful. I wore a micro-mini dress, on which I had sewn small pink 'Carol' roses. We were married in the Registry Office, both of us feeling that we were agnostic, at the time. We knew the registrar, Ivy, so she organised the wedding late, at five thirty. When Mike put on my ring, he was nervous and shaky, and he knocked off my false nail. It pinged up in the air, and everyone watched its descent with great amusement! We drove along the sea-front towards the Grand Atlantic Hotel for the reception, and Mike's mates stood on the sea-wall and waved as we passed. Dad had surpassed himself with the reception, which was brilliant, and, since we couldn't afford a honeymoon, even treated us to our wedding night in the hotel.

I was always into co-ordination. We pretended that we were going to Paris for our honeymoon, and duly went upstairs to change. I had a very pretty French navy dress, which was piped with red. With this I had a red hat and red shoes. I even changed my watch-strap! Mike had worn a light grey suit to our wedding, and, to my mother's horror, grey suede shoes. He had a navy suit and a navy tie and handkerchief, with a red spot, to 'go away'. He flatly refused to change his grey socks to the navy ones. I met his stubborn streak, for the first time!

We went downstairs, with our empty suit-cases, to a tumultuous send-off. Promptly left the suit-cases in the foyer, drove round the block, and re-entered through the staff door. Then we went back upstairs and watched all our friends and family leaving. Great fun. Our daughter was to repeat the family tradition on her first wedding.

Mike's parents paid off the loan he had on his sports car, and his dear Grandad gave us the first month's rent on our furnished flat in Camden Town. Our life as a married couple had begun.

So many lessons were coming my way! I was only twenty years old, and Mike was only twenty three. Yet we set off into our adventure with a light step, and an incredible innocence. It was 1969, and it felt like anything was possible in the Sixties. We were high on life and high on love. And, for the first time in my life, my Mum and I were on the same page!

# Chapter 8

Mercury in the Sixth House: *You are the sort of person who has a very active mental life. Most of the various aspects of your personality, even down to the deepest emotions, come under your close scrutiny. To you, argument is a one-sided thing. You simply take so long to make your point that the other person loses interest! You can accept most points of view, too!*

We had a lovely, one-bedroom flat in Camden Square. It was a great place for young people, convenient for all modes of transport, and we often walked into the West End of an evening. My job, in a clinic, was shift-work. I worked one week for six days, nine a.m. till two p.m. and then the second week for five days, two p.m. till nine p.m. The week when I was working late, Mike and I met in the Park for lunch. We shared our love of London, our sense of humour, and a very positive outlook on life in general, and our life in particular. The first year was hard, though, as we both had a lot of growing-up to do. I had never even boiled an egg! My mother was a very capable house-keeper, and really did not want me in the kitchen when she was preparing a meal. Plus she felt strongly that I would do enough of that after marriage. At school I had not been interested in the Domestic Science subjects, and was thus ill-equipped for the practical aspects of running a home. I remember my first attempts at pancakes. Mike sat with salt and pepper, and lemon and sugar. If it turned out like an omelette, he used the salt and pepper, and if it succeeded in being a pancake, he could use the lemon and sugar! I eventually achieved one signature dish, which I could serve for friends and visiting family. In reality, Mike and I learned to cook together. He loved curries in particular.

At the end of the first year, Mike was to utter the immortal words: "Do you think we could dilute the affection a little?" He had come from an undemonstrative family. If his mother experienced an emotion, she took a pill immediately to stop it. They were not into hugging, in fact every time I met them, we would do this rather strange dance – shall we or shan't we hug? My family were volatile, and definitely dysfunctional, but we did always greet one another affectionately. Mike was not used to being tactile. It was a little like Tom Sellick, who says in 'Three Men and a Baby': "I'm fine with affection, as long as it is disguised as sex!"

So we set about rescuing a cat and scoured the local press. We saw an advertisement for a 'staid lady cat'! It was, of course a typing error, and should have read 'spayed lady cat'. Tammy was in Hampstead Heath, and had been rescued by a Cat Protection organisation. She was neatly dressed in black and white, and we instantly fell in love with her. We were duly checked out, and were allowed to adopt her. Tammy was about five years old at the time, and lived happily with us until she was nineteen. She even moved to America with us. She was anything but staid! She would carry Mike's socks around with her, and talk to them, as though they were her kittens. And she loved curries! Every time that Mike cooked a curry, she would rub around his ankles yowling, (she had a cry like a Siamese cat,) and would beg for her own portion. I became convinced that she had first lived with an impoverished artist or writer, who lived on take-away curries.

Each morning, Mike would sit Tammy on the kitchen chair by the window, so that she could wave him off as he went to work!

We both changed jobs. I took a job in the Daily Express in Fleet Street as a tele-ad canvasser. (Gosh! That toughened me up!) Each evening I brought home the newspaper, and Mike found an advert for an IBM engineer. He applied immediately, got an interview and was taken on. This career move was to change our lives; he did incredibly well, and they even used him on their recruitment adverts in the major newspapers.

With Mike's increase in salary, he became convinced that we should own a property instead of renting. We could only afford £4,500 pounds, so our choice was limited. Much as we would have loved to have stayed in Camden, we could not afford the prices. We found a

Victorian cottage in South Norwood. It was one hundred and fifty years old, and its walls were about two foot thick. It was opposite a lorry park, two doors away from a betting shop, and three doors away from a topless a-go-go pub! My father was utterly horrified! We bought it, nonetheless, and after two years in our lovely flat we moved.

Tammy took well to her new home, which had a tiny garden at the back, and a tinier garden in the front. It was a terraced house, and our neighbours were very interesting. On one side we had an Irish couple. The husband regularly got drunk and, having gone out without his key, would knock on our door, stagger down our hall to the back-garden, and then precariously climb the fence into his own. On the other side, we had a lovely family from Pakistan. Both parents worked full-time, and their children would come knocking to ask for lunch money, since their parents had omitted to leave them any. Further along the road, there was the most delightful old couple. They were Londoners and used to rescue the retired racing greyhounds. They still had a bath hanging in the kitchen, and would take it down and fill it once a week. We have always loved Londoners. They are so friendly and helpful. We had umpteen examples of this when we were in the flat. Young men would help me carry my groceries home, guys would push Mike's car when it would not start, and folk would welcome you under their umbrella at the bus stop. I only have one seedy story to tell. One morning, at the bus stop, a guy opened his raincoat and flashed me. It struck me as being hilariously funny, and my amusement rather 'deflated' him!

In our Victorian cottage, the third bedroom had been converted into a bathroom, and Mike decided to bring the outside loo into the house. He built a somewhat make-shift utility room and now we had a downstairs toilet.

Mike also decided that, since we were now buying our own house and had a second bedroom, it was time to start a family. He longed to be a daddy. Whilst I definitely wanted children, I was not convinced that I was quite ready. I was only twenty two, and had serious misgivings about bringing another soul into this turbulent world of ours. Was I up to the job of raising another human being? Was I up to the job of guiding another soul? It was not the practical details of changing nappies, and feeding which concerned me, although I had never been around babies and had not the first clue, but it was more the philosophical issues. If I was to be a mother, I really wanted to be a good one. Was I ready?

I was always interested in Astrology. Mike is a Leo, like my mother. I was regularly attracted to Leos; they tend to be outgoing and confident, and have a very clear idea about where they are heading. I am a Pisces, and can be indecisive. My two fishes do swim in opposite directions, and I can invariably see both sides of any argument. I do have Virgo rising, and many people take me as a Virgo when we first meet. I like neatness and order. Mike and I learned, early in our relationship, that his fire (Leo is a fire sign) could boil away my water (Pisces is a water sign), and my water could dowse his flames. I could easily dampen his enthusiasm, and he could easily burn through my sensitivity. We learned to give one another space at crucial moments, but we did not always get it right. We still don't. It is a constant balancing act, and is dynamic. People meeting us for the first time tend to believe that I am the noisy, confident one and that Mike is laid back and easy going. This does not prove to be true on longer acquaintance. Mike did not grow up with emotions, remember. The first time I stamped my feet up and down and threw a temper, he burst out laughing! I discovered that it is very difficult to have a row on your own. His attitude was always: 'If it aint broke, don't fix it.' This is fine, but he never did think that anything between us was ever broken, and sometimes I had a different opinion. I was interested in the dynamics of relationships, I was interested in growth, and I was certainly interested in expressing my opinions and being heard. Indeed, it was this very characteristic in Mike that had really made me decide that he was 'the one'. Initially, he listened to me and remembered what I said. It was wonderful. I really felt heard, for the first time in my life. Sadly, as soon as we were married, this amazing trait disappeared. I am sure I am not the first wife to be disappointed by this phenomenon! A friend of ours, Ron, once summed it up like this: "You do not chase a bus that you have already caught!" Mike soon learnt that I am pretty good natured, and that if he waited a little while, normal service would be resumed. And he usually got his own way, I have to say. Regardless of my misgivings, we began to try for a baby.

One decision that I made, at this point, I have never regretted. I wanted a Gemini boy, and a Pisces girl. I got them!

What was I here for at this pivotal time in my life? I was here to learn about becoming a house-holder. Yogis (people who practise yoga,) believe that the first twenty-five years are for education, the second twenty-five years are about being a house-holder and raising your family, in the third twenty-five years you become a teacher, and in the last twenty-five a hermit. I was busy learning about being a house-holder and was soon to experience motherhood.

# *Chapter 9*

Sun squares Uranus: *You won't take either no or yes for an answer. It makes you both unbearable and unbeatable! People either love or hate you. Do you care? No! You know well that all opinions (even your own) are trivial in the end.*

We had adopted a small black and white kitten from a lovely man who was a client of the Clinic in Gerard Street, where I was working. A cat had birthed two kittens in his garage, and my French friend, Giselle, took the boy, while we took the girl. Giselle called hers 'Scooby-Doo', and ours was called Samantha. Tammy took to Mamfi as though she was her own baby, and they became so close, absolutely inseparable. We would take the two cats with us when we went home to Somerset to visit our folks. We did not even put them in boxes; Tammy happily travelled draped around Mike's neck, as he drove. When we arrived at my parents' house, our two would mix with their three cats and two dogs. They never showed any interest in straying.

My first pregnancy, with our son, Tim, was quite a revelation to me. My parents were thrilled to bits. Everyone tells me that it is different when your daughter is pregnant, as opposed to your daughter-in-law. Mum and Dad were already the proud grandparents of Brett and Calum, but they were incredibly excited at the prospect of our baby's arrival. Mum was most supportive, and sympathetic, as I stumbled my way through the first horribly sick three months. I could not stand to cook, any food smells set the nausea off, and yet I was ravenously hungry. I felt as though I had been taken over by an alien! This was, of course, my first pregnancy, so I had nothing to compare it with. I was aware that I was carrying a very strong spirit, and was still unsure as to whether I was 'up to the job'. It seemed such an enormous step, which Mike was very happily taking in his stride, and which I viewed with a variety of different emotions. I had always watched my weight, but after the first trimester, my emotional swings had become so extreme, that I threw caution to the winds and ate everything in sight! Pickled onions became a particular passion. I gained a lot of weight, and although everyone told me that I was blooming, I felt like a blob.

One gentleman who attended the Clinic, confided in me how beautiful he found pregnant women. He told me that his wife was not particularly good-looking, but that she was stunning when pregnant. I asked how many children they had and, with a wry grin, he replied: "Six!"

At this already somewhat turbulent time, my brother phoned to ask if we would take on a German Shepherd, who was desperate for a home. We had both grown up with Alsatians, so without too much consideration, we agreed. Enter Sabre, who turned out to be a very troubled and unpredictable dog indeed.

Mike found himself faced with the unenviable task of dealing with an incredibly volatile and ever-growing wife, a total nut-case of a dog, two delightful cats and an aged Victorian Cottage, badly in need of repair. Add to this the fact that we had no idea how we were going to manage on just one salary, and be able to buy all the necessary equipment for a new-born.

Sadly, all attempts to rehabilitate Sabre were in vain. After he had completely destroyed our home and our peace of mind, the vet proclaimed that it would be impossible to keep him with a baby in the house. He was far too unpredictable, and was capable of violent behaviour. He recommended that we had him put down. So, so reluctantly we had to agree, and then cried for twenty-four hours solidly. Poor Sabre.

My mother arrived unexpectedly one day, catching me on my hands and knees scrubbing the kitchen floor. I was eight months pregnant and absolutely enormous. She was horrified to discover that we had done nothing to create a nursery out of our spare bedroom, and she took Mike to task immediately. In a flash she had him 'by the ear', and marched him down the road to buy a chest of drawers for the baby clothes. She bought the cot and the bedding; Mike's parents were coerced into buying the pram; miraculously we were ready for the event.

I had a lovely young doctor, and a pretty young Health Visitor in South Norwood. They explained that fathers were not allowed in to see the birth at that time, but that some dads showed great initiative, grabbed a white gown and mask, and slipped into the birthing room unnoticed. I was to be in hospital for twelve days after the birth; how things have changed.

I went into labour and off we rushed to Mayday Hospital in Croydon. As is often the case with first babies, the labour was slow to establish, and was stretched over a period of thirty-seven hours. Eventually, Tim was born on his due date at exactly twelve midday! Bullseye. His birth was attended by an elderly, strict and fore-boding obstetrician, and four others, all of different nationalities. It was definitely a multi-cultural event, which I loved. The very English obstetrician, though, demonstrated such authority, that Mike was far too daunted to attempt to sneak into the room. We had a scare at the end of the birth; the cord was wrapped around Tim's neck. They had to cut me to rescue the baby, who appeared blue in the face and distressed. The gorgeous young nurse plopped him down on to my chest, (so important, that bonding moment,) and then they whisked him off to Intensive Care. I fell asleep immediately, and was woken by the young man who had come to stitch me up.

I discovered, much later, on looking in the mirror, that I had burst every blood vessel in my face from pushing so hard. I looked as though I had a bad case of the measles! When the Matron came around, I nervously asked: "Was this permanent?" I was firmly reprimanded, and told that even if it was, I should be very grateful. I had a healthy son and should be only concerned with that.

Mike was like a dog with two tails! Tim was born on June 2nd, and one of Mike's first comments was: "Don't forget Father's Day". He counted his fingers and toes, pronounced him to be the most perfect baby ever, and drove on home in a mist of euphoria. The nurses and I had then the interesting task of teaching Baby Tim to suck. Breast-feeding was tricky to establish, and he developed colic and then, later, projectile vomiting.

In those days, they gave you three nights sleep, taking the baby off into the nursery. I had read that mothers only wake to their own baby's cry, which I found rather far-fetched. However, during the first rather terrifying night, with my new baby beside me, I awoke to his cry. I fed him, changed his nappy, and put him back into his cot. In the morning when I woke, I asked the other six mothers in the ward if their babies had slept through the night. No, all the babes had woken, but I had only heard Tim. This fact made a huge impact on me. In a flash I knew that we were psychically connected. I felt a wave of enormous love for this little scrap of humanity; I recognised that he was my 'raison d'etre'. I had always asked: "Why am I here?" Now I knew. I was here to look after Tim. Immediately, I wanted to go through the whole pregnancy again, without all the misgivings. Or to immediately have another baby, and do it 'right' this time. I set about loving, nurturing and protecting this beautiful being, our son.

We gave him a big name: Timothy Giles Kerton. I was given the very valid piece of advice, shout the name down the garden path and see how it sounds. It sounded great to shout 'Tim'.

My mother bonded with him as though they had shared many life-times together. (As I am sure they have.) He was her most beloved grandchild, always. She bought me a new dress, to come home from the hospital, cut out the size fourteen label, and sewed in a size ten! Mike proclaimed that it was nice to see my ankles again.

We answered an advert for a collie puppy, and brought home Katie. She was the niece of the Black and White collie on 'Blue Peter', and was just beautiful. She chose her pack-leader immediately, Mike, and adored Baby Tim, and the two cats. We had bought a second-hand playpen, and alternated between putting the baby into it, and putting the puppy into it. When Tim was inside, Katie would reach in, grab the toe of his baby-grow, and drag him to the edge to play with him.

Tim was asleep in his cot upstairs one day, when I decided to paint the door of the downstairs loo orange. When I heard the baby wake, I downed tools and went to get him. Arriving back into the kitchen I was astonished to see Samantha, our black and white cat, mincing down the garden path with an orange circle on her backside. She had sat on the top of the tin of paint! Strange to tell, I removed the paint with white spirit, her fur fell out in a circle, and every year on the same date the fur would fall out again.

We were SO hard up. Each Saturday morning, Mike would sweep up our tiny front garden. Oftentimes he would find an envelope, carelessly tossed over our fence, with money left in it from the Betting-Office. We were thrilled; fish and chips that night!

Mike was working very hard for IBM; he became a very efficient trouble-shooter. Each time he licked a territory into order, they would move him to another one. Still, he managed to leave early, work briskly and to arrive home in time to give Tim his bath and put him to bed. Tim was the most adorable baby, interested in everything, very responsive.

After eighteen months in our Victorian Cottage, Mike's nightmares about the roof falling in became so frequent, that we decided to put it on the market. He had been promoted and we could afford more on the mortgage. We were so fortunate. Property prices were on the rise, and we sold the house for twice what it had cost. We bought a lovely little three bedroom terraced house in Carshalton, surrounded by other young families. We were making our way up the ladder.

When we moved in, I was prepared to keep the cats in for ten days. Mike over-rode my decision, stating that they were completely used to travelling up and down to Somerset, so were unlikely to get lost. This proved not to be the case. Samantha went missing immediately. I was utterly distraught, spent hours walking the streets, calling her name, and put up notices on all of the lampposts. It felt as though I had to, in some way, pay for my good fortune. As though being lucky enough to move to a lovely little house, in a lovely area, was not my due, unless I gave up something else which was precious to me. Nine days went by and I was becoming ever more desperate. Now, you will remember that I was an Agnostic, but I decided to talk to God. I made a bargain with him: "I will believe in you, and I will serve, if you will bring Mamfi home safe and sound." The following day, our neighbours from two doors away found our kitten under their floorboards. They had built on a new kitchen, and a hole had been left. Samantha had crawled inside, and somehow managed to survive. We rejoiced, and always after that I kept the cats in for ten days when we moved. And always after that I believed in a Supreme Being, in God.

Tim was the most gorgeous eleven month baby when we decided it was time for another one. In my baby book, which I followed religiously, it said: "Don't leave it too long before you give your baby a play-mate." We asked my parents to babysit for the week-end, and off we went to Paris for a romantic break. I did not actually conceive then, but I 'knew' for sure exactly when I did. At six weeks pregnant I was sewing baby nighties. Mike thought I was crazy, but I knew a baby was growing inside me.

This pregnancy was very different. I did not feel that I had been taken over by an alien! (I wonder now if that was to do with the sex of the baby. Perhaps the female baby was more in tune with my feminine energy.) I was a little nauseous, but that stopped dead on twelve weeks. I carried 'tidily' as my Welsh mother was to say. You could not tell that I was pregnant from the back, and I only put on one stone and a half, in total. A good friend of mine had just birthed her second daughter, and she lent me all her beautiful maternity clothes. (Rather different from my first pregnancy when I had made dresses out of curtains!) When we went to Somerset, to my parents, for Christmas I was six months pregnant and absolutely blooming. Tim had proved to me that I could 'do' this motherhood business, and I was excited to increase our family. I was confident.

I had 'ordered' a Pisces daughter, having already achieved our Gemini son. Mike had been given an award from IBM and was to go to Majorca for several days. The day he was to leave was the day after the baby's due date, and I had rather wondered if he would cancel the trip. My mother came to stay, so that she could look after her beloved Tim. She cooked me a beautiful meal and opened a bottle of Mateus Rose. We had been playing with little Tim in the hall. We had built tunnels with books, and Tim was brumming his cars through them. He was always a comedian, and Mum and I were in fits over his antics. I thought I had wet myself, I was laughing so much, but no, my waters had broken. Mum and Mike were desperate to get me straight to the Cottage Hospital, but I was adamant that I was going to eat my lovely meal first. I did not want to be hanging around in the hospital, as I had done with Tim's birth, and now that the moment had come to part from him, I felt bereft. The contractions were speeding up, and I can still remember Tim's dear little face at the window, waving, when we left.

Now, just as soon as we got to the hospital, the contractions stopped. The young nurse recommended that my husband went home, since nothing was happening yet. There were two staff members on duty in the little Maternity Hospital; a nurse and a Sister. They were run off their feet. They delivered ten babies that night. As soon as Mike left, my contractions came thick and fast. It was by now about midnight. The nurse did find a moment to call home for me, but there was no answer. You will remember that my mother was a deep sleeper, well so was my husband!

The two staff members popped in when they could, which was not often. I rubbed my own back. I had no pain killers, no gas and air, which was the way that I wanted it. There was just me and my baby, trying to be born. At three-thirty a.m the nurse popped her head around the door and asked if I needed the loo. I went in on my own, and locked the door. By the time I re-emerged, it was evident that the birth was imminent. The Sister took me to the birthing room, told me to roll on to my side (so very different to the stirrups of Tim's birth! Clearly a man had invented those!) and, just as our daughter emerged, I asked the super nice Sister if she was a Pisces. She was! Our baby was born on the last day to be a Piscean, and there were three Pisces in the room at the time. I always say that she was 'thrice blessed'. (Some may say that she was thrice cursed!)

At that moment, the nurse was calling for help with a difficult birth. There was not time for checking and

93

cleaning. In fact, I offered to walk back to my room. This was not allowed, but I was thrown, unceremoniously into a wheel-chair, baby roughly wrapped and thrust into my arms, and returned to my room with a phone. It was all really amusing, and lovely, and I just felt enormous compassion and camaraderie with the lass in the next room, giving birth. I phoned my home number, thrilled to bits to have a little girl to go with our little boy. The phone rang fifty times! I counted, thinking that if no-one came on the fiftieth ring, I would phone my Dad. A breathless Mike answered saying: "I came as soon as I heard it"! What was rather sad was that he had missed out on seeing one of his children born. Between Tim's birth and twenty one months later, it had become common practise to have Dads in the birthing room.

Mike arrived shortly afterwards, having put Katie in the back of the car. He looked adoringly at our new baby, and said: "She's a little gem – we'll call her Gemma." My mother had been hankering after a granddaughter called Gemma for years. She had petitioned my sister-in-law through her three pregnancies, but Meg had three boys. I had never been particularly keen on the name, I felt that it sounded like Gamma rays, but exhausted by the birth, I put up no resistance. She could have been called: 'Number Two' as far as I was concerned right then! I was out-voted by my husband and my mother, as often happened, and how right they were. She is a little gem, and no other name would have suited her. I popped 'Louise' in later, for a middle name.

Mike walked our dog, Katie, on the way home, and then left for the Airport. He was later to say that I had a very easy birth on Gemma, but since he was missing for the birth and the after-birth pains, he was not an authority! He was roundly congratulated on becoming a daddy again; his colleagues were most admiring that he had continued with his IBM trip, three hours after his baby was born. Oh Dear! He had become a company man!

I fell asleep when Mike left, and when I woke I looked out at the most perfect scene. There was a beautiful old oak tree, with a ring of daffodils at its base. Three squirrels were playing around in the flowers. Since I had arrived at the Hospital in the dark, I had no idea what was outside the window. For a moment, I thought I had died and gone to heaven! Whenever I see daffodils I think of Gemma.

My poor mum walked the couple of miles uphill to the hospital each afternoon, with Tim in the push-chair. Tim was so handsome, with white blond hair, a little navy jacket and a navy hat with white bobbles. He disliked anything being broken, and if Mum passed a broken down fence on the way, he would say: "Bang!"

Gemma, on the other hand, had jet black hair and emerged with a tan. One nurse asked me if they had two different fathers! The difference between the babies did not stop there. Gem mastered this breast-feeding malarkey immediately. She was an easy baby, as I had been.

Mum knitted her the most adorable little cardigan; it was in peach with a striped front. One of the nurses was appalled, saying that babies should only be dressed in white, but even to this day Gem looks better in bright colours. She wore her cardigan home. So different from Baby Tim – as a very inexperienced, novice mother, I had bought a nought to six months babygrow to take him home from the hospital! It drowned the poor little chap!

It was extra-ordinary arriving home with our new family member. I had left my 'baby', Tim, and when I returned home he was a great big child. At almost two, he was very lively and demanding, and prone to tantrums. I can see now that Tim would have been very happy to have been an only child. My baby book got it wrong; he was not in need of a sibling, a playmate. We did all the right things to introduce Baby Gemma. She bought him a yellow Tonka truck, and he was delighted with that. But he never was keen on this little invader; this intruder into his neat life. He adopted the habit of calling me "Tim's mummy", and would call this up the stairs. Similarly, it was "Tim's daddy" and "Tim's Nana". The inference was that we were his, and not Gemma's. When the baby was just two weeks old, we had just returned from the shops and the phone rang. It was my mother and I settled down to have a chat. Then I heard the awful sound of the baby choking. I dropped the phone, ran into the dining-room, where Tim was innocently eating his bag of sweets. I realised that he had popped one into Gemma's mouth. Immediately, I grabbed her by the heels, turned her upside down, and smacked her on the back. The sweet shot out of her mouth and all was well. Except that, all this time, I had been yelling at Tim: "Don't you ever do that again! You nearly killed her! What are you thinking about?" Poor little boy. Needless to say, he never did share his sweets with her again. He was cured of any such urge for life! Indeed, when they were older, my mother would buy a handful of chocolate bars, and say to Tim: "You choose first, Tim, as you are the oldest." Tim would always reply: "I'll have Gemma's"!

I told them the story of Gemma's birth when they were older, too. I said that it was close run event, that Gem was nearly born down the toilet. Gemma looked at me, all big innocent green eyes, and said: "If I had been born down the toilet, Mummy, would you have flushed it?" "Of course not, Darling", I immediately reassured her. And Tim said: "I would have"! I was never quite sure whether he meant it or not.

There were to be two occasions which reassured me that, despite the fact that clearly Tim would have preferred life without a small sister, he did have the correct values and instincts. When Gemma started Infants School in Chiswell Green, St.Albans, Tim completely blanked her. He would have nothing to do with her at all. But a day came when a boy picked on her in the playground. From out of nowhere came Tim, two years older and fists at the ready! Gemma's teacher was later to say that she did not even know that Gem had a brother in the school. My reply was: "Well, now you do!"

The second occasion was when we were in Nassau. We were living in Kentucky at the time, and used to fit in a holiday on the way home to England each year. The sea was exceedingly lively, and we would take the children into the waves, holding tightly on to their hands. Mike was Tim's buddy, and I was Gem's. We had been into the sea and had a lot of fun, and then returned to the shore. I sat in meditation posture, with my eyes closed, breathing in the prana (the life-force or life-giving energy.) Gemma was busy making sand-castles on the edge of the water. Suddenly, a huge wave came in, scooped Gem up and took her out to sea. She began screaming, and we all rushed to her aid, but Tim got their first. He rescued her, quite heroically, and could never deny that he loved her after that.

So, at the time when I brought Baby Gemma home from the Hospital, Mike's career was taking off. He was working very long hours. No more getting home to bath Tim before bedtime. Tim missed him a lot. He was a Daddy's boy, and Gem was a Mummy's girl. Our health visitor would laugh when she came. I had to tie our dog, Katie, to the washing-line on a long lead, as she was an escape artist. I would just get settled down to breast-feed the baby, when Katie would trip Tim up, and he would land with a bump. Top pulled over baby, I would have to rush out and pick him up. It's a wonder she thrived at all! She never did get a meal in peace.

Tim was medically hyper-active. He was quite a handful, and was accident prone. I used to say that Tim was a demon all day, but an angel all night, and Gemma was an angel all day, but a demon all night. She did not sleep through the night until she was five and a half years old. We disobeyed all the rules, and found that the only way we could get any sleep at all was to have her between us in bed. I was utterly exhausted. Then I found YOGA.

A friend of mine called Eunice used to join Adult Education classes to have an evening away from her two boys. She told me that she was going to a yoga class and I said: "Me too". Little did I know how this decision would completely change my life.

I fell in love with the yoga teacher immediately. She was called Lilla Beksinska, and she had the most delightful accent. My first class felt like coming home, on the most profound level. Lying on the yoga mat for the first time, I connected with my Inner Spirit and felt whole.

Lilla allowed me to go to as many of her classes as I could, each week. I realised immediately, as a young parent, how my coping skills improved. Mike noticed how much more balanced I became. He said that, up until that time, he never knew what he was coming home to. Would I be joyful and euphoric? Or would I be in the depths of despair? Yoga demonstrated to me the line of contentment: I could go up to happiness, but then return to the line of contentment; I could go down to depression, but then return to the line of contentment. I can still remember the day when I spent more time in my 'centre' than out of it. There had been a gradual shift. At first, when a situation would occur, I would react in my normal emotional way, and then later think: "Ah... I should have used my yoga." Then I would be in the middle of the situation, and I would think: "Ah... now I need to use my yoga". Eventually, I could anticipate the situations occurring, and could connect with my centre and engage my yoga skills. Yoga gave me the tools to feel grounded and inwardly strong. (I call this being centred.)

One day, Lilla asked if anyone was interested in becoming a yoga teacher. My hand went up, of its own volition. My yoga class ceased to be a hobby and became my vocation.

Lilla took me under her wing. She was very generous with her time and her knowledge. I adored her. She booked us into a course, where each week we discovered a different yoga, a different expert. The first week we went to a workshop with Ken Thompson. Ken is very well known in yoga circles. He, along with Wilfred Clark, set up the British Wheel of Yoga. Another yoga teacher, who was a friend of Lilla's, came with us. I would drive to Lilla's house, and sit in the back of the car, and then we would pick up Eileen, who sat in the front. At the end of the workshop, we would return to Lilla's house, dropping Eileen off on the way. Thus the front seat was vacant. One time, Lilla began to talk to 'someone' in the front seat. It was a monk. It all felt completely natural at the time. I could see the monk and I could hear their wonderful, spiritual conversation. I was enthralled. But when we stopped in Lilla's drive, I must admit I ran full pelt back to my car and could not wait to get home!

Home-life was certainly more manageable once I found yoga. Gem adjusted to me going out in the evenings, and was content for Daddy to put her to bed. Tim, wise beyond his years, began to alter his diet. He cut out dairy, and his metabolism settled down. I began to listen to my body, and to trust in the wisdom of the children's bodies too. Tim developed an eye problem at this time, and I was to lose my faith in the medical profession.

I had a squint as a small child. At two and a half, Tim developed one too. His eye turned in quite badly. He needed to wear glasses and we began attending the Eye Clinic at the local hospital. The Specialist we saw was somewhat austere, in a good mood, and absolutely terrifying, in a bad mood. She slapped a patch on Tim's 'good eye' and instructed me not to contact her for the next six weeks. I was to go away and to change the patch each day. I remember scooping up Baby Gemma as I left the hospital room, and a nurse said to me: "You have picked up the wrong child. That little boy is blind right now."

Tim reacted very badly to the patching routine. I used to have to wrestle him to the floor practically, and hold him down to change his patch. We all went around the house wearing patches, and all the teddy-bears sported patches, too. Bless him. We read lots of stories about pirates, with patches over their eyes, and to this day he still loves pirates! After ten days I noticed that the other eye had developed a squint; it had moved from one eye to the other. Unsure about how to proceed, and severely daunted by the Specialist, I consulted Mike. He said that since I had received very clear instructions from the medical expert, I should adhere to them. I should continue patching until the six weeks was over. Still undecided, I consulted my other main advisor, my mum. She echoed what Mike had said. We all went through the hell of the next month, and when I returned for my hospital appointment, the Specialist said: "You stupid mother! You should have phoned me immediately!" I learnt a big lesson. I have never taken a medical opinion for gospel since. I query everything. I have a healthy respect for their opinions and training, but a more healthy respect for my own intuition and research skills.

So, what was I learning at this really important time of my life? I was learning self-reliance. I found my way home to yoga. I grew up and matured, becoming a young mother with responsibilities. I discovered the 'light and shade'; I played with the children all day long, but also needed to discipline them and to take care of their greater good. I learned to question the established medical profession. My inclination towards the alternative therapies became more established. Most importantly, I discovered Spirituality. I began to deepen my relationship with the Supreme Being, God. Yoga was opening so many doors for me, and for my family.

# Chapter 10

The Romantic Pisces: *"There's a somebody I'm longing to see, I hope that he turns out to be... Someone to watch over me."* There is something unmistakably Piscean about the sentiment of this lovely Gershwin song. Regardless of your love-life, you already have someone to watch over you. A guardian angel follows the steps of every Piscean. All your close relationships are founded on the basis of caring and sharing.

The peace that I discovered in the yoga class was deep and all embracing. I became evangelical about yoga practice, and remain so to this day. Shadowing Lilla was an absolute delight. She wove a web of magic around her groups; creating a cocoon of peace, love and joy. I studied her approach, and absorbed her wisdoms. She asked me to assist her, and then to substitute for her. When I taught her classes in rooms that I had not visited before, I would arrive early and try to 'feel' where she normally sat to teach. Nine times out of ten I was right. It's a curious aspect of yoga classes that everyone heads for the same space each week. That patch of floor becomes your little home! Sometimes there is a practical reason for this: being able to hear the teacher, or being able to see the teacher, or being close to your friend. But oftentimes it is simply habit and security.

We had lived in our little three bedroom house in Carshalton, Surrey, for four and a half years. I had nagged Mike to knock down the wall between the kitchen and the dining-room, endlessly. He was always going to get around to it, so one day I checked it all out and began the demolition myself! He came home to a heap of rubble, and realised that I meant business! It made a big difference for a while, but still we outgrew the tiny house. I asked Mike to check out with his Manager to see if there were any promotions in the offing, which could mean a move. No, there was nothing on the horizon, so I began looking at other properties. We wanted to move to the best local areas for schools. I found a beautiful, spacious semi-detached house in Carshalton Beeches, and fell in love with it. Our house had risen in value, and we were able to afford a slightly bigger mortgage.

So sadly, two members of our entourage did not make the move with us. Katie, our beloved collie had been run over. She had been out on her walk at the local park with Mike, as usual, and on returning to the car instead of jumping in she became distracted by a motor-bike and chased it. She was killed instantly by a lorry, and the driver was dreadfully upset. Mike's heart was broken. She had always been his dog. We mourned her long and hard.

Tim felt the loss of his play-mate keenly. No more sweet girl, who had gently laid her head on my bump to listen to the baby; and who had stood up so carefully to peer into the pram at Little Gemma. We had a dog-shaped hole in our lives.

Our cute and loving black and white cat, Samantha, had also been taken to Spirit World. At the age of four, she simply died one day. Her brother Scooby-Do did just the same, and a post-mortem showed up a heart defect. She died in a garden opposite ours, and our neighbours told us that another black cat had sat with her for two hours afterwards. This, of course, was Tammy. She was inconsolable. She had lost her baby, and howled for days. Letting-go is a big one for me, and every time one of our pets dies I dissolve. It never gets any easier.

We grieved Katie for a year, and then decided that the children needed a dog. Enter stage left, Biba, who had lived on the streets and had been rescued by a wonderful doggy lady. Carshalton used to be known for growing watercress, and Biba was described as a Watercress terrier. She was a mixture, all right, but a mongrel of the highest intelligence. We brought her home and she jumped immediately on to the dining-room table. We explained that this was unacceptable behaviour, and she never did it again. Biba chose me as her pack-leader, which made it a little easier on Mike. Each animal has such a different personality, and Biba in no way replaced the special being that was Katie.

105

I had a twin-pushchair for the children. As Tim grew, he would want to walk or run alongside. When Tim got out of the pushchair, Biba got in. One day we walked up to Rosehill to do the shopping. I left the pushchair outside a shop with Biba tied to it. The lass in the shop asked me: "Would you like a cat to go with your dog?" I replied that we already had a cat, and she went on to tell me that they had found a stray, and that she was being put down that very afternoon. Of course I took her! We put her into a cardboard box and she travelled home in the pushchair.

The children called her Susie. She was all black and very pretty. Unfortunately, her charms did not work on Tammy, who hated her on sight. No-one was going to take the place of her beloved Samantha. Tammy and Susie spent the rest of their lives ignoring one another. But Biba was very protective towards both her cats.

We moved to our beautiful, spacious semi-detached house in the leafy suburbs, therefore, with two children, two cats and a dog. Tim started at the best school in the area at the age of five and three months, where he settled well, and I enrolled Gem into the local playgroup, which she hated. I was teaching a yoga class in Sutton at an Adult Education Centre, and had made friends already with our super neighbours. We were there exactly five weeks when Mike was put up for promotion, and he got the job. I was devastated. That was a real low point for me. I knew that Mike was right, that if he did not take this promotion another one would not come along. But I was so happy with the status quo at that time. Mike moved almost immediately to Potters Bar in Hertfordshire, leaving me to sell our lovely house. I sold it in half an hour.

We entered a strange time in our marriage. Mike lodged in Hertfordshire all the week, while I ran the homestead. I would look forward to him coming home on a Friday, and by Saturday we would be rowing. I had managed very adequately all week, and Mike would want to come in and reorganise, to take over. We developed control issues! Talking to other wives has convinced me that this is a fairly normal occurrence in this situation, but it certainly put a strain on our marriage.

Mike's promotion meant that we could up the mortgage again and we bought a detached house in Chiswell Green, St. Albans. It was a modern house, on a modern estate, and it had none of the charm of our spacious home in Carshalton Beeches. It did have a number of advantages, though. We were surrounded by young families. The children loved it there. They had lots of friends, and could play outside safely. Gemma loved her new playgroup; Biba found a special friend called Fluff, and both the cats, in their own way, settled in. I was asked immediately to teach a yoga class, which took off as though it was always meant for me to live right there. One class soon grew into many more.

There was only one fly in the ointment. Tim had begun school at age five and three months in Surrey. In Hertfordshire, the children began at age four. He was a whole year behind. Fortunately, Tim had a super teacher, who was incredibly encouraging and positive. Tim read a

107

sixty four page book every night, working very hard to master his words and to get up to speed. Gemma developed a certain look on her face each time she was told: "Shush, Gemma, Tim is reading." It was a mix between resignation, resentment and boredom. She certainly enjoyed getting her own back a year later, when she was learning to read, by constantly saying: "Shush, Tim, Gemma is reading"!

Tim was with a very bright group of children. This particular class was able to pull up the standard of the less able children, and they all soared. We began to realise that Tim was a very clever child. We had always worried about him. He was, as I mentioned before, accident prone. When he was four, my mother and I had been playing with him in the hall. We were all laughing at our silly game, and Tim sprinted past us, tripped, and fell head first through the glass front-door. His forehead was very badly cut open. Now, Mum had always been wonderful in an emergency, but she absolutely fell apart. This was her oh so special grandson, and she kept repeating, over and over again, "I've got Tim's blood on my shoe. I've got Tim's blood on my shoe." I grabbed a flannel, wet it, and placed it firmly on Tim's forehead. Put one of Gemma's cardigans on him, the first garment I could find, threw some toys and some juice into a bag for Gemma, and carried Tim to the car, shepherding the others along with me. I knew that I could not leave Gem with my mum, she was in shock. When I arrived at the Accident and Emergency room, the nurses were wonderful. Within twenty minutes he was in the Operating Room. Now, I had been incredibly strong right until the moment that he was wheeled through the door to the Operating Room, and they ripped his little hand out of mine. Then I fell apart, and it was my mother's opportunity to rally. They did a superb job on Tim's forehead, but he still has a scar now, at the age of forty. Apparently, he went straight to sleep, under the bright light, and they sprayed the finished job with some sort of gold 'glue'. We went home via the Toyshop, and the Assistant there was tremendously impressed. Tim insisted on looking in the mirror, and felt like a super hero. Mum and I sat down, all shaken and in need of a cup of tea, and we could hear some banging. Leaping up to investigate, I discovered Tim jumping off the dining-room table. He was convinced he could fly! With a gold forehead, he must have super-natural powers!

When I had put the children to bed, much later, Mum assured me that I needed a drink. She had brought her gin with her, being very fond of a gin and tonic. Now, I would have the odd glass of beer, or wine, but I never drank spirits. My goodness, I discovered that gin makes me maudling! If crying and being morose is good for shock, then the experience was successful. I am inclined to think now that Bach's Rescue Remedy would have been a better choice.

We had great friends, when the children were small, called Andy and Lesley. Andy had a port-wine stain on one side of his face. You noticed this when you first met him, but within ten minutes you ceased to notice it at all. He had a great personality, and his inner spirit shone through. One day I was talking to Andy about my concerns for Tim – his eye problems and so on. Andy looked at me and said: "You are worrying about the wrong child. Tim is fine. Tim will be fine. Tim will learn to overcome all his challenges. The one to worry about is Gemma. She is just so perfect. She is going to have a much harder time in life." His words shocked me at the time, but I have recognised their wisdom, so often, since the children have grown up. Tim has an independence, a resilience and a special sort of self-reliance which he has acquired from the difficulties that he has encountered in life. Gemma's prettiness and femininity tended to attract the wrong type of boyfriend. People, mistakenly, believed that they could walk all over her and her desire for peace and harmony has, on occasions, fostered that belief.

We did well in Hertfordshire. Mike was happy and successful in his job with IBM; I joined the British Wheel of Yoga and the Friends of Yoga Society, and continued to run my classes. The children did well at the local school, Killigrew Infants. We had lots of friends, a lively social life and felt secure. Then a bomb dropped on us. My mother and father had always had a volatile marriage. After Leigh and I left home, they discovered they had very little in common. Dad was a social creature and spent a lot of time in the pub. He travelled a great deal with work, and Mum became very lonely. She began to realise that she had an empty and unsatisfactory life. She soon grew low and depressed. She had never been an easy person, but then neither had Dad. The lower she fell, the less sympathy he had for her. I began to pick up on the vibes during our phone calls, much as Mum continued to pretend that all was well. We went home for the week-end, and I was shocked when I saw her. She had lost weight, looked haggard, and was shaking so hard that she could not hold a cup. It was clear that Mum was having a break-down. Dad continued on as normal, and when we tried to sit him down to talk about the situation, he stormed out of the house. He said that she had dug herself a big hole, and she could not climb out of it. He was right, and it was clear that he was not going to give her a hand.

Mum left Dad after forty years of marriage. She was in a bad way, and had nowhere to go, so she came to us. Mike went down with a van and collected her possessions. She left Dad, her home, her cats and her dog, at the age of sixty one, and slept on our settee. Dad's last comment to her was: "I do not agree with what you are doing, but I do recognise the courage it takes to do it."

So, Mum left her beautiful four-bedroomed, chalet-style house, her beloved animals, her status and her financial security. She flatly refused to allow one of the children to give up their bedroom, which they would have most happily done, and she continued to sleep on the bed-settee in our lounge. She 'rented' space in Tim's wardrobe, and the bulk of her possessions went into storage.

We rubbed along pretty well together. It was a difficult situation, especially since I had always been a Daddy's girl. He felt that I was taking Mum's side, as she had come to live with us. I saw it as looking after the one who most needed it. She had nowhere else to go. You will remember that my relationship with my mother had never been an easy one. It had improved enormously after my marriage, and Mike was always wonderful with her. My brother, Leigh, was very firmly on Dad's side.

Mike and Mum shared the same taste in movies. They would sit me down between them to watch a horror movie. I hated horror movies. They would then both go to sleep, and I would watch, mesmerised and horrified. When they woke up, and the film was over, they would ask me what had happened, and I would have to go through it all again. I was always a mug!

We were extremely grateful for Mum's presence, when I was taken ill on a holiday in France. This was a medical mystery which lasted for a year. I was nauseous all the time and covered in a rash, except for my back. When it began, in France, I had a very high temperature, and extreme itching. I was being sick all the time. We had gone to the South of France, camping, so we had a long journey home. I was so unwell that I was completely incapable of looking after the children. They had always fought like cat and dog, and they played up dreadfully in the back of the car. Mike always insisted on me beginning the journey in the front of the car, but I would usually end up sitting between them in the back at some point. We would build up a pillar of four pillows to separate them, but still the squabbling and screaming would persist. As Mike drove, with me being constantly sick next to him, the crescendo from the back-seat reached such a pitch that eventually he snapped. He threatened the children with: "If you two don't stop fighting and start behaving yourselves, I shall wallop you both." This was greeted with derision, since he had never laid a finger on either of them. The chaos resumed, to which Mike pulled into a lay-by, yanked Tim out, gave him a resounding slap on the back-side. Then pulled Gemma out and gave her a resounding slap on the back-side. A man standing in the lay-by was astonished, his mouth dropped open as Mike calmly got back behind the wheel and pulled back out into the traffic. The children were completely stunned, and they have never forgotten this incident. We both inclined towards being easy parents, neither one of us was a disciplinarian. But Tim was later to say of me: "Beware the anger of the gentle person." I used to say: "I'm going to count to three..." It usually worked; whatever I had asked them to do was actioned by three. One day Tim asked: "What comes after three?" I had to admit that it was 'four'!

How we completed our journey home is a mystery to me now, but I proceeded to be ill for a year. I had weekly appointments with the doctor, who sent me to every specialist possible. We had an Indian doctor, who really cared, but I can remember feeling very cross with him. We certainly could not have managed without my mother doing the cleaning, the washing and ironing, and taking a lot of the responsibility for the children. She was a star.

The curious aspect of this mystery illness was the fact that I was nauseous and sick all the time, but I could not stop eating. I did not lose weight. I took to chewing gum, something that had always repelled me. Then, one morning after Mike had gone to work, I began to vomit in earnest. Eventually, after hours and hours of vomiting, I passed something black. I was so horrified that I flushed it away. When Mike came home and said to Mum: "Where's Carole?" She explained to him that I had been really poorly. His patience was thin, after all these months of illness, and he was pretty infuriated when he ran up the stairs. But then he saw me. He carried me to the doctor, I was so weak that I could not stand. The doctor said that I should have kept the black item for analysis, but it was clear that I was finally free of it. It had been living and growing inside me. I must have picked it up in France, young wine perhaps. Anyway, I quickly recovered, and never needed to chew gum again.

Mum applied for a job in an old people's home, which she got. It was a lovely house in Watford, and, as the Manager, she had a flat on the top floor. It was hard work and long hours. She did all the grocery shopping and all the cooking. The committee was not easy to work with, but we were proud of her. To go back to work after forty years as a house-wife was some achievement. She stayed there for a while, but it wore her down. She was in her early sixties, and one day when the committee was particularly difficult, I persuaded her to give in her notice. She came home to us once more.

I had seen my father only once during the eighteen months after Mum left the marriage. I would very much have liked to remain close to both parties, and was to attempt this almost impossible feat twice more in my life, actually, but in all cases it was unsuccessful. We had helped Mum with the divorce papers, and given her all the emotional support that we could. Mike and I both endeavoured to remain impartial, but the visit to Dad was difficult. There was a great deal of tension in the room. I remember that his nails were long; he did not look immaculately turned out, as he always had done. He had, by this time, a girlfriend. Someone called Mary. I never met her.

After eighteen months, Mum was out shopping one day, and the phone rang. It was Dad. We had a lovely, easy phone call. I believe he was having some problems with Leigh and his family, and I guess he may have been looking at all that had happened in a different light. He actually asked after Mum, and I remarked that she was not easy to live with. He laughed and said how glad he was to hear me say that. I replied quickly that he was not easy to live with either, and he agreed. At the end of the conversation, he called me 'Darling', and I felt a wave of unconditional love pass between us.

It was the run up to Christmas. Tim had been picked as the Narrator for the School Play. He was desperate to do it, and then contracted chicken-pox. His teacher sent home the script for him to learn, and we recorded it for him to play over and over. He was well and back to school the day before the play. We were all excited as we prepared to leave for the school, Tim looked so smart in his blazer, and I was upstairs getting changed when the phone rang. It was my brother and he asked to speak to Mike. This was so unusual that I realised immediately that something was wrong. Dad had been killed in a car accident. We quickly decided that we must not tell the children, that we would go on with the school play, for which Tim had worked so hard. We left Mum looking after Gemma.

We sat on small school chairs, watching Tim aged eight and so handsome. All I could think about was how proud of him Dad would have been. It was agony to sit there. How could the world go on? My father was dead! How could people behave normally? I developed claustrophobia after this event, so powerful was my desire to run screaming from that school hall.

When we returned home, we told the children the dreadful news. Tim cried a lot, but Gem quite simply did not believe it. She at six was convinced it was a mistake. She never did cry. Mum took it hard. She said that she would have stayed with Dad if she had had any idea that this would happen. I had the sickening idea that perhaps he had not cared very much whether he lived or died.

Leigh identified the body and took care of the funeral arrangements. It seems that Dad had entered into a sort of 'cat and mouse' game on the motorway, with a chocolate brown Rolls Royce. He was driving a nippy little white Sunbeam Alpine at the time. The Rolls Royce overtook him, cut in too tight, and its slipstream drove Dad into the parapet. The young policeman, who was the first on the scene, assured us that his death would have been instant. When Mike was a young man, he had been the first one at the scene of a fatal crash. He described to me how odd it was that the car radio was still playing, but the driver was dead. This is how I saw my Father's crash; the radio still playing, but Dad gone.

Dad was with me for twelve days. I felt his spirit all around me, and felt very loved and embraced. It sounds awfully selfish, but I felt as though, for once, he was just mine. I did not have to share him with anyone else. It was all simple and straight forward; we had a clear channel. At the end of the twelve days he left me. I never felt him again, and I believe that he re-incarnated quite quickly. It was a very different experience when my mum died.

Both Mum and I went down with a horrible bout of 'flu, shock I think which lowered the immune system, and spent Christmas Day wrapped in blankets, so hoarse that we could not talk. In front of the tree were the parcels that Dad had wrapped and labelled for the children. A globe bed-side light for Tim and a doll for Gemma that could be turned upside down to become a different person. I kept one of the labels with my Dad's writing, turned it into a tree decoration, and each year I shed a tear when I put it on the branch. It is now thirty two years since my father was killed.

I borrowed my friend Minerva's skirt for the funeral. There was a wonderful turn-out, which is what we would have expected. He was a popular, a charismatic man. Leigh and Meg hosted the get-together afterwards, and it was all a bit sticky for Mum.

I learned something very important at this time. A really close friend of mine crossed the road when she saw me coming, the day after my Dad was killed. It really hurt. I am sure she felt that she was being sensitive. One of Mike's engineers, on the other hand, simply put his arms around me and said: "I am so sorry." I learnt that it is better to say anything than to say nothing. I always remember this with my students, when they are bereaved.

There were, of course, many repercussions. Dad had left his boat to Leigh, as he and his family had enjoyed many days with him on the water. Mum inherited enough to be able to buy herself a little bungalow in Weston-super-Mare, eventually. As is often the case, even in the midst of the tragedy and really dark days, there were some amusing incidents. Leigh asked us to go down to 'The Dell' and to see if there was anything that we wanted to have as a keepsake from Dad. I took his wooden calendar. I wind it on each day, still, as he always did, and recently I bought a similar wooden calendar for my youngest nephew, Adam, on his fortieth birthday. He delights in changing the date each morning and remembering Papa. There was an abundance of items that Mum wanted to keep, and we returned on the train like a couple of bag-ladies. When we changed trains at Temple Meads, a charming young man asked if he could help. I refused, after all I was married, and my mother said: "For goodness sake, Carole, let him help." We arrived at St. Albans Station, and all I could think of was getting Mike to pick us up. I left Mum on a bench, surrounded by her treasures, to go to the phone. When I returned, she was deep in conversation with a young man, who was showing her his fishnet tights under his jeans! She had never heard of a transvestite, and we were to get hysterical about this incident later. It had been quite a day, with seeing the solicitor and so on. The legal difficulties continued for some time, and were very emotive. The divorce had not been finalised. We wanted to have the animals; dear Minty, the black and white collie, who I had brought home from the beach one day. (We reported him to the Police and so on, but he was never claimed. I had set out with two dogs and came home with three!) And the two cats, Candy and Smokey, who had been kittens from one of Meg's cats. We were told 'No', that Dad's new girlfriend wanted to keep them. I believe she found the expense onerous, and would occasionally petition Leigh for help with their food. I do hope that she made them happy. She was new to Dad's life, and new to theirs.

Many, many years later, my brother was to tell me that my father had an eight year affair, before my mother left him. I was really shocked. I had always seen my father as a man of integrity and honour. Leigh thought it was hugely amusing. She was a woman in one of the places he regularly visited when he went to the Hide and Skin Auctions. I have no idea whether my mother knew, or suspected. I believe, on some level, that she knew the man she had married had let her down on all fronts. They had shared a volatile marriage. They had survived the Second World War together and their letters to one another had kept them going. They had loved one another, and they had both loved us. It was a time of such high emotion, and turbulence. I was thirty years old when my parents split up, and thirty one when my dad died.

119

Christmas behind us, we endeavoured to establish some degree of normality in our lives. Mike saw an advert for an assignment to the U.S.A. on the notice-board, and, on a whim, he applied. He had always wanted to visit America. He went through the interviews, and was on a shortlist of two candidates. I was praying, I have to admit, that the other guy would be successful! We received the phone call early one day, when we were still in bed. I remember Mike holding my hand very tightly. He had got it. We were to move to Kentucky for three years.

This opportunity came at a time when our family had already been under enormous strain. I was very reluctant to leave a secure life in St. Albans at that time. Our children were happy in their very good school, my mother was beginning to piece her new life together, we had good friends, a lovely home, and Mike had a good team. Making decisions about our pets was a heartbreak which I was ill-equipped to face. Dad had died on December the seventeenth, and by the following June the first we moved to Lexington, Kentucky.

We went on a 'look-see' visit. My mother looked after the children and the pets. We flew to Atlanta, and stayed for one night in the Hyatt Regency. When we arrived, we were tired and hungry. We rang down for some sandwiches and beer. Twenty minutes later there was a knock on the door. Standing there was a tall, handsome black man in the most beautiful livery. He held aloft a large silver tray, and on the tray there were elegant sandwiches constructed of marbled bread. On one side of the sandwiches, was every piece of fruit you can imagine, on the other side, every salad vegetable. It was an absolute feast! The beer bottles were chilled in champagne coolers.

The lift to the hotel was on the outside, and was very fast. We went to the rooftop restaurant for dinner, and there was a violinist who asked me what I would like to have played. My mind went blank. The only thing I could think of was the tune which Gemma had been playing on her school recorder: 'My garden bed is ready'! Mike came to the rescue with a request for 'You light up my life', one of our special songs.

Lexington was lovely. It is horse country, all horse farms and white post and rail fences. Mike's new boss, Ted, was absolutely charming, and his family made us very welcome. We followed our usual procedure; always find the best school in the area first. We chose Stonewall, which had a high reputation. A Dutch IBMer was going home, and his wife showed us around her Ranch-style house. She was renting it from a delightful Iranian couple, who became very special friends. We took the house which had a rather amusing address: Ramsgate Court!

We returned home to find Nana absolutely exhausted. My mother had loved looking after the children and the animals, but it had taken its toll. We began to realise that she was growing older. She decided to move in with her sister, Auntie Una. She was a kind lady, and Mum was thrilled to return to Newport, South Wales. It was a sad day when we took her over and said our goodbyes. We knew that we were now going to be parted by many miles, and it was a wrench, our fortunes had been intertwined for a very long time.

We agonised over the decision of what to do with our beautiful dog, Biba. She was always connected to my left heel, and we all absolutely adored her. I knew that quarantine would destroy her, so we finally decided to leave her with our friends, Jan and John. They had two children, roughly the same age as ours, and Biba was particularly fond of Jason. IBM paid for her food all the time that we were gone. We took the cats with us. Tammy was seventeen at the time, and we thought it very unlikely that she would last the three years. We took Susie as her companion. Not that they liked one another any more than when they first met, but we felt that even a cross friend was better than no friend at all!

Gem was not happy at the idea of the move at all. She was settled at school, and her teacher did take me on one side to express her dismay. She said that Gemma was very distressed at the idea of leaving her pets. Gem and I dragged our feet; Tim and Mike were up for the adventure. We rented out our house, and had tearful goodbyes with our friends and with dear Biba.

My yoga students asked me to make a tape before I left, so that they could continue their practice. This I did, and Jan played it one day. Biba rushed around, barking furiously, and looking for me. She was inconsolable once she realised that I was not there, and Jan never played the tape again. Biba had the most endearing habit. When she barked her front paws came off the ground. Many years later, and many years after she had died, I met a clairvoyant who said: "Have you got a dog in Spirit World?" I replied 'yes' and she said: "She is so pleased to see you! Every time she barks her front paws come off the ground."

The cats took the next flight after ours, and we picked them up at the airport. They moved into the house before us. The temperature was a big problem for them and the air-conditioning was faulty. The temperatures in Kentucky would range from -20 degrees in the winter, to 100 degrees Fahrenheit in the summer. Oftentimes it would also be a hundred per cent humidity in the hot weather, too. One day, Susie was very distressed and Tim put her in the basin in the bathroom and surrounded her with ice. He was only nine years old, but he had a tremendous instinct for animal care. That was a turning point for Susie. The air-conditioning was repaired, and she became accustomed to the new climate, as did we.

We had chosen to move in early June since the American children begin their summer vacation then. They have three months off from school. It seemed like a good plan, Tim and Gem could get used to their new, very different life. In hindsight, we realise that it would have been better to have had them start school immediately. We were very lonely. The days were long. We had left our families, our friends, our life, our beloved dog. We endeavoured to put on a brave face for Mike, but it took us six months to get anywhere near settling. Mike bought me a coaster which said: "Bloom where you are planted".

Often we three would be crying when he returned from work, and we would quickly wipe our eyes to greet him.

Mike was having a ball. He loved his job, was surrounded by interesting people, and got home early in the afternoon. Honestly, I did consider leaving him and taking the children home. I constantly worked out the fourteen hours it would take us to get back to St. Albans... we could be there by...

Gemma had wanted to be a brownie. I got talking to a neighbour who gave me the phone number of the Brownie Organiser in our Area. Enter Kathleen Morgan, stage left. Kathleen was an eccentric. She was a Kentuckian, through and through, and was a retired teacher. We adored her. She had me roped in as a Brownie leader, immediately, and a new chapter began in our lives. Kathleen's husband, Charles, was one of the dearest men I have ever met. He was a retired Principal (Head Teacher.) He had been a photographer in the Second World War and had huge respect for the English R.A.F. guys. He told the most interesting stories. In fact, they both did – usually at the same time! They would talk over each other constantly, completely oblivious. The Morgans did not have children, and clearly fell totally in love with these two little English kiddies. We adopted them as grandparents and they proved to be amazing. They would often phone up and ask if they could take the children out for the day. We always knew that the four of them would be having a marvellous time, and could relax. Sometimes, Kathleen would phone and say, in her Kentucky drawl: "Now,

Carole, is there any concept at school that the children are struggling with?" I would come up with something that had showed up in their homework, and the Morgans would sit and design a game to clarify the concept. They would then have the kids over for the day, and play the game for six hours straight. They were just the kindest people ever, and delighted in being part of our 'family'.

When we first arrived in the States it was a culture shock. Mike told me that if I did not take my eyes off peoples' buttocks I would be arrested! They did not all look like 'Charlie's Angels'! It was 1981, and there was very little obesity in England. The Americans would go to a 'movie show' and buy a bucket of coke and a bucket of popcorn. They never walked anywhere. I took a little group of children for a walk from our court, with the parents' permission. After one block, the first mother drew up in her car, to see if anyone had sore legs, and four other cars followed suit!

I was invited to a Newcomers Meeting, and offered free yoga classes in my basement. (Mike's assignment was such that I was not allowed to earn any money.) No-one came, and I learnt an important lesson about human nature. If something is free, then it's not worth anything. I offered yoga classes where there was a five dollar fee for a year's attendance, the money to go to charity, and the classes were full!

This chapter of our lives was incredibly colourful. We learnt about the agony of sudden bereavement. We learned about extreme, fluctuating emotions. I became the

125

designated emotional 'washing-machine' for the entire family. I felt that, in some strange way, all the emotions came to me, and I churned them around and sought to cleanse them. We learned about letting-go of our security, and diving into a new adventure. We learned about culture shock. Our young family clung tightly together through the turbulence of this year, and grew strong.

# Chapter 11

**M**ars in Pisces: *You seldom do things just because you want to. There is usually a strong sense of duty nagging you along. When crossed, you brood for hours, if not weeks, suddenly ferociously explode and then return immediately to your usual, good-natured self.*

We did 'bloom where we were planted'. Indeed, we thrived in America. The pace of life was much slower, it was easy to travel, and the people were lovely. We are still in touch with our Kentucky friends, after twenty eight years. I must say that the post from our friends in Hertfordshire had begun to dwindle after just three years! (Although our lovely friends, Min, Dave, Dominique and Richard, do still send us a Christmas card each year.) We discovered that the Kentuckians were slow to warm to us, but once they take you to their hearts, it is for life. They tended to be suspicious at first of anyone new. Some people had never left the State of Kentucky, and were even suspicious of folk from Ohio!

We were asked some amusing questions: "Are all your streets cobbled?" "Do you have seasons in England?" "Do you have horses in England?" We became something of an attraction at parties!

We made some interesting mistakes, too. I would say to the Brownies: "Please ask your mums..." and they would look blankly at me. To them 'mums' were chrysanthemums, not mothers! I learnt to say 'moms'. I also learnt to speak much slower; not a bad technique for a yoga teacher.

Tim's teacher asked me to go into school and give the children a talk on London, and particularly Buckingham Palace. I told them about the changing of the guard. After I had left, one of the little girls asked Tim how often the guards were changed, and he replied, nonchalantly: "Oh, about every three weeks"!

Tim's teacher took full advantage of having a little English boy in the class. I had told the children that they must stand politely whilst the American children put their hands on their hearts, and recited the pledge of allegiance, each morning. Tim's teacher was fine with this. But, boy, did I have a battle with Gemma's teacher! It took a year for me to convince her that the Stars and Stripes was not our flag, and it would be inappropriate for us to pledge allegiance to it. Our flag was the Union Jack. Mike said I became more and more English the longer I stayed in the U.S.A!

We did miss theatres, and art galleries. We missed our heritage, and our ancient monuments. American history is of short duration. We missed the English sense of humour. The Americans never laugh at their work. If Mike made a flippant, and typically English, jibe about IBM it was really frowned upon. The Americans do laugh, but their humour is different.

My friend, Connie, came to the rescue! Now, Connie is a real Anglophile. She and I connected immediately, and could find fun in anything. Connie lived across the Court from us; she was a relief teacher and had a special rapport with children. She is still a close friend, even though we have been home for twenty eight years. We still write long letters to one another and Connie will tell me whether it is a' two cup of tea letter'; we shared so many herbal teas together. She has a very special place in my heart. It was Connie who looked after Tammy and Susie, when we travelled away on vacation. The cats soon learned to trot across the Court to Connie, when they needed feeding. She remembered everything, and was so interested in all things English. Connie's husband is a real old Kentucky boy, called Shelby. An accountant by profession, Shelby was a very astute business-man.

One particularly snowy day, Mike could not get his Oldsmobile up the slope of the Court to go to work. Shelby wandered over, and said: "I'll sit in the back." Mike had absolutely no notion what Shelby meant, but he duly opened the back-door for him. This time, the Oldsmobile gripped on the ice, and Mike reached the top of the street. Shelby was a big guy!

I had a Pontiac. It was a large estate car, and I could get the whole Brownie Troop in it. IBM gave us a certain figure to buy the family car, and we got a really good deal on the Pontiac. I only once drove the wrong way out of a shopping Mall, when there were no other cars around. Apart from that, we adjusted well to driving on the other side of the road. I used it every day, we drove to Canada to see Mike's Uncle Ted; we drove to Oklahoma to see my Auntie Doris; we drove to Florida to Disneyworld; we saw twenty two States while we were there, and then after three years, because of the exchange rate, we sold it and broke even on the deal!

We started out thinking that we were only going to be there for three years, so we bought furniture from 'thrift' stores (charity shops.) But it did not take us long to realise that three years is actually ages, so we made a home and a life, and put down roots.

Tim joined a soccer (football) team called the 'Cougars', and they won the championship. (We still have his trophy on display!) Gem went to Ballet lessons; Mike took up hiking and Softball; I joined the Cincinnati Yoga Association. My mother came out to stay with us for seven weeks, and really enjoyed our friends and our lifestyle. Pouran and Younes, our wonderful Persian landlords, treated her like a queen. The Americans generally have a somewhat different attitude to life to us; they work hard and they play hard. They always have a holiday to look forward to. Valentine's Day is a big deal, not just for sweethearts, but all the children in a school class will send one another cards, and friends exchange cards, too. It is a Lovefest! Then there is Spring Break, Memorial Day – (the first barbecue of the year, in May) – then Labour Day – (the last barbecue of the year, in September) - Halloween, Thanksgiving and Christmas. The speed limit is fifty five miles an hour, and the Shopping Malls are more leisurely. We seemed to have much more time, when we lived in Kentucky.

We decided that we did not want to be part of an ex-pats group, or to join the English Club. If we were to live in the States, we really wanted to get to know Americans. We discovered that the American energy is much lighter than the British. I did not know a great deal about auras, at this time, but I could pick up on the differences with other nationalities. The aura is the energy field which surrounds every person, every animal and, indeed, every plant. It seemed to me that the American aura was generally wider, and more expansive than the English energy field.

As the European representative, Mike enjoyed his role of host to visitors. After the first year, he was an Englishman, living in America, working for a Dutch boss! There was an interesting incident. Mike's Dutch Boss was over on a visit with his Manager, who was French. The French guy was being somewhat scathing towards the Dutchman, saying: "In Holland, the wives wear the trousers, but in France, the men wear the trousers!" They both turned to Mike, enquiringly, and he said: "Ah. We have a leg each!"

Most of our friends had 'a leg each' too. Pouran and Younes, who owned our house, became extended family. Younes was born in Russia, and his son, Cyrus, was born in the States. They had met in Iran, and told some wonderful stories. The whole family was strikingly handsome, and both the daughters had an abundance of admirers. Pouran was my soul-mate. One day, they phoned us up and asked were we free that afternoon. If so, would we like to see a property with them? If we liked it, they would buy it. Now, Younes was a smart businessman, and he had a number of properties in Lexington, but they lived at that time in a charming house in Strawberry Lane. The property they showed us was stunning. It was a five-bedroom house, set in twelve acres. It had stables, paddocks and a huge barn. It even had central vacuuming! Like it? We were entranced! They bought it, and it remains to me the most beautiful house I have ever set foot in. So many happy occasions were spent around their family table.

Another family who so kindly gathered us in were Roxanne and Vince. They had four children, and were staunch Roman Catholics. We loved holding hands and saying grace before meals with them all. They introduced us to Derby Day, whilst sitting in their Jacuzzi sipping Mint Juleps! Vince was a University Lecturer, and conversation was always lively. These were happy Days.

When Jeannie and Mike invited us around, they said that they only had one regret; that they had not done it sooner! They had a son and daughter the same age as our children. Jeannie would feed the children first, and they would then skip off to play, and the adults would enjoy a leisurely repast. Here we shared wine. Kentucky is Bible Belt and many people were teetotal. We learned, when we had an 'Open House', to invite the non-drinkers first, and then the drinkers later. I am now teetotal, but in those days we used to enjoy American beer and wine. When we left Lexington, Jeannie said: "Everyone will promise to keep in touch and write to you, but I actually will." Unfortunately, she did not!

We met Judie on the soccer touchline. Judie came from Anamosa, Iowa, and has since returned home. Judie is incredibly creative, and her home reflected this in every corner. She and her husband, Ray, became firm favourites. Their son, Jon, was a year older than Tim, and both played on the 'Cougars' team. They went away to camp together, when Tim was just ten. It was a memorable experience for both of them and one they had no intention of repeating! They returned, filthy and covered in mosquito bites. Judie was into folk art, and she taught me some rudimentary techniques. Our home, at Christmastime, is still all about Judie. She made us the most stunning Nativity Scene plaque, which hangs in pride of place.

In our second year in Lexington I took my Friends of Yoga Society Diploma. I thoroughly enjoyed the research involved, and writing the essays. I was required to attend a weekly class, and I chose a class in the University of Kentucky. It was taught by a very spiritual lady called

Shelley. She had studied in Ashrams in India, and was really in to chanting. Sometimes, we held the class outside, which was special. We felt very close to nature, and really experienced the union, which is what the word 'yoga' means.

I attended workshops with the Cincinnati Yoga Association, and made some lovely yoga friends. A Teacher that I very much admired was Jill Mc Connel. She was an Iyengar teacher, and very accurate in the asanas, (the yoga postures.) She taught me a lot about alignment, and was to be one of my Practical Assessors. My second Assessor was Toni, who was bright and joyful. She personified teaching from the heart. My Kentucky friends were very keen to do their karma yoga, when the time came for my Assessments. I was offered several basements as yoga rooms, and the atmosphere in the classes was really light and beautiful. I needed to do two Practical Assessments as I was remote, and a FRYOG Examiner was not available. I was delighted to pass my course with a Distinction, and I still have my Diploma on the wall in the dining-room. It gives me great pleasure to see Pauline Mainland's signature on my certificate. She was the Chairman of the Friends of Yoga Society for twenty one years, and was a very special lady. She was unique, and I have kept all the letters that she wrote to me. We shared a great love of animals; she said that she had been a ginger cat in a previous life. I have a lovely photograph of her, on her yoga mat, with her cats.

I was invited to teach yoga to the children in Gemma's year at school. There were fifty of them in the class, and it proved to be a most interesting challenge. I became adept at moving and separating! "All children whose first name begins with 'C' stand up and change places with someone else." Yes, one of my main challenges was a boy called Charlie. 'Happy Days' was popular on television at this time, and Charlie was 'the Fonz' of this year. He wore his collar turned up, and was generally considered to be 'cool'. One day he brought a letter in from his mother saying that he did not have to practise yoga. I said: "That's fine, Charlie. You sit and watch." He rather imagined that all his peers would follow his example, but that day I did all the strong standing poses: the warrior, the triangle, the half-moon balance, the eagle and the crow. All the boys had such fun, and the following week I had a letter from Charlie's mother asking if he could join back in with the yoga! I have always loved teaching children. I have a number of colleagues who resolutely state that they would never teach children, but to me the changing of the world is down to the next generation. In an adult class, students tend to leave a respectful distance on either side of the teacher. In a children's class, they are on your mat with you! One of my graduated teachers, Mick, once attended one of my Kidz classes as an observation. (Student teachers are required to observe six classes in their last year. It is quite remarkable the amount that they pick up whilst not participating in the practice.) Mick remarked afterwards that it was hard to work out who had the most fun, the children or me! I took this as a great compliment. Enlightenment does not have to be serious.

Whilst we were happily thriving in America, we did not realise that we were growing three years in one direction, while our English friends and family were growing three years in the other. It had been hard to settle in Kentucky, but we had done it. Surely going home again would be easy? This was not to be the case. Gemma had pined when we first went to the States. She lost weight, and looked unwell. We anticipated that going back to England would be all her Christmases come at once! She had been teased quite a lot for being different. Amusingly, most of the teasing was from a Chinese boy! I had a sweatshirt made for her which said: 'Made in England'. I thought it was hugely amusing, and could not understand why she would not wear it. She explained later that she felt different enough, as it was, without underlining it. What we have only just learned is that Tim was terribly badly bullied in his last year in the States. This disclosure came on Christmas Eve, twenty-nine years after these events. We had no idea, and, as Tim said, he did not have the language to explain it to us. The only clue that I remember is that he asked me not to come into school anymore and give talks on England. I thought that was down to mild embarrassment about having his mother in school, and did not realise that there was a deeper reason. The first duty of a parent is to protect their child, and I failed to do this. I did not read the signs, and I failed Tim. His disclosure hit me hard, but the timing of it was pertinent to a situation we were all facing with our grandson, Ben, at his school. He was being persistently bullied, too. I found the picture of Tim, at eleven years old, having to fight for survival against three vicious bullies in the toilets, horribly disturbing. The only reason that they picked on him was because he was English, and I have to admit that this has coloured the way I feel about our time in America. I do know that those bullies will get their karma, probably have already done so, and I do totally respect the fact that the horrible year in Kentucky has enabled Tim to become the wonderfully complete, confident and wise person that he is today. He explained that it took his degree in Anthropology, and this last year of expressing himself through poetry, to fully process and absorb this experience. I will always regret that his view of education became about survival not learning, but his insights enabled Gemma to deal with Ben's situation most effectively. My body 'spoke my mind', and I was so worried about both our boys that I developed eczema on my face and dermatitis on my right hand. It is said that the right side is your past and your father (or the male members of the family), and your left side is your future and your mother (or the female members of the family). The rashes concerned have both been on the right side, thus the past and the male members of our clan are entirely relevant. I see now how this time in Tim's life has affected every choice, every decision that he has made. It is quite clear. He is strong, resourceful, creative and compassionate and we are very proud of him.

We had the opportunity to stay for one more year in Lexington, but we declined. Tim completed his final year at

Stonewall School, and would have moved to Junior High. If we took him home at age twelve, he could move into Senior School with all the other children. This seemed by far the fairest option for him. In hindsight this decision was more enlightened than we realised.

We sent Susie home three months ahead of us, and into quarantine. We felt that she would have served half of her stay by the time we returned. Tammy died in our last year. She was nineteen years and two months old. We had a wonderful vet called Dr. Bill. Tammy was so very old; she had become incontinent, and was bewildered and terribly thin. Twice that week I phoned Dr. Bill and made an appointment to have Tammy put down. And twice she rallied, and I phoned to cancel. On the Friday morning, Mike popped home, and said: "Carole, you have to do it. She has no quality of life right now." I made the appointment. I wrapped her in a beautiful pink shawl, which had been knitted for Gem. Tim sat with her on his lap in the Pontiac, and all three of us cried like babies all the way to the Veterinary Surgery. I carried Tammy in and she yowled at the Receptionist. I sat down, arranging her tenderly, so that she was as comfortable as possible in my lap. When we were called in, I said: "Don't try to fix her, Dr.Bill. She's in distress. Please just give her the injection." He carefully unwrapped her and said: "Mrs. Kerton, she is already dead." God bless her. She had died on my lap in the Waiting-Room. She knew that it was time. I always said that it was Tammy's last joke: doing the Vet out of his fee. It did not make it any easier to bear and I felt terrible guilt at having disturbed her, and taken her out in the car, but Tammy knew that she was loved; that I was trying to do my best for her. I feel now, that all any of us can hope for is to be loved at the very moment of passing. Tammy was certainly loved, and I can still cry for her now, thirty years later. Dr. Bill wrote me the most beautiful letter, saying that he believed that animals passed to Spirit World, and had an after-life. It was a hand-written letter, and I was very moved by it. I still have it, and it restores my faith in human nature.

We buried her in the garden, leaving a little of us forever in Kentucky. We planted yellow flowers on her grave, to remind her of our bright yellow and white gingham kitchen, (where she would watch the mocking-birds and the cardinals on the sun-deck,) and also purple flowers, to connect her with Spirit World.

We had returned to England each year during the summer holidays. One year, we went via Bermuda, which was great fun. Another year, we went via Nassau. For our final trip home, we decided to go to California and Arizona. My lovely cousin, Jill, had settled in the States many years previously. We went to stay with her and her family: Don, her charming Welsh husband; and her kids, Tim and Lucy. We timed it immaculately; Lucy was graduating from Stanford University. It was a time of great celebration. Last Christmas, Don wrote us a beautiful card, describing how Lucy's daughter, Megan, had just graduated from Stanford University. How time marches on.

The day that we left Lexington, Connie came across the court at four in the morning with a tray of breakfast for us. There was never a better friend. It was Connie who played 'Easter Bunny' for our children, leaving a basket of goodies on the doorstep. It was Connie who attended all my yoga classes, and still now, after twenty eight years, practises yoga to my tapes. (She and Dee meet up, just as they always did, and get out their yoga mats. When I 'count' my friends, these two precious ladies are always amongst them.) It was Connie who understood me, who 'got' me. I have a plaque in my kitchen right now, from Connie. It says: "Friends are the flowers in the garden of life."

So we bid a tearful goodbye to Lexington, Kentucky, and a pivotal chapter in our family history was closed. I had discovered the joy of being amongst like-minded people, regardless of nationality and cultural differences. I had taken a yoga Diploma, and had progressed along my yoga path. I had discovered a lovely lady, called Lilias Folan, who was on American television each day. She was my lifeline to the yoga world, and I was thrilled to meet her in Cincinnati. I had begun my life long study of energies, and the wheels of energy, known as Chakras. I had enjoyed having my own yoga room in the basement, and had 'felt' how the energies changed in our home after a practice. I became much more sensitive to my own energy shifts; much more aware of my own Chakras. (The seven main wheels of energy, which run from the base of the spine to just above the crown, are called Chakras.) Of course, the children were miles ahead of me. I overheard Tim saying to Gemma: "Don't ask Mum now. Wait until after her yoga class. Then she will definitely say 'yes'!"

I had faith in my inner strength, as we moved forward into a new adventure in our lives. We were going home!

# Chapter 12

Saturn biquintiles Jupiter: *If there is one thing you do not like the idea of, it is being 'small-time'. Consequently, everything you do has an 'epic' quality to it! You make great plans and normally manage to swing into action with them successfully. You also have a fear of being misunderstood which is why you are keen to keen to grasp any opportunity to explain yourself clearly and persuasively! That is why you make such a good teacher.*

I have always been something of a Pollyanna; more inclined to see the glass as half full, rather than half empty. I returned from the States positively perky! I am surmising that some of my old friends found this a little wearing, but I needed every drop of my positivity to cope with this transition.

Mike was given a job in Portsmouth, Hampshire. The children and I moved back into our house in St. Albans and prepared it for sale. The most enormous joy was our reunion with Biba, our beloved mongrel!

Ecstasy comes close to the emotion, as we reached Chiswell Green to pick her up. She was over the moon! I believe she was beginning to give up hope of ever returning to us. She did not look well. Her claws were very long, as though she was not being walked. Her sparkle was missing, but the joy when we packed her into the car was unmistakable. She was an older dog, but soon was her charismatic self once more.

We made the mistake of going to see Susie in quarantine. Poor Susie believed that we had come to get her, and she was distraught when we left. We waited until her time was served, before going again.

Our house was in a disgusting state. We had let it out for three years, and it was suffering badly with neglect. The children and I set about restoring it. I remember Tim rescuing a coffee table, which I despaired over. It was beautifully carved, but now was covered in coffee cup rings. He lovingly sanded it down and re-varnished it, and we still have it now in our lounge. My opposite neighbour, June, passed on a remark from her mother-in-law: 'The windows are sparkling like diamonds, once more'.

Each week-end we travelled down to Hampshire to house-hunt. Fortunately, I had a friend from Hertfordshire, who had moved to Cowplain. Beryl was able to recommend that Horndean School was the best in the area, at that time. The first house that we chose was beautiful, but after messing us around for a suitable length of time, the owners pulled out. I was becoming demoralised. I was desperate to get Tim into school for the first day of term. Mike found a new house in Lovedean, and we bought it without me even seeing it. He told me, over the phone, that it was near Yoells Lane, and we could call it 'Yoellands'. Since my parents' house was called 'Yeolands', this felt like an omen.

Even buying a new house seemed to take forever. We booked into the Holiday Inn in Portsmouth, because they would take our dog; we were not about to be parted from Biba again! When term started, I would drive Tim to Senior School, and then Gem to Junior School. (They were by now twelve and ten, respectively.) Then I would take Biba for a long walk. We then went back to the hotel to kill time, until I could pick the children up once more. This went on for a month, and I became a frequent visitor to the launderette, getting Tim's rugby uniform washed and ready for the next day. Our week-ends reversed. Now we would be returning to St.Albans on a Saturday. The children became very bored by these long journeys, and soon began to make their own plans. Gem would stay with her friend, Beth, and Tim would stay with Matthew.

Finally, we completed on 'Yoellands', and what joy it was to move into our new home! It was a brand new, executive type house, with four bedrooms and three full bathrooms. The garage was a triple, and it had a lovely long drive. The back garden was small, and a little out of proportion to the large house, but initially this was not a problem.

We set about home making. I had a lot of experience in this regard, and thoroughly enjoyed devising colour schemes and re-arranging furniture.

We were surprised at our children's comments on their return to England. Tim said: "Burn my passport. I will never leave the country again." And Gemma said: "Give me my passport. I'm off to Kentucky, and I'll never come back again." Tim lost his American accent overnight, and never even mentioned to his new friends that he had lived in the States. Gem retained hers longer, and talked readily about her previous 'life'.

We created a new normal. The children settled at school, and the day came when we could bring our beloved cat, Susie, home from the quarantine kennels. Bless her! Was anyone ever so pleased to get out of jail! She made her home upstairs, refusing to pass the landing window as she could see horses in the field opposite.

In an effort to reacclimatise the kids, we had promised them both a new pet on their return to Britain. As if we had not put poor Biba and Susie through enough, we now set about finding a puppy for Tim and a kitten for Gem. We heard of some puppies close by, and without giving it nearly enough thought, we went to see them. Fatal! Try separating a twelve year old boy from a pup, who has just chosen him! The pups were Staffordshire Bull Terrier and Labrador cross. Tim brought home his little boy, and called him Oscar. He was an absolute night-mare, but such a character. On the rare occasions when just 'the Kertons', (Mike, Tim, Gem and I,) are in a room together

145

now, the stories told invariably include Oscar. He was a very handsome boy, with the Staffy diamond on his chest, and Queen Anne legs.

Meanwhile, Gem rescued a stray black and white kitten, and called him Toby. He was one of the biggest cats I have ever seen, once fully grown, and his tail was thirteen inches long and always in a question mark! He was the most curious of curious cats, and he and Oscar became a formidable team. Toby would hide behind a table that we had in the hall, and then ambush Oscar as he passed.

Mike's parents came for the week-end. Gran took it upon herself to teach the puppy to use the garden, instead of newspaper in the utility room. She would stand at the back-door and say: "Come on, Oscar, UP the garden." No response, so she ventured up the sideway to demonstrate the meaning of her command. Oscar then barred the backdoor, growled at her and refused to let her back in!

Gemma proved to be a much better parent than Tim. She doted on Toby and overwhelmed him with affection. When we decorated the house for Christmas, the puppy and kitten were, of course, fascinated by the tree. It went over five times! On the fifth time, Gem was so afraid that I would shout at Toby, that she grabbed her kitten and raced from the room. Little did she realise that Toby had the Christmas tree lights hooked around his back paw. The tree followed her, at speed, across the lounge!

Tim was cutting the apron strings. Understandably, he was on a mission to integrate into a group of English lads, and to be accepted. We had only had one another when we moved to Kentucky, and away from our friends and family. We had become a very tight little unit. Tim was always Mike's buddy, but now he was of an age to break free. He became the youngest member of a group of mods. We did our best to stay in touch with his new interests, and new friends, taking him up to Carnaby Street, and making the boys welcome in our house. It soon became clear that Tim was not going to have time to devote to his puppy, even though he adored him. I use to pay him to walk Oscar!

My plan for me to reacclimatise was to contact all the Colleges in the area and apply for a position as a yoga teacher. My friend, Beryl, had already booked a hall for me and gathered together a group of students, so we had one class off the ground. Petersfield Adult Education Centre offered me a class, which pretty soon grew into four. The Head of Centre there was a guy called John, who was a super employer. North Portsmouth Adult Education Centre offered me a class, which soon grew to be two, and after a while, Cowplain Centre asked me to take on two classes on a Friday, as the teacher was moving. I was off and running. I was on the books as a substitute teacher, too, and got real pleasure from standing in for other teachers. It's a challenge because there is resistance. Everyone is used to their own teacher, and the routine of their practice. It takes a big presence and plenty of charisma to turn them around, and to convince them that all teachers are simply messengers. We are not the message – we are the messengers.

Mike was enjoying his job in Portsmouth when, suddenly, he was moved to Chiswick in West London. There was no way that we were going to uproot again; 'Yeollands' was our eighth home in fifteen years and it was time to settle. So he commuted for a year. He would have left when I got up, and I would have gone out to yoga by the time he returned. We 'caught up' on the week-end.

Our busy life was challenged once more with a phone call from my brother. Leigh had founded a dog obedience security firm called K9 Services. It was very successful in the beginning. His wife, Meg, had started a horse-riding stables. The one business supported the other one, and difficulties had occurred. Leigh was going into liquidation and they had to sell the horses. His youngest son, Adam, was breaking his heart at having to part with his mare, Bonnie, and would Gemma have her? Now, Gem had been going to riding lessons, and the idea of owning her own horse was very attractive. Add to this that we would be doing Leigh and Meg, and particularly Adam, a favour, and the decision was soon made. We agreed to take Bonnie on a month's trial, having never even met her!

I must admit that I was expecting a little dapple grey carousel pony, and was somewhat taken aback when they walked Bons down the ramp from the lorry. She was a horse. She was going to be a handful. Gem was eleven at this time, and it was pretty clear that I was going to be the main stable lass, but nothing daunted, Bonnie became a family member. We now had two children, two dogs, two cats and one horse.

At first, we had Bonnie on part livery at a Stableyard down the lane from us. It was expensive, but it gave us an opportunity to get up to speed on horse management. We could see her in the paddock behind our house from the back bedroom windows. We then moved her across the road to a do-it-yourself Stables called Ashwood. Now, we could see her in the field opposite the front of the house. Gemma's biggest joy was to come out of school, (she was now at Seniors,) cross the road, go down the footpath, and be met at the style by her mother, her two dogs, her horse and her cat! How idyllic was that?

My morning routine was now to get up, feed the cats, walk down the road to the stables, give Bonnie her breakfast bucket and then take her to the field. I loved walking down the road, in the early morning silence, and turning into the stable yard to discover a hive of activity. I then returned home, gave the children their breakfast, made their packed lunches, saw them off to school and then walked the dogs. After giving the dogs their breakfast, I would return to the stables to muck out, and then get myself ready to teach my classes, or to shop, or whatever needed doing.

I had been a fairly confident horse-rider, and soon after Bonnie landed in our family, I decided to take her out for a hack. She was very excitable, I discovered, and unused to being out on her own. For a mare who had impeccable stable manners, I was constantly amazed at how wild and unpredictable she became on a ride. She spooked at everything!

The first part of the ride was relatively uneventful, then we came out on to Lovedean Lane and she bolted. We were galloping down the lane, overtaking cars, with the scenery flashing by! Fortunately, I was able to turn her and I headed her up Rose Hill, which is a steep incline. Once she began to tire, she slowed down and I could breathe again.

After this scrape, I decided to only ride her in company. I went out for a hack with the owner of the stables, Janet. We had one particular hack which we all enjoyed. We called it the three hill gallop. Janet suggested that she and her horse, Carmen, should go first, and then they would wait for us. The first part of the plan worked, but just as Bonnie and I completed the gallop to the top of the third hill, the bridle snapped by the bit. Bonnie tasted freedom and off she went, like the wind. We were hurtling through the country lane, me hanging on to her mane for grim death. The hedgerows were zipping past me, and all I could hear was the pounding of her hooves. I knew that we would soon emerge from the lane on to the road. There were often lorries coming around the corner, and all I could think was that Gemma would never speak to me again if her mare got injured. I chose a soft looking spot and disembarked! Bonnie hurtled on for a short way, and then noticed that she had lost her rider. She stopped, and, quite nonchalantly, began to eat the grass. The side that I had landed on was very sore for a while, and my spectacles were damaged, but we had survived another adventure!

Tim was home for lunch on this particular day and, seeing me limp in all covered in mud, he said: "I suppose it was that horse again." Mike was permanently wanting to sell her. He was into Health and Safety for his family, and she was definitely a liability. She never passed the risk assessment! But, strangely, she behaved beautifully when being schooled, and was no trouble at all when we took her on a hack with Gem on board and me beside. Gemma was only eleven when she had Bonnie, but we did know that, if we had taken a smaller pony first for her, I would never have been able to part with it. So, it made sense to encourage Gem to grow into her. The miles we went with that mare! We would often do a fifteen mile hack, with Gemma riding and me walking.

Another adventure that we had with Bonnie has proved a fun story to tell at parties. We had been to the Orthodontist, and both Gem and I were wearing skirts. Tim happened to remark upon this, when we said we were going to the Stables to groom Bons. We did not anticipate any difficulties. We led her out of her loose box, but someone else was using the hook to which we normally attached her lead rein. So we tied her to a huge trough, which sat outside the entrance to the stables. Bonnie loved being groomed, and was perfectly happy until a fly landed on her nose. She jerked up her nose and, in so doing, realised that the trough moved. That was it. She was off. She blazed out on to the road, dragging the trough after her. I hurtled after her, and in my ignorance and arrogance, honestly believed that, by adding my eight stone of weight to the trough, I would stop her flight. It did not work! I was also dragged after her; the whole front of my body being painfully scraped along the road's surface. Fortunately, at this point, the lead rein broke, and Bonnie trotted up the road, quite undeterred. I shouted at someone to open the gate, and she casually went in to the field and began to graze. Our neighbour, and great friend, Patsy, was hugely amused. She had been driving up the lane, to come home, when she saw Bonnie fly out of the stable yard. Then she saw the trough fly out after her, quickly followed by Carole. It was like something from a Carry-On film! It took five men to lift that trough back into place! I was grazed and sore for several weeks, and, again, Mike wanted to sell the mare.

So, despite our early efforts, Tim and Gem became stereotypical. Tim was into scooters, and Gem was into horses. Often our garage would be home to six lads all stripping down their scooters. Mike and Tim would talk about engines, and Gemma and I would talk about clear rounds. On Mike's fortieth birthday, we decided to get him something that he always wanted. Our cats had all been black or black and white, and he had expressed a hankering for a ginger kitten. Obligingly, our next door neighbour's ginger cat, Candy, gave birth to two kittens, and we took one at six weeks for Mike's surprise. He called him Roger –'Ginger Rogers'!

This kitten was the cutest creature ever. He was so tiny that he could sit on the palm of my hand. Gem was terrified that Oscar was going to eat him. He did lick his lips every time he saw him! We kept them separate for a while, and then I would take a high stool into the lounge, place it behind the settee, and sit with Roger in my arms to watch television. Oscar viewed him, suspiciously, from a distance. Oscar had proved to be volatile and unpredictable and he was particularly aggressive towards other dogs, which can be a Staffordshire Bull Terrier characteristic. In all other respects, he was adorable and was actually a perfect gentleman with our dear old bitch, Biba. Oscar had learnt respect for cats early on. Susie, our well-travelled black kitty-cat, always believed that she was boss. Indeed, she behaved as though she was an 'only pet'. Oscar, as a small pup, had encountered her in our narrow hallway. She faced him squarely, and pulled back her paw to strike. As she landed her blow, he dodged and cracked his head on the wall. His face was a study. The 'balloon' coming out of his head clearly said: "My word, that cat can pull a punch!" The day that we decided to introduce Oscar to Roger formally, we waited till Gem had gone to bed, then we placed the kitten in an armchair. Mike, Tim and I stood guarding him, with rolled up newspapers, and Oscar approached. He put his nose close to the kitten's face to sniff him, and Roger gave him a good slap. From that moment on they became the best of buddies. They were inseparable. Toby took Roger under his wing, curling up and sleeping with him, and Oscar was his very best friend. Now, we had two children, three cats, two dogs and one horse.

One day, having followed my usual routine, I was out walking the dogs and I thought: "I haven't seen that kitten for a while." I ran home and switched off the washing-machine, just in case he had sneaked in there. I searched high and low, calling his name, and eventually heard a pitiful miaow. He had jumped out of Tim's window and landed on the conservatory roof eight foot below! He was fine, and once I had climbed up the ladder and retrieved him, I was fine too. We had a lively and interesting household.

I learnt a life-changing fact at this time in my life. Everything is yoga. It's not just going to a yoga class, sitting on your mat for the posture work, breath-work and meditation; everything is yoga. Cooking dinner for your family is yoga. Walking the dogs is yoga. Grooming the horse is yoga. Phoning my mum is yoga. Every breath taken is a yoga breath. My yoga students became extended family. The love that you feel in a yoga class nourishes you on a very deep level. I began to realise just how powerful prana is. (Prana is life-force, life-giving energy.) When I looked around me, at my peers, I realised that I had more energy at my disposal. I lived, breathed and loved yoga. Yoga is a way of life, and it was my way of life.

**Top**: From left – Dad, Mum ( with Carlo), Grandad Frank, Auntie Margaret, Uncle Ron.
Front row: Cousins Lesley, Diana, Frank & Stella.
**Bottom Left**: Grandad Frank ( with his Scottie) and Dad.
**Bottom Right**: Mum & Dad in love and in 1938.

(1)

Dad and Carlo                                                    (2)

**Top:** From left – Mum, Auntie Una, Dad, Gran (Elizabeth Davies – my mother's mother).
**Bottom Left:** Uncle Joe, my safe harbour.
**Bottom Right:** Our family, outside our house in Bristol.

(3)

**Top Left:** Our family.
**Middle Left:** Mum and me.

**Top Right:** Sharing my apple with the cat, (18months old).
**Middle Right:** Leigh & me on the Isle of Wight.

(4)

**Top Left:** Leigh was always on my back !! **Top Middle:** Mum and me. **Top Right:** "oddly thoughtful"!
**Middle left:** After my swim. **Middle Right:** Leigh with Kim ( left ) and Bob ( right)
**Bottom Left:** A trip to London to see the Coronation decorations, June 20th 1953.
**Bottom Right:** Leigh and me with Whiskey, Ginger and Bob.

(5)

159

**Top Left:** Bob with "Puppy". **Top Right:** Me on holiday in Newton Ferrers, Devon 1957, ( aged 8 ).
**Middle:** Me.
**Bottom Left:** Striking a ballet pose. **Bottom Right:** In the front garden of "Yeolands". (6)

**Top Left:** "Yeolands"   **Top Right:** Mum & Dad in Jersey on a business trip, ( June 1959).
**Middle left:** Me riding Dolly.   **Middle Right:** At the Zoo, (from left ) Keith, Leigh, Chris, Mum & me.
**Bottom Left:** On the ferry to the Isle of Wight, me, Dad, Chris, Leigh & Keith.
**Bottom Right:** Lucky, me and Russ ( who came from Russ Conway's brother).   (7)

**Top :** Growing up. ( From left ) Me, Leigh, Keith, Mum and Chris with Lucky and Russ. ( Outside "Yeolands")

**Bottom:** What and advert for vegetarianism! My Grandmother, Nana Clara Williams at the age of 80.

(8)

"Sauna Girl" the photograph that Mike had on his wall. (1968).          (9)

Don't look now,
but we're married!!
( August 30<sup>th</sup> 1969)

(10)

**Top Left:** Mike with Sabre. **Top Right:** Expecting Tim.
**Middle left:** Mike with Samantha, me with Baby Tim & Auntie Lo with Tammy in South Norwood.
**Middle Right:** Mum, Tim ( aged 11 months), me, Mike & Katy.
**Bottom:** Me with Baby Gemma.

(11)

**Top:** The five grandchildren – ( from left), Adam, Calum, Brett, Gemma & Tim.
**Bottom Left:** Gem & Tim on holiday in France.
**Bottom Right:** Tim & Gem at the campsite, France (1977).   (12)

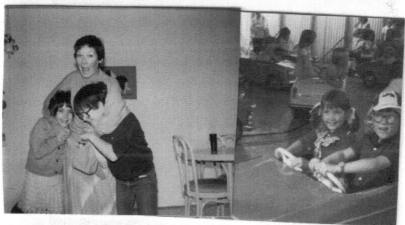

**Top Left:** Me with the children & Biba outside our house in St.Albans.
**Top Right:** Mike and me on holiday in France, ( Tim took this photo ).
**Bottom Left:** Me with our gorgeous kids, ( in the kitchen in Kentucky).
**Bottom Right:** Gem & Tim, (still in France). (13)

**Top left:** Mum & the kids in our front garden, Lexington, Kentucky. **Top Right:** The Kertons at Disneyworld, Florida.   **Middle Left:** Tim, Gem & Mum at the Kentucky Horse Park.
**Middle Right:** Gem, Mum ( seated on a deck chair!), and Tim in our pool in Lexington( 1982).
**Bottom:** Gem & Tim, Daytona Beach, Florida.                                                    (14)

**Top:** Tim with baby Oscar.
**Middle:** Oscar & Toby.
**Bottom:** Bonnie & me.    (15)

**Top:** My brother, Leigh, with Mum in the Hospice, ( June 1990 ).
**Bottom:** Mum with Leigh & Meg's three son. ( from Left ), Adam, Nana, Brett & Calum, ( in the Sue
Ryder Hospice). (16)

**Top:** Mike and me at Neyyar Dam near the Sivananda Ashram, Kerala.
**Middle:** me with Jamila, our Fruit salad lady on Kovalam Beach.
**Bottom:** Tim & Beth share a joke In the boat on the Kerala Backwaters.(17)

171

**Top:** Me with Dr Ananda, ( son of Swami Gitananda), at a Retreat.
**Bottom:** Swami Govinda at the Sivananda Ashram, Neyyar Dam, Kerala, South India.     (18)

**Top:** The four Kertons on
Santander beach ( August 2009)
**Middle:** Gem & Tim, Santander.
**Bottom:** Cate and me at
Gem's Hen weekend ( Jan 2004). (19)

**Top Left:** Mike and me ready for the Bollywood Party. **Top Right:** Tim & Bethan ready for the Bollywood party.
**Bottom:** Clive and Gem at the Bollywood Party ( my 60th Birthday celebration )          (20)

**Top left:** Meg and her lovely husband, Simon.
**Top Right:** Meg and Si ready to party , Indian Style.
**Bottom:** Mike, Rudi and me, ( at our static caravan " Lazy Days"). (21)

*Carole Kerton*

**Top Left:** Essence of Mike
**Bottom Right:** Essence of Carole.  (22)

# Chapter 13

Jupiter sextiles Sun: *You like to live according to a high moral code.*

My mother loved Bonnie. She had loaded the mare into the horse lorry, when Adam was eventing. She loved to come and stay with us. Sometimes, Mike would whisk me away for the week-end, and Mum would move in and take care of the household.

One short break we took in France found us in Carcassonne. We were walking around the castle when I experienced a strong feeling of deja-vu. This was closely followed by a past-life flash. I was a Cathar, and we were being besieged. The Cathars were an heretical Christian sect that flourished in Western Europe in the 12th and 13th centuries. We knew that we were going to be wiped out, and many of us chose to throw ourselves off the battlements, to our death, rather than be captured. I was one such. Later, on reflection, I realised that this explains one quirk of my personality. I do not like to approach the edge when high up on a mountain or hill-top. I do not have a fear of falling, but rather the desire to jump is very attractive, and desirable. I have to give myself a good talking to, and need to convince myself that I have not finished the work of this life-time yet!

Gemma discovered boys. She was always a very pretty girl, and had no trouble attracting the opposite sex. At some point in our family history, Tim moved from being the big brother with an annoying little sister, to being on the parental team. I do not remember this being a conscious decision, on anyone's part, but it was a most effective shift. The three of us concentrated on bringing up Gemma, and Tim kept a close eye on her boyfriends. Ian was a year older than Gem, and as blond as she was dark. He was a very handsome young man, lots of fun, and very willing to fit into our family. He was absolutely sweet with my mother, and was just as happy washing the car, as mucking the stable. He would go out on hacks with Gem; she on her horse, and he on his bike.

Bonnie was still excitable on a ride. Gem loved to take her to Lady's Mile. I would walk there with them, Gem would set off at a frantic gallop, and Mike would drive the car to the other end of the lane and park across it, to stop Bonnie's flight! She was a mare with a lot of opinions, and Gem did very well to handle her. They used to go off to Clear Rounds, and sometimes Bonnie would behave impeccably. Sometimes, she found it more amusing to put her head down at the last second and watch Gem take the jump without her! We booked them into dressage lessons, with a very knowledgeable young man. Sometimes it went really well, and on those days it was sight to be seen; Gemma so pretty, and Bonnie so graceful. They were a stunning sight; Bonnie was half Anglo-Arab, and she certainly stood out in a crowd.

We were out on a hack one day, when Gem heard a cat crying. On searching around, we discovered a small black kitten, abandoned in a field. Yes, of course we took her home! Mike made a firm pronouncement: "We have three cats already, and we are not having four." Mike does not put his foot down often, but when he does, we all remember. Daisy, (for so Gemma named her, since she had been found in a field in Day's Lane,) spent the first night in the stable. We spent the next day searching for her owners, in vain, and Daisy spent her second night on Gemma's bed. We now had four cats. Roger took to the role of Big Brother, and although Susie remained aloof, you would often see Daisy, Roger and Toby all squeezed in one chair together, in the conservatory.

Oscar did not bat an eyelid at having a fourth cat. He had become the self-promoted policeman to all cat fights. The moment he heard the low yowl of an imminent scuffle, he would hurtle towards the backdoor. He actually did what you see on cartoons: he revved up and started running on the spot. As soon as ever you opened the door, he would fly up the path, barking ferociously. Our cats just stood their ground: "Oh, its only Oscar," but the other cats would run for their very lives. It was a great game!

Another favourite trick for Oscar involved an empty kitchen roll tube. I would blow the soldiers reveille and he would appear, like magic. He sat up, puffing out his chest, and then would proudly receive his cardboard tube, as though he was receiving his orders, and then belt off with it, thrilled.

He and Tim spent hours chasing one another around. We had a circuit in 'Yoellands', as it was open-plan. Tim would 'set it up' by catching Oscar's eye, and then they would be off, blazing round the furniture at top speed. It drove Mike completely mad. Years later, just after Tim had left home, I came back from yoga to find Mike and Oscar hurtling around the furniture. Expressing my incredulity, Mike said: "Well, someone had to do it!"

Dear Biba got older. Her chief job was to greet me when I returned from my yoga classes. When she became very deaf, Oscar would wake her up to tell her that I was home. Then she would run down the hall, barking, with her front paws coming off the ground. He never took over the job. Biba was my girl; Oscar was that most unusual of dogs, a family dog. But Tim was always his favourite.

We decided to build a stable for Bonnie in the back-garden. It seemed like a really good plan at the time. It would save all the walking up and down; it would be good security to be able to see Bonnie; we would have everything 'in house'. We endeavoured to buy the land behind the house from the builder, but he was not going to part with it. Nothing daunted, we built the stable in our rather small back garden, beside the shed, which became the hay-store. Mike built a lovely little post and rail fence around it, and we had our very own Kentucky Horse Farm! I could not wait to send photographs out to my great friend, Connie, In Lexington! Connie had already met Bonnie, and loved her. She came to stay with us for a most memorable holiday. Whilst here, and holding Bonnie, the mare jerked and broke Connie's finger. We took her to Casualty, where she promptly fell in love with the doctor, and kept insisting that she could pay with Mastercard. She loved telling that story, and her crooked finger was always an excuse to tell tales of England.

There was only one problem with this gorgeous little stable set-up. Bonnie would not pass through the garage and side-way to get there. We tried everything. Our friend, Tania, and a Shetland pony called Pinto, to the rescue. Now, Pinto would do anything for a bucket of pony nuts, so we enticed him in and Bonnie followed him. We were overjoyed. Bonnie then was very happy to be in our garden all winter, but once she went out nights on May 1st, she would not come in again for the whole summer. Unfortunately, Pinto would! I would hear a shout from the garage: "Mum, Pinto's in the drive, the garage, the side-way, the back-garden!" He would escape from the field and head straight for us: "Mmm. I know where good pony nuts can be found." He would shuffle by bits of engine, umbrellas, ladders, you name it, and there he would be, nose contentedly in bucket. We had some rough journeys getting him back to the field. On one occasion, he pulled me right through a hedge, with Mike looking on, helpless with laughter!

It was a special ceremony at nine o'clock each evening in the winter, when Gem, Ian and I would go out through the conservatory, give Bonnie her apple, skip her stable out, and give her a hay-net for the night. We always kept her in on Christmas Day, and it was such a joy to see her blinking her long eyelashes over the stable-door, while we ate our Christmas lunch in the dining-room. Very often, you would glance out and see Roger lying along the door, keeping her company.

On one memorable day, we were grooming Bonnie in the garage. Daisy was up in the rafters and made her way along till she was right above the mare. We suddenly looked up, and realised exactly what was going to happen. We had visions off Bonnie rearing up and hurting herself, out of fear, when the cat landed on her. To our utter amazement, though, when Daisy jumped down on to her back, she did not even flinch. I am sure that animals operate on a telepathic level. We had four cats, but Bonnie never stepped on any of them. She would lower her head, put her nose really close to their faces, and gently snort. Even Susie, who at first would not come downstairs because she could see the horses in the field opposite, learned to love Bonnie. Unfortunately, she never learned to love Gem! Gemma would bend down to speak to her, and Susie would grab her on both sides of her head, and give her a good shaking!

Susie always slept beside my bed. I would open a drawer, put a blanket over the contents, and there she would sleep all night. Indeed, all of our animals slept in our bedroom. Biba would be on my side of the bed, Oscar on Mike's side, Susie in the drawer, Roger on my head (just like a Russian hat!), Daisy cuddled into the crook of my arm or the back of my knee, and Toby would stretch his full length between us. Finally even Mike's good nature snapped. He said that if I could get Bonnie up the stairs, she would have been in the bedroom, too. He issued an ultimatum – it was either him, or the animals. It was touch and go there for a bit (!), but eventually we compromised. The cats slept in the lounge, and we kept the dogs in the bedroom.

Tim is highly intelligent. He has a high I.Q.; in fact it is in a band occupied by only two per cent of the population. Unfortunately, it was not 'cool' at that time for a boy to study. He made no effort to revise for his G.C.S.E.s, and suddenly decided to leave school at sixteen. His close friend, Andy, had applied for a Shipwright's Apprenticeship at the Dockyard in Portsmouth, and Tim decided to do the same. I was horrified. I had always envisioned Tim doing 'A' levels and going to University. I could not bear the waste of his great potential. Mike instructed me to back off. He said that if I kept nagging, I was going to lose the kid altogether. Now, in hindsight, I realise that school had developed into a survival test, rather than an attractive opportunity to explore learning, and I fully understand why he was so eager to leave.

Mike had suffered when Tim had broken away on our return from the States, but we had always endeavoured to keep the communication channels open. Mike reasoned that he could do a lot worse. This was a sought after Apprenticeship, and it would be excellent training. So, Tim left school, got through the interviews and went to the Dockyard for a four year training. He commuted there each day on his scooter, then a motorbike, and finally a Harley-Davidson. He continued to have a wide and loyal group of friends; he continued to compartmentalise his life; he continued to read good classical books avidly; he was a very good kid and he followed his own plan for education.

How good he was showed up when his Nana was taken seriously ill. My mother developed cancer of the cervix. She was still living in Weston-super- Mare, and her doctor recommended radiotherapy. She was desperately sick, and literally stopped eating all together. Being sick was hell to my mum. I had travelled up to see her, in the snow, one day, taking my dog, Biba, with me. It is so sad to see your mother going downhill and growing older. She had been a very strong lady; strong in her opinions, and strong in her constitution. Eventually, responding to a plea from her neighbour, I managed to overcome her desire to retain her independence, and brought her back to our home. She was in bed for three weeks, while I took her little delicacies to try to tempt her appetite. We were all thrilled when, after three weeks, she got up and dressed. She still looked frail, but her spirit had not given up yet.

Mike was insistent that we should move Mum near to us. Her Welsh family were against the idea, but Mike was very concerned at me driving all the way to Somerset, in hazardous conditions, whilst emotionally churning and not knowing what I would find on my arrival. We considered buying a house with a Granny Annexe, and looked at several, but Mum was not ready to make that jump. She found a bungalow which was a half a mile down the road from us and bought that. We had three happy years with her, when she became incredibly close to Tim and Gem.

Lovely people lived in her little cul-de-sac, and they made her very welcome. Gem would announce that she was going to stay over on a Saturday night with Nana; they would have a beautiful meal together, and then watch a movie. We now do this on a Friday evening with Gemma's oldest daughter, Lizzie. She loves historical dramas, and we watch Charles Dickens, or Shakespeare, Jane Austen or Oscar Wilde. We all so look forward to our Fridays; just as my mother did to her Saturdays with Gem.

Once, when Gem was staying with my mother, they invited me over for lunch. Now, Biba was a very old dog by this time, and she could not make the walk. Oscar, on the other hand, definitely needed the exercise. So, I decided to put Biba in the wheel-barrow, and trundle her down the lane. I tied Oscar's lead to the handle, put blankets in the bottom of the barrow, and off we set. Of course, the problem came when Oscar sniffed a particularly enticing odour, and strained to the side. Then we were in extreme danger of all capsizing. My only regret is that I did not get sponsored. We were such a hysterical sight that I feel sure

185

we could have raised good funds for charity! My mother thought it was hilarious, but Gem refused to walk back with me. I was a total embarrassment to a fifteen year old!

Mum developed a cough, which was persistent and painful. Finally, the doctor diagnosed secondary cancer; this time in the lungs. There was nothing that they could do, and I remember holding Mum so tightly, as though the force of my own will could reverse the inevitable outcome.

They took Mum into St. Mary's Hospital in Portsmouth. She soon made friends in the ward; she was always a character. Tim was a free spirit and I knew that I could not make him do anything that he did not want to do. But as I said, he was a good kid, and he would turn up at the Hospital, on the way home from work. In he would go, take his crash helmet off, and sit down for a good natter with his Nana. She loved it, and so did all the other old ladies in the ward.

We wanted to nurse Mum at home, but she was adamant that she would go to Bordean House, which was a Sue Ryder Hospice in Langrish. It was a beautiful house, and she loved it there. Most of the staff were superb. Gem and I would arrive, and there would be no occupants in the bedrooms that we passed on the corridor. They would all be in Mum's bedroom; it was like a permanent coffee morning!

This was the poem that Gem wrote for Mum at this time:

*'Nana, you've lived a colourful life,*

*You've been a daughter, a sister, a mother, a wife.*

*You've travelled the world and seen lots of places,*

*You have so many friends and know so many faces.*

*You've raised dogs and cats and a goat called Sam,*

*And have been a much 'tidier lady' than certainly I am!*

*It's been a pleasure to have you just down the road,*

*And to watch the garden grow that you carefully sowed.*

*You'll always be part of our family,*

*For all the grandchildren, A B C, T and G.*

*Yes, you've had four grandsons, but only one granddaughter,*

*And I turned out the best, even though I'm much shorter!!'*

*Tim wrote: 'You're a brilliant Nana, and we all love you. Keep smiling... Who can describe a grandmother's love? It is such a special thing... Love, Tim.'*

Mum decided to knit Gemma a complete layette for her first baby. She took to this task with a will, and produced the most exquisite baby clothes. She then packed them neatly in a suit-case, to await the day when they would be needed. Gem was only sixteen. We carefully stowed the suit-case away, and with what mixed emotions Gem opened it, seven years later, when she was eight months pregnant on Lizzie. It still smelt of my Mum! That beautiful clean fragrance that was my mother's signature. We were all to smell it often, as Mum visited us from Spirit World, and we would know she was with us still. Gemma proudly dressed Lizzie in Nana's hand-knitted garments, then Amy and finally Ben. Then she lovingly washed them and stowed them away for either Tim's babies or Lizzie's.

This was the poem that I wrote in mum's Visitor's Book:

*'Together we've lived and laughed and talked;*

*Together we've cooked, gardened and walked;*

*Together we've watched Tim and Gem grow –*

*And have shared with them whatever we know.*

*The family goes on, as families must,*

*But even this will not separate us.'*

The last week of Mum's life was agony. Mike would sit beside her bed, listening to her breathing. She was breathing so rapidly; her lungs were like colanders. She was in a coma. For the last five nights, I slept in her room with her. No more 'coffee mornings', no more Gem and Ian dancing round the room to make her laugh. Her sisters, nieces and nephews had all been wonderful, and had visited. At the end, I made myself very unpopular by denying any more visitors. She was like a broken doll, and she would have hated anyone to see her like that. One of the nursing Sisters asked me if it was hard to be away from my family. I replied that 'no, it was hard to be anywhere else, but right beside Mum.' I had given Mum 'permission' to leave. She had confided in Mike that she was ready to go. She was knocking on Heaven's door. The

Sister convinced me to go home for a night as she said this could go on for another three weeks; they did not know.

How extra-ordinary to go home! My world, even in that short time, had become one special room. I received a rapturous welcome, though, and I suppose I needed to be jolted back into our everyday world. I had continued to teach my yoga classes, even when I was staying in the Hospice. The following afternoon, we received a call to say: "Get here quickly". Mike left immediately, and I left shortly afterwards. I believe that Mum waited, firstly for me not to be there, (I was holding her back, even though that was the very last thing in the world that I wanted to do,) and secondly, to fit in with my yoga schedule. I know that sounds bizarre, but she was so convinced that my yoga helped people, and she cared. Mike was there for her last breath. They had always had such a close relationship, and she could not have had a better son-in-law. When I arrived, Mum's spirit was no longer in the room. We had shared unconditional love, at the end of her life, and my heart ached for her.

I taught my yoga class that night. It was one and a half hours after Mum died. I knew that was what she wanted me to do, and I dedicated the class to her. Gem and Ian came to the class, and we had stopped off at Tim's friend, Justin's, to give him the news. One dear friend, and long-time student, Patricia, still remembers that class. She has been with me for twenty-seven years. After the class, I remember Ian saying: "I cannot believe that you tell people to breathe, and they do." My mother was no longer breathing, and my life would never be the same again. Nevertheless, I counted my blessings, and will always remember that I was very fortunate to experience unconditional love with both of my parents at the end of their lives.

Yoga is a way of life. It is not just a weekly class; it is a perennial philosophy. Being a yoga teacher is who I am, and the best of who I am sits on the yoga mat. Dedicating a practice to some-one has a profound affect. I believe in the power of collective thought. We have seen the effects of this, time and time again. My early Monday class could all tell you stories of poorly, premature babies, pulling through after the yoga class; and depressed folk suddenly finding a reason to live; and those fighting their passing suddenly relaxing and surrendering, peacefully, to their death. Students from the classes always report 'feeling sudden warmth, or lightness' when we send them healing and they are unwell. One lovely student, Louise, even attributes a successful Art Exhibition to the yoga class's good thoughts! There is so much more to this practise of yoga than meets the eye, and there is always a reason for someone choosing to join a specific class. At this time, I had a friend in my yoga classes called Lyn. I looked at her on day and saw that she was wearing a helmet, and that she had a moustache. I knew in a twinkling that she had been a Cathar, too, and that she had jumped to her death next to me. Its hard to describe these past-life experiences, other than to say that there is an inner knowing; a soul recognition; a realisation.

# Chapter 14

M ars sextiles Jupiter: *You can be a reassuring person to have around in a crisis. If there is no crisis there is every chance that having you around will bring one on!*

The funeral went well. Mum had always said that Leigh would be late for his own mother's funeral, and so it proved! I did really feel his support that day, though, and we had a long talk, leaning on Bonnie's post and rail fence. The service was led by our local Vicar, Chris, and he did a splendid job. Mike rang the bells at All Saints Church, Catherington, so we knew him well.

It was dear cousin Sally who came down, with her husband Bryan, to help scatter Mum's ashes and to see her stone in place. Out of my twenty six cousins, Sally is my favourite. I do keep in gentle touch with six others, (Christmas cards mainly,) but Sally has always been a good friend. She wore the brooch that Mum had picked out to give her. She asked me to bring her jewellery to Bordean House one day, and we sat on the floor while she allocated her special pieces for her favourite people. Funny to think that I had twenty six cousins, our children had three, and our grandchildren have just one.

So the painful task of sorting out Mum's possessions and the bungalow began. Mum had expressed regret that she had not had time to do this for me. Bless her! She need not have worried. As Gem had said, in her poem, my mother was a very tidy lady. Each drawer was like a filing cabinet! Her wonderful neighbour, Mel, who had bought Mum the Visitor's book for the Hospice, gave me sound advice. She said: "Carole, when you reach the point when you just cannot bear to go through any more poignant memories, place the stuff in a box, and put it up in your loft. The day will come when you can face it again." Perhaps the most poignant find was the newspaper announcement of my parents' wedding, and the ornaments from their wedding cake. Mel and I kept in touch until her death; always sending one another cards on the anniversaries of our mothers' deaths.

Tim continued to work at the Dockyard; Gemma changed boyfriends. We got to know Scott, Terry, Mark, James (who was the vocals in a band) and then she met Gary. They met at a night-club in Southsea, and it was love at first sight. Gary was four years older than Gem, very good-looking, and he was a Trainee bank Manager, so he had prospects. It was not very long before they had got engaged and then bought a lovely little terraced house in Southsea. Gem was doing her 'A' levels, and planning to go off to University. There was one evening when we all met at a restaurant in Southsea, and at the end of a lovely meal we parted company outside, and Gem and Gary walked away, hand in hand. They were a strikingly good-looking couple. Gem had very long hair at that time, in a French plait. As they walked away, Gem looked back at us, over her shoulder. There was something in that look... I knew for certain sure that wherever her life took her, and whatever decisions she made, she would always be a family girl. She would always look back over her shoulder.

With Gemma going to University, I began to realise the full impact of me being the only stable lass. I would be unable to exercise Bonnie. She was a very volatile mare, and, as a yoga teacher, I could not handle a broken limb! We decided to find a suitable field to buy, and to retire her. Mike studied the newspapers, and eventually found a beautiful field in Steep, near Petersfield. When Gem, Mike and I went up to see it, we knew immediately that it was the right place. This was to be confirmed later, after building the stables, when we saw a double rainbow over the loose-boxes. I had inherited some money from my mother's estate, and I knew she would be delighted to contribute to Bonnie's retirement home. Eventually, we installed her, and after one false start, we found her a suitable companion. Gossie entered our lives. She was a liver chestnut Connemara pony; a tremendous character, very bossy and very jealous of Bonnie. But, as the vet said: "Better to have a bossy friend than no friend at all."

It did not take long for me to realise that travelling up and down the motorway to attend to the horses was not a good use of my time. I pushed for a move to be closer to them. We drew a circle around the field in Steep, and looked for property within a half mile of the horses' field, which was called 'Foxfield'. We still needed four bedrooms, although the children were imminently leaving home, we did know that they would come back. We also needed good parking. We made an appointment to see 'Fyfield'. The house was in need of love and care, but it was light and bright and ticked a lot of boxes. Mike was very reluctant to leave our large house in Lovedean, but ridding ourselves of our mortgage was a successful temptation. After three attempts, we sold 'Yeollands', and moved to Fyfield. We have lived here now for almost twenty years, the longest that I have ever lived anywhere in my life, but I can still remember our moving day as though it was yesterday. It was a complete disaster!

In all the rushing around, Oscar had managed to escape into the front drive. He attacked a passing dog, and bit him quite badly. We, of course, paid for the vet's bill, but it was not a good start to the day! Our buyers arrived in their lorry, long before we were ready to evacuate, adding to the pressure. It was December the twenty-first, and Mike was horrified at moving just before Christmas, but I knew that it was then or never! (We had our Christmas decorations up in 'Yoellands', and were expecting Mike's folks for the holiday.) Mike and Gemma left to go up to the other end. Tim and I finished up, packing our special items in his Volkswagen Camper and my estate car. I had our dog, Oscar, the three cats, and a clock, which had been a wedding present to my parents, and which was too precious to be entrusted to the Removers. I set off, believing that Tim was following. His camper van promptly broke down at the bottom of the drive, blocking all exit and entrance! Meanwhile, Mike and Gemma had discovered that the folk who owned 'Fyfield' had neither handed in their key, nor moved out! The couple who owned it were in the middle of an acrimonious divorce; she had agreed the sale, he had not. The house was full, and our Removers eventually ended up moving the contents out on to the front lawn and then moving our furniture in. It was chaos. There were vehicles everywhere, the neighbours were not pleased, and we were beginning to realise just what a state our new house was in.

Our first night was bitter. The boiler was broken, and just before Christmas was not a good time to be looking for a heating engineer. We argued over who was to have Oscar on the bed, to keep us warm! In the morning, Mike and Tim got up, washed in cold water, and went off to work. I was going up to the stables, walking Oscar with me, when Gem asked: "What shall I do, Mum?" Now, the whole house was filthy and full of packing-cases, so I replied: "Just pick something." I was unprepared for what she chose. When I came back from the stables, she had put up the Christmas decorations!

Little by little, we cleaned and repaired. Tim bought us a book for Christmas entitled: 'Doing up a dump'! Mike's parents came up trumps; they came only for Christmas day, and his Dad made a beautiful log fire while his Mum rushed around making everyone cups of coffee. In early

January, the new boiler was fitted, and we made plans for new windows, carpets and so on. I never regretted the move. I loved being just a short walk from the horses, and just a mile from Petersfield. Mike did look over his shoulder often. He missed his gorgeous large garage, and new modern house, but he threw himself enthusiastically into field management. His first task was to join the farmers' union!

The A272, at that time, was not nearly as busy as it is now, but we did have concerns about the cats. Our dear old Susie had developed a tumour, and I had made the decision to have her put down. I could not bear that she was in pain. She had been the most faithful of cats; had been to Kentucky and back; and how I missed our 'love-ins'. I buried her in the front garden at 'Yeollands'. Biba, my beloved Watercress Terrier, was buried in the back-garden. We knew the end was nigh for her, and prepared a beautiful plot, beside the stable. My two special old ladies were much grieved. When we moved to Petersfield, we had two young adults, two horses, one dog and three cats.

A short while after our move, Gemma and Gary ended their relationship, and she was heartbroken. We were very proud of her. She handled finishing it in a very mature way, but she grieved for a year.

Tim completed his Apprenticeship, got his indentures, and was presented with his Diploma by the Admiral. He worked for one year as a Shipwright, learned a lot of practical skills, and then decided to take voluntary redundancy. He had renovated a Volkswagen camper, and decided to travel around Europe. As he said to me at the time: "I don't think I like Ships, Mum." He left on his twenty first birthday. Now, we have never been allowed to celebrate Tim's birthday with him. He just simply cannot handle the fuss! He loves being part of our birthday celebrations, but is mortified by being the centre of attention when it is his own. On his eighteenth birthday, we went out for a meal to celebrate, and he went out with his friends. We knew he was home when we heard the balloons popping, at the end of the drive. Even his last one, his fortieth, he arranged to go away with his mates. We did organise a very small celebration, with Gem and family, and my lovely sister-in-law, Meg, and her super husband, Simon. This we did the week before his birthday, and we got away with it. But it came as no surprise that he was leaving us to travel on his twenty-first.

Tim saw seven countries on his trip, and we drove out to meet him in Italy. Gem, and her friend, Teresa, flew out for one week, too, and we had an excellent holiday, although Gemma was still nursing her broken heart. Tim had read extensively during his trip, and had grown intellectually and spiritually. On his return, he decided that he had the travel bug, and promptly planned to back-pack around India and Nepal with his friend, Steve. It was October. Gemma left to go to Southampton University on the Saturday. We drove her over to the student house, and had a very tearful goodbye. Then we drove Tim to the Airport on the following day, to go to India. I remember being so determined not to embarrass Tim by crying; I kept a British stiff upper lip! But Steve's Mum and both his sisters had a good sob. Coming back in the car, I was still talking inane rubbish, when Mike interrupted me and said: "You're going to have to cry sometime." The 'sometime' arrived when we reached home and Gem phoned. We both sat there, clinging on to the phone, sobbing our hearts out and totally incapable of speech. I had lost both my children, in the space of two days, and it was an empty nest, indeed. Mike missed his kids, but basically he rejoiced. He could have the remote now! He could choose the television programmes! He could sit in his favourite chair! I went into a decline meanwhile, and grieved and mourned my loss for six weeks. Only my yoga pulled me through.

After six weeks, I reluctantly adapted. I found that I had time to read; what a luxury! I read yoga book after yoga book. My classes were going from strength to strength, and I was learning so much. Each new student brings a different energy to the group, and there are always new health conditions to research.

I have this theory that we are born with a cut-out shape already prepared for us in the world. It is like a jig-saw piece. As we grow, and learn; as we become more intuitive, and have greater insights and realisations; as we realise that this journey of ours is endlessly fascinating, and never-ending, we fill this shape a little more. Eventually, if we fulfil our full potential, we fill every corner of this jig-saw piece, and it is then that we merge into the whole, and the bigger picture becomes clear.

I have always used my intuition. I love that word, intuition –'teaching from within.' I began to examine my own yoga practice in greater depth, and to examine my yoga classes in a different way. I began to enquire. Yes, that works, but why does it work? The Colleges I worked for began to ask more from us. They wanted us to provide them with 'learning outcomes', and 'aims and objectives'. One of my Colleges wanted me to do a thirty four week lesson plan, in advance. At first, moving yoga from non-vocational to vocational study seemed absolutely ridiculous, but one of my Heads of Centre explained to me that I was assessing my students all the time, anyway. This I did instinctively, storing my observations in the back of my mind. They were simply asking me to write them down. I had never been an administrative sort of person, but I was beginning to appreciate the point of well documented research.

My joy is in never repeating a class. I also never repeat a workshop. I continue to grow. I am not in the same place ever again, so my energy, my realisations, my growth has moved on. I might repeat sections of classes which work well, but nothing is repeated in its entirety. This obviously makes for more work, in the planning, but I hope that it keeps my teaching fresh and alive. I began to realise that some of the aspects of my class, which had just simply 'come to me', were based in ancient yogic traditions and philosophy. I began to appreciate that I was being guided. Indeed, it was at about this time, that I actually felt my Spirit Guide being replaced by another one. I had been promoted!

I believe that yoga teachers are the communicators for the Earth. We filter down the messages from the Spirit World which are necessary for humanity's progress. Often I will be talking to another yoga teacher, half-way through the week, and we will discover that we have been using the same theme, and even the same set of postures. I am sure, as I mentioned before, when the Council sits, the wise ones say: "Pass this message to the Yoga teachers. They will get it around." I feel that we are here to bring balance, understanding, and to reconnect humans to their hearts and souls.

I had more physical time, at this point in my life, to turn inward and to get to know the 'real me'. I began to understand that yoga is a journey of self-discovery. I was being offered ways to learn more. For instance, one day I was driving back from yoga in the car. I stopped at a roundabout, and to my left there was a dog with his owner, returning from his walk. I became the dog! I know that sounds bizarre, but for a brief moment, I was that dog. I could feel exactly what it was like to be that little soul. I knew his mind, his breath, his heart. This is called 'shape-shifting', and it is practised by Shamans, (Native American Indian medicine men.) It happened on another occasion when I was passenger in a car. We passed an elderly gentleman, walking with a stick. I became him. I filled his body, and 'knew' every ache and pain, in every joint. I also found that I was more and more aware of people's auras. This is the energy field that surrounds every being. I had been able to 'see' auras for a long time, but now it was becoming difficult not to 'see' them! My wonderful first yoga teacher, Lilla, had written a book about auras. I had been talking to a close friend on one occasion, and the subject of auras came up. Her book literally jumped out of the book-case!

One beautiful student, who came to my class in Alton and was moving away said: "You have a unique ability to make everyone in the room feel special. I will miss seeing that in action." I was very pleased with this comment. It made me feel humble, because I knew that I was 'channelling'. I was 'open' to receiving information so that I could know each person, and hopefully help them, in some small way. I often receive a nudge at the end of a practice: "Go and see so-and-so. They need a hug". I always act on the information, and it is invariably correct.

My depth of experience, at this time, was growing. I was filling out more of my jig-saw piece.

# Chapter 15

Jupiter in Capricorn: *Some of your friends are chosen particularly because they are of the esoteric kind.*

There is an old saying: "Tell me who you have been with, and I'll tell you what you are." My friends are yoga people, spiritual folk. The friends who have come to me through my classes are very special indeed. Tricia became a firm favourite for our whole family, she has a beautiful energy; and dear Inge, a Danish therapist with a big heart and delightful sense of humour; Theresiu, who is Dutch and ethereal, and is married to an exceptional Homeopathic doctor; Jill, a close buddy who has been to India with us, and who is a soul-mate; dear Yvonne, who has shared wonderful week-ends at the Krishnamurti Centre with me. These are the friends who have supported me on my journey. Later, I was to make more strong connections with colleagues in the Friends of Yoga Society, and then those most special of people, my graduated teachers. These friendships have stood the test of time.

Most of my friends are vegetarian. Tim was the first in our family to become a 'veggie', followed by Gemma and me. I was a vegetarian for well over twenty years, and then took a further step and became a vegan. As one of my graduated teachers, Sue, remembers, I told my student teachers that: "I love my grandchildren, but I don't want to eat them. I love animals, and I don't want to eat them either." The first rule of yoga is AHIMSA, non-violence. (Please see the introduction.) You cannot eat a slice of cow without killing the cow first of all. This is violence. I once went to a yoga week-end led by a rather well-known yoga teacher. I happened to sit next to her the first night at dinner, and she tucked into roast beef! I could not take anything that she said after that seriously.

Mike was to give up meat later on, after our first visit to an Ashram. Mike was an 'armchair yogi'. He fully acknowledged and observed the changes that yoga had brought about in me. He read all the books, and completely agreed with all of the philosophy, but he did not attend classes. I feel that, on some level, he believed that if I was a practising yogi, it was good enough for both of us! The Universe was soon to dissuade him of this idea.

I used to teach a triple on a Monday evening for Highbury College. The first one was five till six thirty, then the second was six thirty to eight, and the last one was eight to nine thirty. One Monday evening when I got home, everything was wrong. Mike was not there to greet me, Oscar was in a state and his bed was in the dining-room. There was a horrible hush to the house. I found a hastily scribbled note on the breakfast bar. Mike had been 'blue-lighted' into hospital with a suspected heart attack. Now, Mike's grandfather died of a heart attack, and so did his father, so there is a genetic proneness of which we were both aware. I immediately phoned the hospital, and heard that he was comfortable. After a host of tests, it transpired that he had a virus in his heart-wall, which had manifested as a heart attack. We both had to face our demons at this time. Both the children were away, Tim in India, and Gemma in Southampton. Gem came home immediately, but we decided not to tell Tim until he returned. Mike was making a steady recovery, and was being very sensible about addressing his stress level.

Indeed, this was the time when Mike announced that he was going to join a yoga class; that he needed to de-stress urgently – not like I had ever mentioned that! I whole-heartedly embraced the idea of Mike joining a yoga group, but I was ill-prepared for it to be one of mine. I was not sure how I would feel about having him there but I need not have worried. He slipped into the back of my Petersfield class, having impressed upon me that he did not want a 'fuss'. I was not to announce our relationship. Funnily enough, six weeks later, one of my students in that class, called Shona, saw us in Petersfield, holding hands. She looked at me, askance. It was not until the end of term, when my class was asked to fill in feed-back forms, and I said: "I cannot really ask my husband to evaluate me!" that Shona breathed a huge sigh of relief and said: "Oh, he's your husband. I did not think you were the type to have an affair!" Had we known that this was the rumour, we may have kept them guessing for a little longer!

It was enriching for our relationship to have Mike as a student. He fitted in beautifully, and became a popular member of the group. He has now been practising yoga for eighteen years. At first I felt that it was a box ticking exercise, but soon I could tell from the questions that he asked that he was taking it on board. He saw another side to his long-term wife. He began to respect the philosophy that is yoga. He began to see that the best of me is what sits on the mat. Up until then, my yoga teaching was my 'little job', and was treated like a rather interesting hobby. But now Mike could fully appreciate the benefits, and had a new respect for me. I discovered that there was only one drawback to having him present: I could not demonstrate balance postures! For some extraordinary reason I could demonstrate, successfully, all week, but at Mike's class I would founder. What was even more amusing was that he was very good at them!

Mike had always been a good breadwinner. He paid all the bills, and took care of our finances. We supported Gem through University, and she worked her way as a cashier at Waitrose. No student loans for Gem. My 'little job', my yoga, bought the extras. I paid for the horse feed and bedding. I had paid for the children's driving lessons. (They had both passed their motorbike tests, and their car tests.) I paid for Christmas presents and holidays. But now my income was increasing with the extra classes, and I became more of a contributor.

Tim returned from India, and we met him at the Airport. I will never forget that joy! We have a wonderful photograph of Tim and Gem reuniting! He had a marvellous experience, and we never tired of hearing about his adventures. We threw a welcome home party; Steve's parents catered for the meat eaters, and we did the vegetarian food. This proved to be much more popular with the young people, and we learned to provide only vegetarian food from there on. The party was a bit 'low key'. After five months away, and a completely different pace of life, Tim and Steve were completely disoriented. Mike and I became ever more enthused at the idea of going to India, ourselves. Tim had, as was often the way, been the trail-blazer!

We asked Tim what he intended to do now and he replied that he fancied training as a Tree Surgeon. He applied to Sparsholt College, and was accepted for a one year course. I found it a little more difficult to rev back up to being a full-time mum than I had expected. We loved having him living at home again, though.

Gemma got her degree in Theology, and took a post-graduate course in education. She is a born teacher. Her course was in Chichester, so she moved back home, too. During her time working at Waitrose, she met a new boyfriend. He was tall, dark and handsome and very smitten with her. This young man had experienced some difficulties in life, but he came over as a gentle giant; Gem found his vulnerability appealing. We had always believed, as a family, that love conquered all. We never turned away a needy puppy or lost kitten. The new boyfriend's stories were poignant and we opened our hearts to him. Mike had reservations when they became engaged, but Gem dispelled them in a very moving letter. They chose for her to wear her Nana's beautiful diamond ring as her engagement ring. It was not long until he had moved in, too. I hoped that living for a while with us would make him feel welcome in the family. After all, they were both very young, and it was a big step. We wanted them to feel supported. So, we had three young adults, two horses, one dog and two cats at this time, under our care. We were still grieving the loss of wonderful, whacky Roger, who had lost his life on the road. Our opposite neighbour's daughter found him. She was desperately upset, and Mike took him immediately and buried him up at the field. I found this difficult, not that I wanted to see his dear little dead body, but just that I could not accept that he was gone. I kept expecting to see him run in, tail held high. Many more of our animals would join Roger in our pet cemetery, over the years.

It was a very busy time. I would cook two days meals at a time, and seemed to be constantly changing between stable clothes and yoga clothes. Gemma had grown up through all the Children's yoga classes, and had then moved on to my adult classes at age fourteen. Even when she was away at University, she came home for my workshops. Now she involved her young man, feeling that yoga would be good for him. He did attend some workshops, but found the philosophy behind our vegetarianism challenging to his cultural background.

Gemma and her fiancé decided to get married in the April before she finished her post-graduate course. Added to all my other duties, was planning the wedding. It took about a year, but it was a real fairy-tale affair. We wanted everyone to have just what they wanted. Mike wanted to travel to Steep Church, where he rang the bells and still does, in a white Rolls Royce. Gem wanted to travel from the church in a horse-drawn carriage, and her fiancé wanted to 'go away' in a Jaguar. Steve's mum worked in a Bridal store at that time, and she found Gem the prettiest dress. She looked absolutely beautiful. We had the Reception at the Langrish House Hotel, just up the road from Bordean House, where my mother died. A string quartet played on the balcony as we entered, reminding us of the many concerts which we had attended at Gem's school. (She was first flute in the school orchestra, and once played with the Royal Marines.) Then we had a disco later. One hundred friends and family attended both the ceremony and the Reception, and a good time was had by all. My brother was not talking to me at the time, unfortunately, so he and his family missed out on this occasion. We gave the young people the deposit for their flat in Petersfield for a wedding gift, and treated them to a night in the Langrish House Hotel. The next day they went to Cyprus for their honeymoon, and Tim immediately stripped out their bedroom, re-decorated and moved in!

The photographs from the wedding were stunning, especially the ones taken with the horses. Gemma's four bridesmaids had worn lilac, and we bought white head-collars for the horses with lilac lead-reins. Having Gem just up the road was delightful, and our house had a little more space, but we missed her.

Tim completed his Tree Surgeon's course, successfully, and then told me: "I don't think I like trees very much, Mum." I replied: "Oh, okay, Tim. What are you going to do now?" He decided to go to University, and to take a degree in Anthropology! I could not have been more delighted! All my Christmases had come at once. So, off he went to London and I was to have two children with 'ology's'.

It was back to Darby and Joan, again. Suddenly, I had more time for my yoga career and I applied to Pauline Mainland to become an Area Officer for the Friends of Yoga Society, (FRYOG.) Pauline was absolutely delighted, and encouraged me to gather the troops. Mike and I had attended a yoga holiday in Lesbos, Greece, in 1996, shortly after Gemma's wedding, and we now continued with a series of holidays at Cortijo Romero in Spain. This was a New Age Centre, and we absolutely loved it. We would get a house-sitter for the horses, dog and cats, and spend an idyllic week practising yoga and tai chi, and eating the most wonderful vegetarian food.

It was on one such holiday that Mike decided to 'retire' on a Friday. He had taken the voluntary redundancy package from IBM and was working as a manager in the Health service. He was at the Royal South Hants Hospital, and then at Southampton General. It was a stressful and very demanding job, with a variety of different challenges, but he enjoyed it. He was always exceptional at managing projects. Being at home on a Friday, meant that I could teach three classes during the day, and he would be there for Oscar and the horses. We entered a rather lovely phase. I would come home on Friday afternoon to find the stable work done, the dog walked, and my delicious dinner cooked. We had a conservatory built on the back of the house in 1997, and here we would sit to enjoy a leisurely meal and a glass of wine. Often, we would sit over the meal for hours, discussing philosophy and how to make the world a better place.

Gemma was unfortunately unable to get a job as a teacher, but did become manager at Hargreaves Sports Store in Petersfield. She was about to make the world a better place – she was pregnant. It was a little early in the marriage, and heaven only knows how they were to manage, financially, but we had been faced with the same dilemma when we were expecting Tim, and we had muddled through.

I began to have a series of dreams, about a 'Golden Baby', even before I had heard the news of Gem's pregnancy. In these dreams, I was the only person who could save this special babe. The dreams were technicolour and James Bond-like; real adventure stories. I always succeeded in saving the baby and spiriting her away to safety.

Since I had been alone to have Gemma, I was determined to be there for her when labour began. When her waters broke, we all rushed down to Queen Alexandra's Hospital. I took my knitting, and was ready to sit it out, however long. Late in the evening, though, the nurse sent us home. She was sure that it would follow the first baby pattern, and the birth would not take place until the morning. She was quite right. Enter the world Elizabeth Clare, and our lives were never the same again. It had been a long haul for Gem, and her young husband was famously to say: "Well, at least you were lying down"!

The first time I picked up Lizzie and laid her across my lap, she melted into me. I felt a very strong soul connection, and I know that we have lived many life-times together. We are very close. I knew that she was the golden baby of my dreams, and that I would guard her with my life, always.

I endeavoured to help Gem as much as possible, by taking around meals for her husband, and doing his laundry while she was in hospital. Once she came out of hospital, I was on call to take over if Mummy and baby had a bad night. Tim was delighted to be an uncle, and to welcome another Gemini into the family. Lizzie's birthday is June 1st and Tim's June 2nd, and Gemini's are known for their mercurial temperament. It was not long till Lizzie had us all wrapped around her little finger. She was a demanding, but utterly delightful child, and I was ready to bore everyone with my grandmother's photographs.

Tim had always compartmentalised his life, so we were delighted when he brought home his girlfriend, Sally. She was just lovely, rather like a bouncy Labrador pup. Sally loved the horses, and liked nothing better than coming to the stables with me, and helping out. She became a most welcome house-guest, and we really enjoyed seeing Tim with a partner.

When Lizzie was just three months old, Gemma had to go back to work. I could not bear the idea of this dear little baby being put into a nursery, and so volunteered to have her for half of the week. Although I loved my time with her, it was a nightmare. There just were not enough hours in the day. I still had to walk the dog, care for the horses, feed the cats, teach my yoga classes and run my home. Oscar was unreliable and I had to keep him away from the baby, which made life even more complicated. I seemed to spend a lot of time barricading the pram. I hated driving her up to the nursery, and used to sing: "You are my sunshine, my only sunshine", all the way there. I endeavoured to put on a brave face for Gem, as she was under pressure too, but it was an awful time. I had previously been super- efficient at Christmastime, but that year I picked up little Lizzie, after doing the horses, took her back to the flat and collapsed into a heap. Gem came home from work to find me sound asleep on the settee, with the baby sound asleep on my chest. Nothing had been done. Gem brought me a huge bouquet of flowers, and bundled me back home, where Mike and Tim had come up trumps. They had put up the tree and had all the pressies beneath it. Oscar had taken on his customary role of guarding the Christmas tree from the cats, and the guys had cooked the dinner. It was Elizabeth's first Christmas, and it was 1997.

Gem and I realised that this routine was unsustainable, and she gave in her notice. She decided to train as a yoga teacher, to my absolute delight. I would take care of Lizzie one day a week, as she studied and wrote her yoga essays. She was working three jobs, to make ends meet, as well.

Her husband was Deputy Manager in a high street store, and as they had definitely outgrown their flat, they moved to a nice house in Waterlooville. He got busy with re-decorating, filling in all the cracks. The cracks in the marriage, though, were not so easy to fill. We began to realise that all was not well, more because of what Gemma did not say, rather than what she did. I would call in at lunchtime, between classes, and Gem would look tired and strained. She had always believed that she had said her vows, and that was for life, for better or for worse. Then one final happening convinced even her placid and giving nature that they could not continue. She appeared home one day before Christmas, complete with baby and suit-case. I saw the postman carry her bag up the path, and I knew that our lives were taking a dramatic new turn.

Gemma proposed a two week trial separation, a cooling off period so that they could take stock, but it was not to be. She was left with an old banger, rather than the nice family car which we had given them, and it was amazing how quickly their home and their life together dissolved. I drove to the house the day after she had left, and picked up their dear little rescue cat, George. Oscar did not notice one more black and white cat entering his premises!

213

Elizabeth was eighteen months old, absolutely delightful, but suffering with night terrors. We had two broken dolls to repair.

The emotions at this time ran high. I was constantly afraid for Gem and for Lizzie. Every time they went out in the car, I prayed for their safe return. I was living on a knife edge, and I felt very alone and very responsible. Lizzie would wake up several times a night, screaming. She would not allow us to enter the room, or to hold her and comfort her. Gem and I would sit, forlornly, cross-legged on the landing carpet, chanting. Eventually, the screaming would die down, and we would all retreat back to bed. It was not until we discovered a marvellous Cranial Osteopath that Lizzie had any respite. Frequent visits to him were a necessary expense, a life-saver. Even so, we all dreaded bed-time. We just could not get little Lizzie to sleep. I would climb into bed with her, she would finally drop off, it would take me twenty minutes to slide silently out of the bed, only to have her say: " Is it Mummy's turn now, Nanny?" when I reached the door!

This was a time of dark and difficult days. I felt very responsible, and very guilty. Was there something I could have said to Gemma to prevent her going through all this heart-ache? Was it somehow my fault? Had I failed her? Then one day I was walking home from the field, with Oscar on the lead. All these thoughts were passing through my mind, and suddenly I was surrounded by a golden light. I stopped in my tracks and distinctly heard the words: "You have played your part. You have played your part well. All has transpired exactly as it was planned." All worry left me, instantly. I felt that I was held in a state of grace. I recognised, on a deep level, that Gem had worked out her karma. This episode in her life, and ours, had to take place. It was decreed, and the enormous reward from all the angst was Lizzie. I walked home in a golden bubble.

Gemma had passed her yoga diploma with a Distinction, and was working in the evenings. Mike would have to get home, after a long and stressful day, and baby-sit while Gem and I taught our yoga. We worked very well as a team, despite the many challenges, and became a functioning commune. Gemma and Lizzie had the two bedrooms at the end of the landing; we put a baby-gate across the corridor, so they had their own little flat. We converted the conservatory into a play-room. Our lives revolved around Lizzie. She called Gem 'Mummy-Nanny', and me 'Nanny-Mummy'. One day, Gem texted to say that she had been offered a substituting job at a yoga centre in Fareham. It would only work if she could give Lizzie to me at the end of my morning class. So, we duly met up in the car-park. Lizzie was none too pleased to be handed over so unceremoniously, like a package, so to coax her I said: "Never mind, Darling, we'll have a mini-picnic in the car." I gave her a packet of Hula-Hoops, and she proceeded to put them on her chubby little fingers, and then to suck them off, and eat them. I looked over at this beautiful child and felt a rush of overwhelming love for her. (Any grandmother reading this will recognise the feeling.) Without looking up from her fingers, she said, in a very matter-of-fact way: "Nanny loves Lizzie". She felt that wave of love. How wonderful to be so connected, and to know that we are loved.

When Gem had announced that she was pregnant, she had asked me what I wanted to be called. She had rather wanted me to be 'Nana', but my mother was such a wonderful Nana, that I felt it was an imposition to take her name. I suggested 'Nanda'. It has a lovely yoga vibe, and I was Nanda for the first twenty months of Lizzie's life. Then, one day, Lizzie called me 'Nanny', and that was that. Mike had joked that he was not about to be called 'Panda', but he was 'Gaga' until Lizzie was five! It was a similar situation with her own name. Gem was adamant that she would be called 'Elizabeth', but she soon dubbed herself 'Lizzie', and we all followed suit. She is such a complete 'Lizzie'.

Oscar had learnt to adore our little granddaughter. She would toddle over to the dog-food cupboard and get out his box of biscuits, then feed them to him, much like posting letters. He thought she was wonderful. She was not so kind to Georgie. This poor little cat had experienced a terrible life, before Gem had rescued him. He had been a street cat, badly dehydrated, and had obviously had a broken leg which had knitted crookedly. He had the sweetest nature, and Gem loved him dearly. She always believed that he would get better, and she religiously took him to the vet, once a week. I must admit that I tried not to get attached to him. I knew that he would not be on this earth for very long, and my emotions had taken a resounding battering, as it was. One day, I was washing-up in the kitchen, when Georgie limped in followed by Lizzie. She had discovered that if she scooped his good leg form under him, he would fall over. She thought that this was hugely amusing. I did not, and I told her off. She took no notice, and repeated the action. Without thinking twice, I scooped her leg from under her, and she fell over. She cried loudly, and her Mummy came running. I was in big trouble! But to this day, Lizzie has never been unkind to another animal.

Gem and I would do our Monday morning yoga planning sitting on the floor in the hall. I was discovering the depth of awareness. For instance, I would get a headache in a certain part of my forehead if I was dehydrated, and in a different part if the room needed oxygen. Our home ran on yogic lines, and we lived a yoga way of life. We both taught children's yoga classes, and Lizzie was a natural yogi. All our friends practised yoga. Gemma bought me the most beautiful 'Bhagavad Gita' for my fiftieth birthday. Gandhi was never without his copy of the Gita, and found solace in its pages no matter what was occurring around him.

It would have been easy to allow my fiftieth birthday to slip by unnoticed, coming as it did just three months after Gem came home, but I determined we should go to Center Parcs. We all needed a break and a change of scenery. Lizzie had never been on holiday, but she knew from the way that we talked about it that it was exciting. When I arrived home, after teaching my three yoga classes, I told her that I must just go up and do the horses, and she said: "Not horses, Nanny, holiday!" I loved the week-end at Longleat. We had a Sunday brunch with a jazz band playing, and for a very brief time our troubles faded. Tim came with us. He has the wonderful ability to be truly present. We may not see Tim frequently, but when we do see him he gives us his full attention.

A year passed. We eventually gained some stability and Gem and Lizzie healed. I had always proclaimed that no-one would ever be able to fool me with a surprise party, I was far too observant! How wrong I was. Gem used e-mail to organise a lunchtime gathering for my fifty-first birthday. Mike took me to a lovely hotel in Midhurst on the Saturday night, so I believed this to be my treat. I was bowled over, when we returned, to find 'Fyfield' full of dear friends. Even our friends from Cornwall had come! This began a really special year for us. I felt strongly that the girls needed holidays. We went to Portugal in the May half-term. We rented a friend's villa, and Tim rode over on his motor-bike to meet us. The beginning of the holiday was marred by a dear little cat being stuck up a tree, but I threw my weight around until it was rescued! In the July, we went to Disneyland, Paris, and then on to a Eurocamp, where we stayed in a static caravan. I remember taking Lizzie to the playground there, and spending long hours playing in the sandpit.

It was in this year that we had an opportunity to go to India. I loved yoga, Mike loved curries, we both loved travelling, and we had long held a dream to spend time in

India. We had thought to wait until Mike was retired, and then to go for six weeks, but this opportunity felt too good to pass up. Swami Satyaratnanda Saraswati had been the Diploma Board Officer for the Friends of Yoga Society, and she had found the job somewhat onerous. She approached me to see if I would be prepared to take it on. I was already enjoying being involved as an Area Officer, and we had successfully held a number of 'Celebration of FRYOG' days. I took on the job and became part of the Executive Committee. Ernest Coates had taken over as Chairman, after our beloved Pauline Mainland died, and he was taking a yoga group to Kerala, Southern India. There were two places left, and we felt that they had our names on them.

The first week we went to the Sivananda Ashram in Neyyar Dam. Ernest had impressed upon us that the accommodation was basic. I was ill-prepared for 'dirty'. I could not unpack my suit-case. I had envisioned a tiny little cell, all painted white. The state of my room brought tears to my eyes, but it was a good deal cleaner at the end of our week!

The Ashram experience was truly magical! The temple chanting in the village would begin at five o'clock. We would get out of bed, and out from under the mosquito net, at five twenty. We would then put our meditation shawls over our shoulders and silently make our way to the Large Hall. It would be dark, and silent figures moving slowly into position gave the moment a special significance, a shadowy glimpse of our community. We would sit for meditation, for about an hour, and then the chanting would begin, led by Swami Govinda. At the end of, the chanting would come the Arati, the ritual of the flame, followed by a sweet delicacy. We would all disperse, to wash and change, and would appear to the summons of the bell for the asana practice. The Sivananda system uses the same twelve postures all the time, and always begins with twelve rounds of Salutation to the Sun, (Surya Namaskar.) All the Sivananda teachers wore yellow tee-shirts, and white asana pants. The teacher of the day would teach from his mat, beginning the practice with an opening chant, and two other teachers would walk amongst the rank and file doing corrections.

After the first two hour yoga class, we would have the first meal of the day. The food was, of course, vegetarian and we would eat in silence, sitting on the floor on long rush-mats. While we gathered and waited for the food, we chanted: 'Hare Krishna, Hare Krishna, Krishna Krishna, Hare Hare. Hare Rama, Hare Rama, Rama Rama, Hare Hare.' If we dared to talk whilst eating, a loud 'Om' would go up to remind us that silence was the rule.

After rinsing our plates, we would go to do our karma yoga. Mike and I were on the bins, which involved taking some rubbish for recycling and some to the tip outside the Ashram gates.

Now, Tim had finished his relationship with Sally, and formed a strong bond with Bethan. They had moved out to Sri Lanka, where Beth worked for a charity and Tim wrote his novel. They decided to come and join our group at the

Ashram. So it was that one day, while I was taking the rubbish to the tip, complete with my rubber gloves, I saw three figures approaching up the lane. It was Tim, Beth and a young Indian guy, who was also on his way to the Ashram. We had not seen them for five months, so you can imagine the reunion, and Tim was to remark that it was business as usual – me wearing rubber gloves!

Ernest made our youngsters most welcome. They joined in with all the activities, and we all particularly enjoyed the lectures given by Swami each afternoon. It was at this point that Mike gave up eating meat. Swami Govinda explained that prana is life-force and it is only present in animals while they are alive. Once they are killed, the life-force stops immediately, so eating meat means that you are receiving no prana. Killing animals for food breaks the first rule of yoga, which is Ahimsa, non-violence. He also explained that animals eat vegetation. We can eat the vegetation 'first-hand', receiving all its nutrients, rather than having it 'second-hand', once it had been digested by the animals. I had become a vegetarian very easily, Mike had held out longer, but now he made the transition and stuck with it. I was very pleased.

This is an excerpt from a piece that I wrote about the Ashram experience. It was published in the Spring of 2003: *We were told that there would be a walking meditation on the Sunday morning. At 5.00 a.m the devotional music played out over a loudspeaker, resonating around the village, the lake and the Ashram. The loud bell rang out at 5.20 for us to rise and we struggled out from under the mosquito nets, washed in cold water and wearing our meditation shawls around our shoulders, we met outside the Ashram entrance. It was still dark and when we had all gathered, the tall French instructor led the walk. He headed left towards the village and we followed the edge of the lake. We walked in silence, in threes and fours across the roadway. We became aware of the stones and dust beneath our feet and the folk walking on either side of us. As it became lighter, we saw the small homes with the families rising. The mothers were already in their beautiful saris, so we saw flashes of red, green and purple. The children were dressed in immaculate school uniforms and were cleaning their teeth, while the fathers were lighting wood fires. They would heat the water for the woody, smoky, herbal tea which began the day. We walked on in silence in the half light and just as we turned a corner, we saw a man lovingly bathing his cow in the lake. Just at that moment I had the overwhelming feeling that I was not alone – that somehow all my family, friends and yoga students were with me, as though in some strange way I was representing them. We came to the edge of the village and the instructor turned and climbed a rocky hill. We all followed suit, and finding a rock on the hill, we sat cross-legged. We faced the hill from behind which the sun would rise and then the magical sound of the three 'Oms' resounded across the lake, the village and the hills. The chanting began. The instructor sang a line and we repeated it back to him. Across the lake, the lions in their park, roared back to us. Gradually it became lighter and lighter, and finally the sun rose and bathed us in its first rays, its pink-gold glory. The chanting stopped and we sat in perfect stillness, in perfect silence, in perfect harmony. Then, all too soon, the instructor moved back down the hill and, devotions over, we were allowed to talk. So, we fell into gentle conversation and straggled our way back through the village. We saw again the humble homes, some with cardboard front-doors, and the children were fascinated by the strange sight of this large body of assorted folk. Some of them smiled, some waved, some were just bewildered. We passed chickens, and beautiful cows, and old men talking. Then one of the instructors pointed out a Puja which was taking place. A Puja is a religious ceremony; men dressed in black had been fasting for 49 days and were preparing to climb the mountain. It was a colourful and moving sight. We went back to the Ashram for Chai (Indian tea) at 7.30 a.m. Of all the excellent meditations which we did in our fortnight in Kerala, Southern India, this will always remain my favourite.*

I was very sad to leave the Ashram and felt like I would have benefited by another week. Evy, who was a member of the group, felt the same way. I admit, though, that it was wonderful to reach the Samudra Bay Hotel for the second week. What luxury! Air-conditioning, clean bedrooms, and a very short walk to the beach. Tim and Beth found a room, just over the wall from us, at a fraction of the cost. They were both well-travelled in India, and knew all the tricks. We had a good week and Ernest taught each day, outside. It was hard to hear him above the roar of the sea, but there was plenty of prana!

Mike fell deeply in love with India. Lying on wooden beds, watching the huge waves splash into the shore, drinking lime sodas, and having a different curry each evening, he was in heaven. I was thrilled to see 'Oms' everywhere, and to bump into Swamis at each corner. I loved all the saris, and the Indian folk are just so friendly and welcoming. We had come home. We were to return to India five more times.

We had been so impressed with Cortijo Romero that we had invested with them. After visiting India, though, and discovering how easy it was, we knew that Kerala would be our destination of choice for the future. I did, however, agree to teach with Ernest in Ibiza. He and I are very different people, and very different teachers, but we did work well together. We were a good team. We took three groups to the lovely hotel in Ibiza and a good time was had by all.

Gemma met Clive at a neighbour's dinner party. They clicked immediately. Clive took Gem out for the evening, and then asked if he could take both the girls out the next day. Every time he bought a bouquet of flowers for Gem, he bought a posy for Lizzie. He courted them both. I remember that when he met Mike, for the first time, he said: "I believe we call you Gaga!" They decided to move in together, and looked for a house near us so that Lizzie could attend the excellent village school in Stroud. They embarked upon a baby, and Gem was busy painting the new house complete with bump. Lizzie was permanently in her overalls, (which Grandad had bought her at the

Tractor Show), up on a step with a paintbrush in her hand. Their new house was just one mile up the road from us, but I still cried a lot when Gem and Lizzie left!

The day that Gem went into labour on Amy, she phoned me at five in the morning. I drove over immediately to take care of Lizzie, and sat chanting 'Om Namah Shivaya' until she woke. Pauline Mainland had told me that if you chanted this mantra five hundred times, and then made a wish, that the wish could not be refused. I wished for Gem to have an easy birth.

Gemma had a water birth, and Clive was there throughout. They named the baby Amy, and when Gem asked me about a middle name, I suggested 'Louise', as it is Gem's middle name. Thus Lizzie was named for my maternal and paternal grandmothers, and Amy carried on her mother's name. I must admit to having ambivalent feelings towards this new-comer. I felt that if I loved this little one, I would in some way be disloyal to Lizzie. I also felt that she was Clive's baby, she belonged to his family. I guess I felt that since I had been privileged to be so involved with Lizzie's early years, that it was only fair and generous to give Amy's babyhood to Clive's parents. I called her 'the baby'. I noticed also that Gem was very possessive towards Amy; I believe this was because Lizzie had chosen both of us as carers, and when she came home to Fyfield, she did not lose a parent, she gained one. Gem, Mike and I were Lizzie's parents. She had no contact with her biological father, (although he and his mother always remember her birthdays, and remember her at

225

Christmastime, too.) I believe that Gem wanted to 'own' her new baby, and who could blame her?

I was asked to have the two girls when Clive and Gemma went away for the week-end. The baby was in the study in her cot, (actually the same cot that Tim and Gem had; I repainted it for Lizzie.) She woke in the night for her bottle, and I sat in front of the long mirror to feed her. I was wearing my mother's dressing-gown, and it was almost dark. As 'the baby' glugged her milk, I suddenly saw my mother standing behind me. Mum had been in Spirit World for eleven years by then. She wrapped her arms around me, and around Amy, and welcomed her into the Sisterhood. It was as though she claimed her. From that moment on I called her Amy, and I loved her. There is no rationing with love; there is always enough to go around. Love begets more love.

Amy was also to 'claim' me. One day Gem came in through our front-door, clutching her baby, and as she passed me, she grabbed my sweater and swung out of her mother's arms. Gem said: "Well, there was no mistaking that gesture!" I have a very good relationship with Amy. She is enormous fun, and is a very organised young lady. She is my granddaughter, though, and because of our history, Lizzie is a mixture of granddaughter and daughter. I remember our neighbour, Martin, saying that I could have been Lizzie's mother, when she was little. However, we came through a lot in the next four years, and I definitely looked like Amy's grandmother!

This was a time of rapid spiritual growth for me. I was fully aware that my pathway was entwined with that of my daughter, just as it had been with my mother. The 'Sisterhood' took on a new significance for me, and we welcomed Tim's partner, Bethan, into our group. My classes were ever growing. I taught thirteen per week, and my Teacher Training Course moved from a fortnightly meeting in my house, to a College Course held at Highbury College. My involvement in the Executive Committee of a well-known Yoga Society had opened my eyes to the yoga politics. I was learning and growing. The Bhagavad Gita tells us that it is better to follow your own path, no matter how badly it goes, rather than to follow someone else's, no matter how well that goes. I was very aware of the path that was in my blueprint this time around. Why was I here this time? I knew, on a soul level, that I was here to serve others: my students, my family and the larger yoga community.

# *Chapter 16*

Venus in Pisces: *Sometimes you do more for people than you ought to, and sometimes you do more for them than they need; depriving them of a chance to find out the hard way which of their ideas are bad and which are good. But always your motives are sincere, your results are impressive and your admirers manifold. The only people who do not like you very much are the grumps and pessimists who feel shamed and confronted by your open, friendly manner.*

I attended a host of yoga and spiritual workshops. One springs to mind immediately. Inge had given me a leaflet for a day with Willy Lone Bear, as she knew that I had read a lot of Native American wisdom. I booked up for Tim, Gem and me. Inge and Phillipe (her lovely husband) went, too. Willy Lone Bear appeared in full costume, and was quite a character. His mother was a Canadian Indian, and he had a wealth of knowledge and soul wisdom, but his father was from Southampton and he talked with a Hampshire accent. At one point he did a drum meditation.

As soon as he started to play, I began to sob. The sobs came from deep inside me, racking my body. The moment the drumming stopped, so did the sobs. It was instant. I have no idea what I released that day, but I do know that it opened a pathway. I began to get past-life flashes.

Patanjali, in his sutras (please see the introduction, where the Eight Limbs are explained,) tells us that it is bad to seek out the yoga 'Siddhis', but that if they come to you, it is good. The Siddhis are psychic powers gained by yoga practice and they may be transient or permanent. I was never seeking supernatural, or extra-ordinary gifts, but from my dedicated and diligent practice I had experienced 'shape-shifting', aura reading, premonitions about students' health issues, messages from Spirit World and I was now to be given a lesson in past-life experiences. When I have talked to friends about this, they have asked me: "How do you know that this was a past-life flash? Could it not have been your imagination?" I can only reply that there is an 'inner knowing'. I check it out with my soul.

I believe that we are here to live this life. These past-life flashes are to shed light on a current situation. It would be very tempting to wander off the path, and to become distracted by journeys into former incarnations, but that is not the purpose of the exercise. My first past-life flash shed light on my relationship with my son, Tim. We had lived as a married couple in North America. He was a very handsome brave, and I was his squaw. We were young, and newly-wed. I can still see him, quite clearly, in my minds' eye, stripped to the waist with a feather in his long hair riding a beautiful chestnut horse. Our tribe was being attacked, and he was a brave warrior. He told me I must guard the village and the elders and he galloped away. I watched until the dust from his horse's hooves was no longer visible, and I never saw him again. He died bravely, and I was completely heart-broken.

Tim once told me that I was afraid of him. I am not, but I used to be afraid that one day he would leave and never come back. I was afraid that I would say something wrong, and he would go, never to return. I have always cried when Tim departed. He and Beth came to a yoga holiday in Valle de Vida, Spain, five years ago. I taught upon a yoga platform, a quarter of a mile up the mountain. It was a beautiful group, and a beautiful week. When Tim left, I cried. The other group members were somewhat astonished, but I told them: "He is my son." When we left him in India, I bawled. When we left him in Portugal, I remember that awful moment when we turned into the Airport, and he was no longer in my rear view mirror, on his motor-bike. He waits to see my eyes mist over, when he gives me a goodbye hug! The past-life flash explains 'why'. Since Tim's fortieth birthday, I have noticed a shift. He is on a spiritual journey, and is writing a lot of poetry. We are both always growing and learning.

My second past-life flash concerned Gemma. In this lifetime I was the husband. We had found the perfect relationship. We understood one another on the deepest level, and lived in complete harmony. We lived for one another, and although we loved our children, they came second to our feelings towards one another. Our souls were united as one, and we had established the state of Samadhi (bliss). One of our children in that lifetime was my father from this lifetime. He felt resentment, and jealousy. He felt that he was not 'heard'. Certainly Gemma is completely devoted to her children, this time around. She is a wonderful mother, and the children absolutely come first. I completely support her in this and, as grandparents, we are on call constantly. I believe that we are 'atoning' for our rather selfish life-time together. To atone means to bring to oneness – At One.

Lizzie and I believe that we were sisters in Egyptian times, and my good friend and colleague, Kathleen, remembers a time when we were together in Tibet. Past-life flashes for me always bring clarity about a current situation.

Mike's parents did not believe that there was life after death. I tried to talk to them both about it, but they were convinced that your last breath on earth meant that it was all over. This resulted in them 'clinging' on to life, and having great anxiety about their health. Mike's Dad had always said that eighty years was enough. We made a big fuss of his eightieth birthday, all arriving with a buffet, balloons and presents. It was a beautiful, sunny day and I remember Mike, Tim and Arthur sitting on the steps of their conservatory and laughing together. He died four months later, in the March, having become very confused and anxious. He believed that his neighbours were plotting against him, and that his electric meter was faulty; his electric bill would be thousands of pounds. Mike's mother wrote one line in her diary: "Arthur died suddenly."

We were all there for the funeral, and I did the reading. Mike's mum had been worried that Tim would not wear a suit, but of course he did, and looked so handsome. He made a connection with Mike's cousin Sheila's son, David.

Mike is an only child, so the responsibility of taking care of his mother fell to him. She had never enjoyed robust health, and Mike would drive to Somerset every five weeks to do whatever needed doing. His mother, Joan, had a nasty fall and was taken to hospital with a broken hip. Coincidentally, (although I do not really believe in coincidence, but rather that nothing happens for no reason,) it transpired that my brother was in the same hospital. I was alerted to this fact by my cousin, Judy. She phoned and said: "Carole, if you feel disposed to make a gesture, it had better be quick, because Leigh is dying."

Leigh had not spoken to me since Mum's will had been read. You will remember that he fared better in Dad's will, and that Mum (who, very sadly, had lost faith in Leigh at the time of her death,) had favoured me. Well, Leigh had developed bowel cancer, and had been very seriously ill. Due to complications, his leg had been horribly infected and he had suffered blood-poisoning, septicaemia. We went to visit Mike's Mum, and then went to find Leigh. He was in a private ward, sitting on the edge of his bed. I would not have recognised him. He had lost an enormous amount of weight, and Meg had cut his hair short. If I had been going to a yoga workshop, I would have thought that he was the Guru, (the teacher – one who leads you from darkness to light.) He was surrounded by spirit. He had almost died, and had an ethereal air. He did not look at me, but rather his eyes slipped over my face and rested on Mike's. Indeed, he greeted Mike like an old mate. They had known one another long before Mike and I became an item. Leigh began to talk nonsense, giving us explicit instructions as to how we were to pick something up for him, and to be sure to say that Leigh had sent us. We did not stay long, but it was important that we had visited. We met Meg outside in the car park, and she cried and gave me the biggest hug.

The next time that we visited, Leigh was in a General Ward. Meg was on one side of the bed, and got up immediately to embrace us. On the other side of the bed was their oldest son, Brett, who did the same. I looked down at Leigh, in the bed, and his face was awash with tears. I bent down to hug him, and I cried too. We were reunited. Leigh made a fairly good recovery, although it took a long time. Later, I paid him the money that he felt I 'owed' him. I talked to Mum, in Spirit World, about it and she left it to me to decide. Mike was very supportive of my decision, and Leigh and Meg sent me the most enormous bouquet of flowers. We were friends for about five years, and they attended our Coral Wedding Anniversary, which was a great source of joy to me. We had missed a great deal of one another's family histories, but I was to catch up in the years to come.

Any past-life flashes with my brother, I hear you ask? We had always had a volatile relationship, and clearly we had karma to clear. I had an experience during a meditation, which explained a lot. It was a past-life flash of the most vivid variety. Leigh was burying me alive. He was very angry, and his face was puce from his efforts. He was ranting at me, and seemed to believe that I stood between him and what he most wanted in the world. I was afraid, and I could feel the weight of the earth on my chest, crushing me. Finally, I could not breathe. You will remember that I had asthma as a small child. I believe that this is why. I also realise that this sheds light on my fear of my brother's temper. I read recently that anger is fear announced. I have a huge, and sometimes disproportionate, response to bullying. It presses my buttons. I remember coming out of The Petersfield School on one occasion, after teaching two classes. There were two boys of about fourteen fighting. One boy crashed the other one to the ground and proceeded to kick him, viciously. I waded in immediately, separating them and remonstrating loudly. When I recounted the incident to Mike later, he was a little horrified and said: "They could have both attacked you." It had never crossed my mind; my instinct was to save the victim.

I have bouts of severe insomnia. Curiously, each time that they occur, they are followed by a spiritual awakening of some kind. My sleep pattern was disturbed after Gemma's birth. She did not sleep for the first five and a half years, and having one little dear up all night, and the other little dear being boisterous and hyperactive all day, took its toll. It can take me hours to get to sleep. I have made quite a study of it over the years. Of course, the Restless Leg Syndrome does not help. When I have had a bad night, I wake up feeling nauseous and light-headed. It as though I am not earthed, not grounded. I believe that it this which opens a door-way to spiritual awakening. Do not get me wrong! I am certainly not recommending lack of sleep, but I do find for me that there is a reason for it. This is somewhat comforting, although there is nothing as frustrating as tossing and turning, while your partner snores, happily! Meg and I have discovered that we often pass through patches of insomnia at the same time. We believe that we are psychically linked and pick up on negative vibrations. Often these bouts of sleeplessness coincide with specific family anniversaries.

Mike retired in 2003. Gemma and Clive threw him a surprise party in their garden. It was a huge success, and he suspected nothing. Tim and Beth played their parts well. The little girls wore T-shirts proclaiming: 'Hospital Manager retires to become full-time Grandfather!' Mike had plenty of work to keep him busy at home. He had bought a tractor, an old Ferguson, which he loved. It had no brakes, and he had to turn it up the hill to stop. Of course, no-one else was allowed to sit on it. He is still very much an 'only child' when it comes to his toys! Mike took care of all the hedges at the horses' field, as well as the topping and the fertilising. We worked very well as a team; I took care of the horses, and he took care of the land. We had approximately five acres. Gemma was busy with her two little girls, so we would call in 'Animal Aunts' to care for our horses, dog and cats while we were away.

Meanwhile, Mike being retired freed him to visit his mother in Somerset when he was needed. These visits became more frequent, as she became increasingly frail. He also took a part-time job working for 'Compassion in World Farming', a charity close to his heart.

Oscar had become a very old dog. He was still an absolute dear, but he was tired and stiff. The day came when he asked to go out into the back-garden, and he fell five times on the way from the backdoor to the lawn. Each time he manfully struggled up, but it broke my heart to watch. I made the dreaded appointment, and I phoned Tim in London. He immediately said: "Okay, Mum, I'm coming home to pay my last respects and to bury my dog." It still makes me cry to remember it. He was as good as his word; Oscar was buried at the field, and joined his friends, Roger, Toby and Georgie in our Pet Cemetery. Georgie had died at home, and Toby was to follow just a week later. We mourned the passing of our animals deeply. They are family members, much beloved. The energy you share with your pets is unconditional love. They are all such characters. Our animals have enriched our lives and have taught us compassion, responsibility and loyalty. I am always slightly suspicious of people who do not like animals, and instantly feel a bond with those who do. At this time, we just had our little cat, Daisy. She was a home-body, never straying from our garden. She was very affectionate, except when I had to brush her, when she would turn into a cougar! We did not plan on getting another dog, but the Universe had other ideas.

One year when we visited Cortijo Romero, the excellent Personal Development centre in Spain, we met a beautiful canine. She was called Freddie, and she belonged to the Course Tutor. Freddie was a Norwegian Buhund. I loved her personality, and her somewhat independent air and self-confidence. I told Gem about her, when we returned, and she looked the breed up on the Internet. There was a Norwegian Buhund bitch looking for a home in Lampeter, in Wales. We went to see her, and we both felt that she was special. Pip was a golden colour, very pretty and, initially, very quiet. Lizzie was thrilled to bits with her, as they were the same age. Daisy was less delighted, but set out to lay down the house rules, and to impress upon Pip who was boss.

We walked Pip up to the field twice a day to do the horses. One day, a car stopped and the dear lady within exclaimed: "You have a 'Bu'!" She owned two Buhunds, and was a great fan of the breed. Her friends in Lythe Lane, Colonel and Mrs. Sime looked after dogs. Diana Sime explained that they took in 'Day boys and Boarders'! Another day when we walked up to Foxfield to do the horses, we met a gentleman, who again exclaimed: "You have a 'Bu'!" He was always known as 'The Author', and he too was a fan of the breed. We began to realise how unusual they are, and Pip was certainly a conversation starter. I loved her foxy looks, and her curly tail. We had taken her on at the age of three, and she had quite a few vices. She barked hysterically at the front door. If someone was invited in, she would continue to bark at them for half an hour. We tried everything! I had my Teacher Training group coming to the house at the time, and dear Cate came up with all sorts of ideas, but nothing helped. Dayla did best, rolling around the floor with her, which was a wonderful and loving distraction. Strangely, if she was out and returned to find folk in her house, she did not mind at all and proceeded to greet them quite normally. When my Teacher Training Courses returned to our house, after years with Highbury College, we bought a motor caravan and Mike would take Pip out for the day. Her favourite place was West Wittering. She would just take off along the beach, and walk for miles. She was a very opinionated soul and hated the hoover. It was 'the enemy'! She would attack it viciously, and rip the bag. We went through a number of hoovers, while Pip lived with us, but it was hilarious to watch! Mike and I would be in fits of laughter. She also hated the window-cleaner, and would tour the house after him, throwing herself at the doors, and barking her head off. She would be hoarse by the time he left. We asked the lovely young man to come early, while we were at the stables, and the problem was solved. For all her idiosyncrasies, we loved Pip dearly.

At this stage of our lives, we had a dog, two horses and a dear little cat. We had our son happily settled down with his partner, Bethan, in London. Tim had gained his degree in Anthropology, and then a Post-graduate certificate in Criminology. He then followed the obvious career path and became a motor-bike courier, in Central London. I tried not to think about this too much, or I would have been a nervous wreck. I trusted Tim, and his judgement, and wrapped him in white light, so that the angels would protect him. We loved Beth; I always said that if we had been into arranged marriages, she would have been the girl I would have chosen. She was very loving, really into yoga, most intelligent, (she has a degree from Cambridge,) and she was busy changing the world. Beth worked for various different charities, and often travelled to India, making a huge difference to the lives of many struggling families. They lived in a neat flat in Stoke Newington, and it was not too long before they had adopted a beautiful cat, Tilly, who then proceeded to birth the cutest kitten, Moley.

Gem and the children lived just a mile up the road, in the next village, Langrish. We enjoyed the social life of all three villages, Steep where our horses resided, Stroud where we lived, and Langrish where Gem had put down roots.

My mission at this time was all about training good yoga teachers. When two large groups enrolled for the course at Highbury College, I requested Gemma as my deputy Tutor. The College readily agreed, and we very much enjoyed working as a team. I trained eighty teachers in total, and I am still in touch with a good number of them. Six still attend my weekly classes: Claire, Chris, Deirdre, Lynne, Becky and Tania. Six stay in gentle contact: Cate, Connie, Donna, Sara, Perminder and Delphine. Some stay connected by e-mail and text: Vicky, Mel, Lucy, Vicky, Ineke, Kate and Stuart. Several more

239

attend our Park Place Pastoral Centre Retreat each summer: Jean, Sue, Jayne, Dayla and Nigel. Some lovely graduated teachers, like Celia, Sara, Lucy and Claire, also attended my Post-graduate Course: 'How to teach yoga to children'. Dear Sara took over this course for me. I was to call upon many of my graduates to help, while I was on the executive committee for the Friends of Yoga Society. One of my aims, as a yoga teacher, was to take yoga into schools. There was a wonderful Government initiative which paid yoga teachers to go into schools in Havant, Hampshire, and to teach during the lunch-times. Cate, Jeannette and I took this on. I also offered classes at The Petersfield School, where the pupils could choose it as an option. Gemma has done a wonderful job of taking it into the school where she works. It is actually now on the curriculum. How I would like to see yoga in every school in Britain, before I die! Gem has also become a Teacher Trainer; she is much beloved and her graduates are busy changing the world.

It is a great source of pride to me that my daughter is equally committed to yoga. Who knows? Perhaps one day there will be three generations of teachers upon the stage at Park Place. When Lizzie was four years old, Clive asked her: "What are the colours of the rainbow, Lizzie?" She reeled them off: Red, orange, yellow, green, blue, indigo, violet, and then he asked: "How do you know that?" Lizzie replied: "Because they are the colours of the chakras!" That is a yoga brat for you!

Gem and Clive married on February the fourteenth 2004. It was a very pretty wedding; Gemma wore a red dress, the design of which was actually called 'Gemma'! It was a lovely, simple, classic design and we used the piece that was taken off the hem to make a sash for Lizzie's bridesmaid dress. She and Amy made beautiful attendants. They took the children to Center Parcs for their honeymoon, and later had a barn dance for friends and family in Horndean School, which both Tim and Gemma had attended. Everyone dressed Western-style, and it was enormous fun.

Two of Gem's friends organised her hen week-end. I was rather dreading it, but actually it was marvellous fun. For the first evening we gathered at an Indian Restaurant in Port Solent. We wore Salwar Kameez, (Punjabi Suits,) and bindis on our fore-heads. Then we went to Brighton. Gem was sharing a room with Beth, and with her University friend, Kylie. I was sharing a room with Cate, one of my graduated teachers. The theme was 'Angels or Devils'. I was, of course, an angel!

We did a good tour of Brighton, and ended up at a Night Club. It was super good fun, and what particularly impressed me was the way every one of our group of eleven looked out for one another. The hotel was excellent, and Cate and I spent a long time that night laughing and crying. I sent her a card later saying that: 'You may forget the people you laugh with, but you never forget the people you cry with!'

Mike and I had planned to go to Phuket, Thailand, in January 2005. We had looked through all the brochures, selected our hotel, and were very excited at the prospect of our adventure. Gemma asked us to cancel our plans, though, as she was expecting a baby and we would be needed to look after the girls. Certainly we would have been involved in the Tsunami, had she not made this request! This is such a wonderful example of the Universe looking out for us. I do sincerely feel that we are guided constantly. As it was, Gem had a miscarriage, but later carried and birthed Benjamin Robert in June. We were delighted to welcome another Gemini into the family! Ernest and I had planned to take a group to Ibiza for a yoga holiday. Ben was due the day before we left, but very obligingly he appeared early. Gem told friends: "I either have to birth this baby now, or keep my legs crossed for ten days till Mum returns!" It was very hectic. We had the two little girls here, took them out for an Italian meal to round off our three days together, and then home to Mummy, who had just been discharged from hospital. I then had precisely one hour to pack, and to clean the house before the Animal Aunt arrived! Amazingly, my packing that year was perfect, and it was great to know that Gem was safely at home with her little gang. She had spread her children out very well; there is four years between each of them. The first time I picked up Ben, I swear he looked at me and said: "You may be my Nan, but I'm my own man!" He certainly is. I used to rock him to sleep to a Jack Johnson C.D. until he wised up. It is very different having a grandson, after two granddaughters, and they are all strong characters. I often say to new grandmothers in my classes: "Being a grandmother is the best job in the world!" and I bought my sister-in-law, Meg, a tee-shirt which read: 'If I had known what fun it would be to be a grandmother, I would have done that first!'

Life was busy. I was a full-time yoga teacher. I was a Tutor, offering Teacher Training Courses. I was running an Annual Retreat, and taking groups to India, Ibiza and Spain. I was Diploma Board Officer on the executive committee of a well-known yoga society. Indeed, FRYOG was the first yoga society to offer Teacher Training. When Ernest retired from the Chairmanship, I stood for the post. I was voted in and we formed a strong committee. I felt that it was my path, and that I had a great deal to offer the organisation. I burned with the passion of mission. FRYOG was growing; yoga politics were changing; there was much to be done. For the next five years, I devoted all my energy, love and enthusiasm to our growth and re-organisation. Every day I performed a task for FRYOG. Every day I had fresh ideas. Every day I communicated, connected, coaxed. Mike and Gemma were wonderful supports; family members, but both yogis too. They made excellent sounding-boards.

I am here to serve. At this time, I was seeing approximately three hundred people a week. I needed to remember their names, their ailments and their concerns. My yoga students are family to me, and I love them all. I was determined to grow the FRYOG membership to five hundred, and I was on call from each and every member. I made myself available to my student teachers; pastoral care is a big part of this role. I was serving as a grandmother, as a mother and wife, and as a stable- lass. I was interfacing with other yoga associations. There were times when my head was full of faces, and sleep was slow in coming. It is really important to me to feel that I am contributing, that I am a useful member of society, and my yoga community. They say 'if you want something done, ask the busy people.' This was certainly my experience. In hiring new officers in the Society, I found time and again that it was the busy ones who would say 'Yes'. I wrote this poem and it was published at about this time:

MY YOGA JOURNEY

*I came into this life with yoga beside me.*

*Sat in meditation pose at the age of three.*

*I was given asthma to focus my mind on my breath.*

*Always understood that there was no end in death.*


*Met my teacher at just the right time –*

*Found her teaching and her philosophy sublime.*

*Then I practised and I taught and I grew,*

*So much fascinating knowledge to pursue.*


*Each student had a tale to tell*

*Of how yoga had in some way made them well.*

*I have never doubted my path,*

*Nor finished honing my craft.*


*And then came the call to teach teachers, blessed day!*

*So many eager minds to guide on their way.*

*To see the groups bond gladdens my heart.*

*Each one with fresh insights to impart.*

*I love my student teachers and hope to plant seeds,*

*To nourish their soil and help eradicate life's weeds.*

*And then, when they've blossomed, passed the course and flown,*

*I know they're busy with cultivation of their own.*


*And when we meet up, hug, share and talk,*

*I know from their challenge they do not baulk,*

*But push on, with yoga flag unfurled,*

*Passing on Patanjali's wisdom to the world.*

*I know my mission and smile with delight,*

*As the snowball grows ever in might.*

*It gathers speed and size and on and on*

*Till the world is changed – we have begun!*

# *Chapter 17*

M oon in Virgo: *Work, play, duty and pleasure merge in your mind. Deep down inside you feel incredibly guilty, but you do not know why! You flog yourself mercilessly through a series of self-imposed penalties in an attempt to assuage this inner disquiet. The ridiculous thing is that you have not done anything to feel guilty about. You simply have your moon in Virgo!*

Gemma cried when each of her children started school, as I had also done. I remember her tearful comment the day that Amy went to school: "There's no little person skipping along beside the push-chair!" Tuesdays were always 'Grandmother's Day'. Gem would come and we would go supermarket shopping, and have lunch together. As Ben grew, he entered into the family rituals with gusto. Tuesday afternoon, I would have Lizzie and Amy for tea. Lizzie was never an adventurous eater and I would introduce her to new tastes gradually, and ask for her feedback. We kept a 'New Tastes' journal. Lizzie took up the flute, following in her mother's footsteps, and, later,

Amy took up the clarinet. Lizzie went to Ballet classes and Amy attended Tap classes. They both loved our horses, and were keen members of the Kidz Yoga classes. I mentioned before that one of the differences between teaching children and teaching adults is that the adults leave a space around the teacher, and the children are on the teacher's mat! They love singing and so chanting is always popular.

It has been my experience that children brought up in yoga families turn out to be giving, loving and fun. The atmosphere of a children's class is non-competitive, and all inclusive. Spitefulness and bitchiness does not occur, and each child is communicative and resilient. When I was teaching the Postgraduate Course 'How to teach yoga to children', both Gemma and Becky 'lent' me their children as guinea-pigs. I taught the class here at our house, and the classes were held in my conservatory/yoga room. I remember on one occasion that we were colouring in mandalas. A mandala is an aid for meditation, and the colours that the children use to embellish their design tells you a great deal about their personalities and growth. Ben was still tiny; at three years old his colouring was somewhat random! Becky's son, Sam, on the other hand, was very precise. Sam was ten years older, at thirteen. Ben had his finished in three minutes, but was fascinated to watch Sam as, with endless patience, he produced a master-piece. There was only the central circle to complete, when Sam made the most generous gesture I have ever seen. He glanced at Ben and invited him to complete the mandala, and to colour in the circle.

Instinctively, the little chap knew what a great honour this was, and he tried so hard to do it beautifully. When the task was complete, Sam took the mandala over to show it to the ladies who were training. He stood with his hands behind his back, and Ben stood next to him, with his hands behind his back, too. The ladies asked questions about the choice of colours, and Ben beamed from ear to ear when it was pointed out that he had contributed. This little cameo sums up a children's yoga class beautifully; Sam so very generous, and Ben so determined not to let him down.

Sam's twin sisters were always keen yogis, and have stayed friends with Lizzie through the years. Recently, they all went up to the Yoga Show together. They are so natural, so loving, and so completely themselves. I believe that yoga children have the tools and techniques to weather life's storms. They have a support system, and a deep understanding of their Inner Spirit.

We were all called upon to use our yoga strength when both Pip, our lovely dog, and Mike's Mum were taken ill. Mum had a variety of falls and injuries, and then had suffered a Central stroke. Mike, being an only child, had shouldered all the responsibilities of selling the bungalow and getting Mum into a good Care Home. I had recommended finding a family run Home, and one with a pet. This he had accomplished, and Mum became fond of the little cat called Treacle. Mum had developed pneumonia, and was not expected to last the night. Mike drove immediately to Weston to sit by her bedside. At the same time, Pippin became desperately ill. She had severe vomiting and diarrhoea, and it transpired that she had three tumours around the liver. One of them was larger than the liver itself. We had a wonderful young Vet at the time, who was Spanish and was also a Homeopathic Vet. I sat beside Pip's bed and Mike sat beside his Mum's. I was alone to make the dreadful decision, the one that all pet owners dread. It was April, and very cold. There was no way that I would be able to dig the grave from the frozen earth at our field, so I made the decision to have our beautiful 'Bu' cremated. Mike came home to be at the Vets with me. His mother had survived, for a little while longer, but we had lost our canine companion. She was only nine years old, and we were so not ready to say 'goodbye'. I cried for three weeks solidly. I remember sobbing to Mike: "When will I stop crying?" So many special friends sent cards, e-mails and support. I have a beautiful Indian box in the hall full of sympathy cards. My dear friend, Jill, brought me a shrub, recommending that I plant it where my little friend used to play. A lovely New Zealand couple, who had house-sat for us on a number of occasions, sent us an exquisite card made from a photograph of Pip that they had taken. She was sorely missed.

Mike had extracted a promise from me that when our current animals died we would have no more. He wanted to travel; to be less tied to a daily schedule. When I gave my word, I was ill prepared for Daisy to die and then Pip to follow so young and so closely. I had taken Daisy to the Veterinary Surgery as she was being very sick. They assured me that all was well, but I knew better. I had seen enough animals reach the end of their lives to know that she was slowly declining. I knew that she had a tumour, as it became increasingly difficult for her to get comfortable. I felt absolutely wicked when my legs started to jump, after she had cosied down on my lap. She took to sitting on the pouffe at my feet, so as not to be disturbed, and it was here that a Vet called Sarah eventually put her down. Daisy was our last cat. She had entered our lives as a stray, brought home from a hack with our horse, Bonnie. She was my constant companion, and we always shared a 'love-in' each morning. She had a special little 'chirrup', which I can still hear in my head. Daisy was buried at the field, along with her friends Roger, Toby, Oscar and Georgie. Pip's ashes were scattered there, too, beside the stable which she had 'helped' me to muck-out each day.

So we had no pets in the house and it felt very empty. As we planned our trip to India that winter, we only needed to set up cover for the elderly mares. They needed special attention as Bonnie had a proneness to eye infections and Gossie had skin problems. As my Auntie Kate used to say: "You can't grow old gracefully!"

We were looking forward to this yoga group travelling to Kerala, in South India. There were dear friends amongst the yogis. We would again stay at a small hotel in Kovalam, which had only twelve bedrooms. We preferred to feel that we were part of the community, rather than being remote in a grand hotel. The word would go round as soon as we arrived, and we would be fondly greeted not only by the hotel owner and staff, but also by Sanjeev who put out our deck-chairs on the beach, Jamila who was our fruit salad lady, and the local traders. This time, Mike and I were allocated the best room in the hotel; very simple and basic, but with a lovely view. Our routine was always the same: up early for silent meditation and yoga practice; breakfast, taken all together in the tiny hotel garden; then either an excursion or free time to visit the beach, attend an Ayurvedic doctor, or do some local shopping; then yoga class in the afternoon, on the roof terrace of the hotel; and then we would go out as a group for our evening meal. There are superb vegetarian restaurants in Kovalam, and each group soon chose a favourite.

We had a dream to take the whole family to India one day; this has not yet come to fruition. We did broach the subject, though, of taking Lizzie away for a short break in the October half-term. We came up with the scheme that once the grandchildren became ten years old we would invite them to choose a city in Europe to visit. Gem felt that she could part with Lizzie for just three days, and that she was grown-up enough to go away with her grandparents, and Lizzie chose Florence as our destination. She loves all things Italian, food, scenery and culture. All three of us were very excited as we set off on our adventure. We flew straight into Florence, and our hotel was right in the centre of the beautiful city. Lizzie immediately allocated the temporary bed to Grandad and she and I had the comfortable divans! Lizzie loves to shop and she was mesmerised by the beautiful pashminas and masks. We walked the city, enjoying the Boboli Gardens, the Uffizi museum, the statue of David and the view from the top of the Duomo. It is easy to be a vegetarian in Italy, and the restaurants were superb. We made a lot of memories, and it was just glorious to have Lizzie all to ourselves. As I say frequently to Gemma, she makes beautiful children!

The run up to Christmas was busy as usual. Amongst my own weekly classes we had developed an annual ritual. We would wear red and green, and would have a more light-hearted class on the last day of term. Sometimes we would have partner work, or a Laughter Yoga session, or sounds and chanting. I strongly support the idea that enlightenment does not have to be serious! I have been teaching yoga now for thirty seven years, and for many of those years I would write a Christmas poem, make copies and give one to each class member. When I worked for the Colleges, they would happily enter into the spirit of the enterprise, and would assist with the copying and the art-work. I am interested in Colour Therapy and have attended some workshops on this subject. At Christmastime the red hue is for love and the green is for peace and harmony. When Lizzie had such dreadful difficulty sleeping, as a little one, her bedroom was yellow. Gem took her away one week-end to Alton Towers, and I got busy with my paintbrush. Changing the colour of the room to blue made a noticeable difference.

We used to take a day out in December to travel to the family to deliver our Christmas presents. It was a special day, and I always felt embraced by warmth. We usually went to Mike's Mum for lunch, then popped in to see Leigh and Meg, and then on to Cousin Sally and Bryan. This Christmas was a little different. Mike's Mum was in the Care Home, and was now not communicating at all. Bless her; she just lay in bed with her fists firmly clenched. I believe that she was clinging on to life. It was quite painful to visit, but the staff in the home were very kind. Our visit to Leigh and Meg was not a happy occasion either. Meg was in a lot of pain with a broken pelvis, and Leigh was very busy with his taxi business. We did not know, at that stage, what was around the corner, but we could pick up on the tension in the air. Seeing Sally, Bryan and the family was always a delight, and this served to soften our day. Bryan is a builder and he built their beautiful timber house. Their previous cottage is just a step away and their second son, Rhys, and his wife, Maria, and their children live there. They overlook the stables where their daughter, Sarah, keeps her horses. They are a very involved family, all constantly helping one another out. Rhys's dog, Milly, would wander over and spend time with Sally's pets. Their house is always a buzz of visiting grandchildren and animals. We recently went up to celebrate Sally and Bryan's Golden Wedding Anniversary. There were some thirty people and six dogs present. They have now built a new timber house, with Bryan being the craftsman and Sal being the labourer. It is gorgeous, just like a giant sauna bath, and it is just behind their previous home. They are still on hand for the horses.

Late in December Meg left Leigh, after forty one years of marriage. This was, of course, history repeating itself as

Mum had left Dad after forty years. It was a difficult time for all family members, and inevitably rifts occurred. My relationship with my brother had never run smoothly, and although he had my compassion, our communication channels broke down. No-one could have foreseen that Meg and I would become very close at this point, and that Leigh would cease speaking to me entirely. As with my Mother, we gave our support to the one we felt most needed it, and since Leigh had previously agreed that Meg could share me as a sister, sisters we became. Meg is an only child, as is Mike, and I had always wanted a sister. Meg refers to me as 'Little Sis', and her lovely new husband, Simon, has fitted beautifully into our family.

On Boxing Day Mike's Mum died. The funeral was arranged for the day before we went to India. We had Tim's cats staying with us over Christmas, while Tim and Beth went to her parents in Wales. They came back for the funeral, and we hired a large taxi and travelled to Weston together. It was a bitterly cold day. I had chosen to read a lovely poem at the service in the Crematorium; one that I felt Mum would have enjoyed. The six of us went back to the 'Nut Tree' pub, and were joined by Mum's sister-in-laws, Joyce and Doris, and Joyce's husband, Ken. We were very grateful that day for the support of Tim, Gem, Clive and Bethan. We did wonder if Leigh would come to offer his respects, but he did not.

It was an extra-ordinarily emotional time. We left for India, leaving a competent horse-sitter in place. I was not concerned about teaching this particular group, as I knew them all well. I knew the hotel and the yoga roof space, and I was looking forward to seeing all our old friends in Kovalam. Kannan was a particular favourite, he had run a restaurant on the beach for years, and was now managing an apartment block. Indeed, when we alighted from the bus which had brought us from the Airport, I felt excited to share our India with these lovely yogis. It was always amusing to watch the reactions of those who had never been to India, when we first arrived! Trivandrum Airport itself is an experience, and as you come out into the baking sunshine to find the bus, your senses are assaulted. There are so many colours, sounds and smells, it is literally sensory bombardment! Lovely, handsome young Indians gather our suitcases, writing 'Sandybeach Hotel' on them with chalk. They then stack them, precariously, on top of the roof of the bus. We pile into the bus, becoming welded together in the heat as we squeeze into our seats. Everyone cranes to see out of the windows, and as we pass wooden huts and little market stalls on the roadside, gorgeous little Indian children wave to us. Everyone is fascinated by the constant honking of the horns, the antics of the rickshaws and the motorbike's which carry whole families.

Arriving in Kovalam, the porters set off with our suit-cases balanced on their heads. They are barefoot, and yet they smartly outstrip us. On this occasion, I was so tickled at pointing out places of interest to the group, that I neglected to look where I was going. Unfortunately, my foot went down a hole in the road and I sprained my ankle badly. I was to teach the classes for the first week with my

255

foot in a bucket of cold water, and was to hobble painfully around Kovalam for the entire fortnight. Both Mike and I were in a highly emotional state, and in that first walk (and then limp) along the beach, to reach our hotel, we both knew that this was going to be our 'goodbye' to India. It was a long and sad 'goodbye', but there were many high spots on this trip, too. It was Stuart's birthday while we were away. To mark his special day, we all clubbed together and raised a substantial sum for our fruit salad lady, Jamila. She had confided that she owed a lot of money for health bills, and had no way of paying it. Her face when we presented her with the cash was a wonderful gift to Stuart. He went for a swim, along with Jenny, in the high rollers off Kovalam Beach. I had warned them of the sea's power; every year we saw someone drowned on this stretch of sand, despite the sterling efforts of the Lifeguards. (I had swum with Tim and Beth three days running, perfectly safely, on one occasion. The fourth day, I went in alone and the sea decreed that I was becoming a little too confident. It picked me up, threw me over several times, and then lobbed me into the shore. Fortunately, I am not afraid of the water, and I came up laughing and spluttering, with all orifices jammed with sand! Mike had watched, helplessly, from the water's edge.) Stuart saw a huge wave approaching and turned his back to it with a large grin. The sea punished this arrogance, churning him as though he was in a washing-machine, and then throwing him unceremoniously on to the sand. He had a very sore back for a few days, and had to take it easy in yoga.

I was talking to Stuart one day when a curious vision occurred. I was looking into his face and suddenly a different face was transposed over his. It was a laughing Mexican, and it was someone that I knew. It was fleeting, but very vivid, as my past-life flashes usually are. When you meet someone and there is an instant connection, there is every chance that you have known them before.

I was endeavouring to rest my ankle as much as possible, so that I could give the group the two yoga sessions a day, for which they had signed up. We took each group to the Sivananda Ashram, Neyyar Dam, and also to an elephant sanctuary to bath the elephants. That year, Mike took the group on his own. I was sad to miss these outings, but I was able to go on the Backwaters trip. One of the happiest days of my life was boating along the Backwaters with Tim and Beth. The crafts are hilarious. Our first experience was in a very dilapidated wooden boat, with four aged dining chairs just placed inside. The dear boatman was toothless, but cheery and smiley. Our guide, who had become a friend, was called Sam. He supplied us with delicious fried pink bananas in newspaper. It is so peaceful on the Backwaters. You see kingfishers and sea-eagles and egrets. You pass by tiny wooden huts, almost completely hidden by the trees and foliage, and glimpse a snippet of the way the Indians live. You see the most stunning blooms. The quiet is something very special and it was a joy to share this experience with firstly Tim and Beth and then each of our groups.

Most of the folk that year were delightful, and co-operative, but there are always group dynamics which occur. On this particular trip I felt very emotional. We had just buried Mike's Mum, my sister-in-law had left my brother, and I had sustained an injury on arrival. I have a firm belief that a yoga teacher is a professional, and that the 'show must go on' regardless. We needed to put our own grieving and processing to one side, and devote ourselves to the job at hand. I was to discover, however, that personal lessons continue to be learned, and you cannot 'postpone' your own growth. I have learned my buttons over the years and one of them is loyalty. One member of this group had always fallen under the heading of 'friend'. I felt that we had a rather special relationship and I was certainly not expecting any disharmony from this quarter. However, my disloyalty button was pressed firmly, and I felt the hurt keenly. Because of my role as group leader and my heightened emotional state, I decided that confrontation or discussion was inappropriate. It was a hard lesson for me, but inevitably an important one. I remember reading that you cannot teach honour and integrity. It is either there or not. Of course each person has their own version of what constitutes honour. My belief system is that we are here to give love, to serve, and to promote harmony. My mind knows that I should not have expectations, but my heart is still hurt when people I value are disloyal. I remember the light-bulb going on when I recognised that two people seeing an aura will pick it up slightly differently. We all look through our own auras. Life is the same, we look at every situation through the lenses of our past culture and experiences.

After the evening yoga session, we would all change and then go out to a restaurant for a delicious meal. On Stuart's birthday, the waiters asked him if he would like fireworks. The Indian lads love to set off fireworks, and have no concern for Health and Safety! It was quite a spectacle, and a lovely evening. We had witnessed 'fire-eating' with one group; it was entertainment which, quite literally, had you sitting on the edge of your seat, ready to call the ambulance! We had also witnessed the antics of the Indians on Christmas Day. They, quite rightly, reclaim their beach, but then drink cheap home-made alcohol, and take boats out on the wild sea. They are a fascinating race; so beautiful, so spiritual, so joyful, and yet capable of being incredibly irresponsible. We learned to book in to the Sea-Face Hotel on Christmas Day, and to spend the day off the beach and around the pool. It was also sensible to keep a low profile on New Year's Eve!

We had some amazing trips to India, and shared some incredible moments with our yoga friends. Dear Cate and Ian; dear Nigel and Jill; dear Barbara, Patti and Rachel; dear Lynne, Annie, Jenny and Stuart; they are all etched in our memories and smile from our photographs. But Mike and I could feel that Kovalam was changing. The energy was different. There were rumours abroad of the changes that were to come to our special beach. When we left that time, we knew that we would not return and that we were changing, too.

As a yoga teacher, I have a strong bond with India. Yoga postures were depicted on cave walls five thousand years ago. Yoga originated in India. At first it was passed down by mouth, from Guru to Chela. (Guru, you will remember, means to move from darkness to light, and your Guru is your teacher. A Chela is a student.) Then, in approximately three hundred years B.C. Patanjali set down the Eight Limbs of Yoga. All classical yoga classes are based on Patanjali's teaching, and it is still so relevant today. Often people ask if yoga is a religion, and, of course, the answer is 'No'. Yoga is a philosophy and a way of life. There are certainly references to Hindu Gods, and beliefs. These are inevitable, as yoga originated in India, but anyone can practise yoga, no matter what religion you adhere to. I have found the Indian people to be so attractive and friendly. Their idiosyncrasies are delightful, and I love the colours, the sounds and the smells of India. That last visit, though, gave us a glimpse of an undercurrent. Kovalam had become more commercial, and there was a feeling of getting the most possible out of the tourists. We felt exploited, although our hearts broke open at the plight of some of the beggars, and we dug deep to help where we could. Quite simply, we felt less at home, and perhaps our rose-tinted glasses steamed up a little.

The emotions of this trip and this time felt magnified. I believe that we were grieving on many levels. Grieving the loss of Mike's Mum, and indeed the deaths of all of our parents; grieving the breakdown of my brother's marriage; and grieving the passing of our direct connection to India. I am not a victim type; I am generally a confident and empowered person, but the issue in our group had felt like the last straw. It felt, since it had in a minor way involved Mike too, that it had kicked me while I was down. The kicking was not to stop there.

# Chapter 18

Rising sign in Virgo: *Your self-effacing style just isn't strong enough to hide the attraction of your natural insight. No wonder the whole world comes to you with its problems!*

We arrived home that year tired and worn, whereas normally we returned energised and fresh. I was back immediately to the day today running of FRYOG, my classes and the stable work. Our horses were getting older; Bonnie was now thirty four and Gossie thirty three. I scheduled their annual check-up with the Vet for the half-term in February. We had a wonderful horse vet, a young lady called Charlie. She had seen Bonnie through all manner of eye infections, and felt like one of the family. We were even on hugging terms. Bonnie's worst eye infection had seen her wearing a contact lens, being confined to the loose-box for weeks, and having a sunshade rigged up on the outside of her stable to keep the sun out of her eyes! The family joked that all she needed was a Pina Colada, or Pony Colada! A friend of ours, Alex, had come to give Bonnie healing. I was despairing that she would ever be allowed out in the field again, and Alex said: "What have you got to lose? Let her out for a run." We did, and Bonnie immediately rallied. The next day when Charlie came she pronounced Bonnie much improved, and said that we could put her out. I tried to delay, as I knew she would realise that this was not a horse who had suddenly had her freedom restored. Bonnie had done all her pirouettes and heel kicking the previous day! Charlie laughed, and told me that I was sneaky.

It so happened that Charlie brought a trainee with her to do the horses' annual shots and check-up that February. She was going to rasp Bonnie's teeth, but she said that she would just check her eyes out first. She explained Bonnie's medical history to the trainee, and got out her bright light. Now, Bonnie had been her usual gentle, gorgeous self that morning, but as soon as Charlie shone the light into her eye everything changed. She flew to the back of the stable and began to let out the most horrible noise. She then charged Charlie aggressively, and it became clear that it was not safe to be in the stable with her. She had had the bright light in her eyes so many times before, when Charlie checked her for infection and irritation, and we were all mystified as to what was going on. We decided that the best course of action was to let her calm down, to carry on with Gossie's check-up, and to get Charlie back the next day to see to Bonnie.

We let Gossie out into the field, when her treatment was complete, and Charlie and the trainee vet left. Mike and I endeavoured to calm Bonnie, to put her rug on and to let her out into the paddock. Now, Bonnie and I had always been very close, but it became clear that she wanted me nowhere near her. It was as though she was schizophrenic; this was an entirely different horse. Bonnie had never exhibited any sign of aggression at all, but now she had become a demon. Finally she was in the field, and seemed to be more normal when we left. Charlie meanwhile consulted with her colleagues. No-one had ever experienced this radical change of behaviour in a horse, simply by shining a light into their eyes.

We got through the day, attempting to convince ourselves that the light had simply surprised her, that she was ill-prepared for it. When we returned to the field to get the girls in that afternoon, we could convince ourselves no more. She charged directly at me, and she looked like she was out to kill me. She could not tolerate me anywhere near her. We could not get her into the stable and although Mike managed to bravely remove her New Zealand rug, we could not replace it with her stable rug. I was in shock. I fully recognised that Bonnie was an old horse, and that one day she would die. I was prepared for that, but not for this complete mental breakdown. I was compelled to realise that she had lost her mind. Charlie came back with another Vet, but they were unable to approach her. They decided that the only course of action was to call in a Vet who was trained to use a tranquiliser gun, the following morning. This was one of the most awful traumas of my life, and I now had the unenviable duty of phoning our daughter, Gemma, and of breaking the terrible news that her beloved mare had lost her mind and would have to be shot. The Bonnie that we knew and loved was already gone.

As Bonnie's main carer, it grieved me sorely that she spent the night wandering around the courtyard, cold with no stable rug, and not tucked up in her cosy loose-box. Gem got up at five o'clock in the morning and drove to Foxfield to say 'goodbye' to her precious girl. We had always said that we would stand on either side of her when she was put down, but even this was denied us.

A previous Vet from our horse practice, and one we were very fond of called Malcolm, shot the tranquiliser into Bonnie's rump and Mike led her, quiet now, up the path. He held her while the deed was done. He said that she knew, at the end, that it was the only option. Charlie cut a piece of her beautiful white tail off for me to keep, and Bonnie was cremated. Her ashes are in a beautiful casket, and her photographs and her painting remain in pride of place. The grieving for your animals is somewhat different to the grieving for your family. With animals you share complete unconditional love. They are your day to day business and they need you. Your animals do not care how you look, or if you have had a bad day, or have made a poor decision. They love you, anyway. It still gives me great pain that our beautiful Bonnie's life ended in this horrible way, her demise was truly horrendous. My friend, Theresiu, explained that there is a term in Homeopathy which is called 'Madness by bright light'.

We limped on for a little while tending to Gossie each day, until we realised that she needed horse company. We returned her to her previous owner in Alton, and Joyce was delighted to have her Connemara back. We later went to visit her, and she was overjoyed to see us. Sadly, she died in the May, just three months after Bonnie. No-one could have predicted that we would lose both horses so closely together. When Bonnie passed to Spirit World, I petitioned my Mum to look after her. Immediately, I saw a vision of my mother leaning on Bonnie's stable-door at our old house, 'Yoellands'. She was wearing a blue-checked shirt, one that she was always very fond of, and looked as though she was very happy to take over the virtual horse management for me. My mother's big smile was a huge comfort to me; I knew that Bonnie would not be lonely; and now Mum welcomed Gossie, too. I am confident that she looks after all our beautiful animals, in Spirit World.

Life was very strange with no routine, and no beautiful pets. Mike sold the field. He said that we were in the unusual position of being able to downsize without moving. He had managed our five acres and stable buildings for sixteen years, doing all the hedging, ditching, trimming and repairing. It was a wrench for him to sell the Ferguson tractor and the topping equipment at the Farm sale, and for the longest time we could not walk up the lane where our horses used to live.

Partly to distract Mike and to keep him busy, we organised a yoga holiday in Spain. It was at an exceptionally beautiful place called Valle de Vida, and we took a group of nineteen. We stayed in tee-pees, and the one which Tim and Beth shared had a stunning 'Om' in the tiled floor. This was a yoga retreat to remember. We were able to book in for therapies, and I had one with the owner, Robbi, who was an Osteopath. It was superb. His wife, Kerry, could not have been kinder, and their cook, Amanda, served us the most amazing vegetarian food. Robbi and Kerry had two large, black pups called Bill and Ben. We would make our way up the mountain, a quarter of a mile climb to the yoga platform, in silence, each morning for meditation. The dogs would be restrained until the meditation was over and we began our yoga practice. Then, free at last, they would hurtle up the hill to greet us. One morning, they made off with one of Stuart's socks, holding it between them and blazing down the hill, thrilled with their treasure! Needless to say, the sock was never seen again!

Cate and I thought it would be a great idea to chant in the steam room. The acoustics were amazing! It became an hilarious occasion, beginning very seriously with the 'Gayatri Mantra' (which is the most famous of all chants,) and finishing with 'I'm Enery the Eighth I am'! It was a wonderful coming together, with much laughter. Enlightenment does not have to be serious, and the fun that we have had with our groups has certainly raised our spirits. We all remember Denise's wonderful, infectious laughter; Delphine doing her morning practice in her pyjamas; Sue's birthday when Vicky looked stunning in a Spanish dress; and the nightly discussions around the dinner table. Mary made a beautiful keepsake album for

Denise at the end of the holiday, and when they showed it to me, later, the memories came flooding back.

There was only one disadvantage to this marvellous Retreat; the yoga platform was on the top of the hill, and it was windy. I had to strain my voice to be heard, and on the last day it deserted me completely. It was missing for a month after our return, which is a real problem for a yoga teacher. Your voice is your stock in trade. It was also cold, and only Tim and Beth were brave enough to get in the pool. However, the group was very special, and this was certainly our favourite yoga holiday. We did not realise at the time that it would be our last.

The lack of a voice was tiresome. This was a challenging time for me, professionally. One of the toughest aspects of being Chairman to a large yoga society is the 'hiring and firing'. The organisation is run by volunteers, and I would spend a lot of time on the phone looking for replacements for Officers who were stepping down. I had trained eighty teachers, and many of them stepped up to the mark and helped me out. That year I was busy organising the 'Kidz Day' and the Park Place week-end Retreat. I was unable to find any help in the run-up to these events, although good folk such as my dear yoga friend, Swami Satchidananda Ma, turned up on the day and were invaluable. The saying that 'it is lonely at the top' certainly proved true for me. I gave a great deal of pastoral care to my students and to FRYOG members. I was constantly on the phone, answering e-mails and texts, but it seemed impossible to find a colleague to whom I could turn. That summer, I really felt 'up against it'.

The smallFRY junior members' yoga day was a great success, and we raised a substantial sum for the Indian Orphanage which Satchi sponsors. I was tired afterwards, but faced a hectic week, as it was the annual retreat the following week-end. I remember spending two full days planning practices, and laboriously filling in the lesson plan sheets. It is close work, and the phone never stopped ringing, so I was constantly disturbed from my task. The way that I plan the Retreat is that I choose a theme early, often at the end of the last session at the Park Place the previous year. I then allow that to play at the back of my mind. Ideas come at the oddest moments, and I jot them down and build on them later. For me, inspiration must be allowed to emerge in its own time, in its own way, and in quiet moments. I might sit down to plan, but if my mind is disturbed precious inspiration does not arrive. At this time, I was frustrated and feeling drained. The class for the last day did not feel right, and I was running out of time.

Our lovely friend, Delphine, was emigrating to Australia. Delphine trained with me and I was determined to see her before she left. On the Wednesday evening we drove to Southampton to Stuart's house to say our goodbyes. It was a really bright sunny evening, and I omitted to take sunglasses. I was the map-reader, and I was aware how uncomfortable my eyes were becoming. I tend to over-ride discomfort, and to operate on will-power when under pressure, and this was to prove a foolish mistake. Our goodbyes said, we proceeded to buy the fruit for the week-end, on the way home, and then to bag it up. (We supply each student at the retreat with their own fruit-bowl, so that they can snack healthily.)

On the Thursday morning I was teaching an amalgamated class, my students and Cate's. It was quite a strong class, and I felt good. I walked out with my friend and student, Frances, and when we reached the car park, I realised that my eyes were seeing different images. Having always had eye problems, since the age of three, I shrugged it off as over-tiredness. I went to the Hairdressers and closed my eyes while she cut my hair. When I opened them again, I could see only purple with my left eye. I drove home to Petersfield with my left eye closed, which was not the most sensible decision I have ever made. Especially since my right eye has always been the weak one. When I arrived home, I told Mike that something had happened. I said that I had a horrendous headache and that I could only see purple with my left eye. I suggested that it might be a migraine, as the symptoms seemed to fit. Mike gave me paracetamol and we waited for twenty minutes to see if they took effect. The pain at the end of the twenty minutes was so incredibly intense, that it became clear that Medical aid was required. There was no doctor available at our surgery, and so Mike took me to the small Petersfield Hospital. The nurse there was very sweet, and began playing around taking my blood-pressure. At this point my normally equable and co-operative husband began to jump up and down with frustration! "I know my wife", he declared loudly, "and she is not a malingerer. She is in intense pain, and needs help NOW!" At this, the nurse had a light bulb moment and phoned the Eye Department at Queen Alexandra's Hospital in Cosham. They instructed her to get me there immediately. It was the worst twenty minutes of my life, as Mike drove me to the Hospital. I have never experienced pain like that, and every bump in the road was torture. Waiting to be seen, I had to lean against the wall with my head as low as possible. The nurse took one look at me, declared suspected Acute Angle Glaucoma, and within two minutes I was lying down and on a drip. The Specialist later told me that in another twenty minutes I would have lost the sight in my left eye completely. The pressure had risen from the normal, below twenty, to fifty eight. I was hospitalised. It was Thursday evening, and I was due to lead a Retreat for fifty people the following afternoon. Mike phoned Gemma and said: "I have bad news. Your mother is in Hospital, and you're running the Retreat!" The kicking had not finished yet.

I slept for three days. The hospital staff was amazing. They regulated the pressure in my eye with laser treatment and drops. The Acute Angle Glaucoma had been caused by too much pressure and not enough space. And that is exactly how I felt! There was too much pressure in my life, and not enough space. My eyes had always been my weak spot, and the lesson that I needed to learn manifested itself here. The doctors did all the treatments to the right eye as well as the left. My eyes are small and almond shape, somewhat Tibetan, and there was every chance that the right eye would follow in the family tradition.

Mike shared his time between the hospital and Park Place Pastoral centre, where the yoga Retreat was being held. Gem found the conflict emotional and exhausting. She wanted to be with me, but she knew that I would want her to run the retreat. On the Saturday afternoon, where the session is not mandatory, I had planned to read and discuss the 'Upanishads'. These are stories with morals and teaching. They are part of the Vedas, the ancient philosophies of India. On the way to the Hall, Gem bumped into my dear pal, Jill. She asked if Gem was alright, and she immediately burst into tears. Jill said: "Okay. I'll handle this one. You go and have a nap." That's a true friend for you. She served me and my daughter at the same time.

Gemma did a wonderful job that year. It was a big ask as she was only in her early thirties. Lovely Sara was the other teacher on the platform, and she gave her support to Gem. Granted I had prepared and organised it all, and I took comfort from that, but being responsible for fifty people is a big deal. Patti, who trained to be a yoga teacher with Gem, told her that she could feel the practices which were planned by me and the ones that felt more naturally her, the ones planned by Gemma herself.

We had a tearful debrief on the Sunday afternoon, when the Retreat was over and I had come home from the hospital. For three weeks, I did very little. I was putting thirteen drops a day into my eyes, and my sight was permanently blurred. When I climbed out of bed to go to the loo in the night, Mike would get up too, to make sure that I did not stumble and fall downstairs. He had been retired for five years by this time, and was completely happy running the kitchen, and doing the shopping. We got into 'talking books', and our lovely friend, Yvonne, kept us supplied. Many yoga friends were helpful and supportive, and we found the truth of the statement that 'you find out who your real friends are, when you are in need.'

Mike endeavoured to keep my daily life gentle and peaceful, and to ensure that I got plenty of sleep in order to heal. I have always had patches of insomnia, but at this time I was so exhausted on all levels, that sleeping was all that I wanted to do. So it was that, three weeks after my eye trauma, I was sound asleep when Mike had an odd turn in the night. I eventually awoke to find all the bedroom lights on, and Mike sitting up in bed. I assumed, quite wrongly, that he had indigestion, and I sleepily made my way to the nursery to sleep in one of the grandchildren's beds. He came after me and was really angry. Apparently he had what he described as a 'white-out'. He suspected that he had suffered a heart attack, and he demanded my full attention, and right then! So off we went to the hospital again, and they kept him in for tests. Now, I had not driven for three weeks, and with blurred eyes it was not the best plan, but drive I did. Tim came home that week-end, expecting to see how I was doing, and found himself instead visiting his father in the cardiac ward. Fortunately, it was not a heart attack, and the doctor was able to reassure us that all the tests had shown up negative.

Mike is an engineer at heart, and has always said, of our relationship, 'if it's not broke, don't fix it'. I am the one who is constantly fascinated by human dynamics. We have observed, over the years, that I feed him with energy. If my energy is low, for whatever reason, he will go down. This time was a perfect example of just this. I had my three weeks of recovery, and now it was his turn for some attention!

That term I taught from the chair, and Mike, very kindly, drove me to my classes. Wonderful Jean substituted for my groups when I had hospital appointments, and would not allow me to pay her. I had been diagnosed with Adie's Syndrome in 1977, which simply meant that my left pupil was larger than my right. After the trauma, the left pupil became fixed, and therefore did not adjust to light and dark. Night-driving was horribly uncomfortable. Eventually, my wonderful surgeon replaced my own lenses with plastic ones, in an operation like a cataract procedure. He squeezed the left pupil down as much as he could which has helped with bright lights. He endeavoured to create twenty-twenty sight for me, but the end result was that my left eye became slightly short-sighted and my right eye slightly long-sighted. Once my brain adjusted to this, which took a while, I was exceedingly happy with the result. Indeed, I feel that I am the luckiest person on the Planet. I could have been blind in my left eye, and seeing little with my right eye, (which had a squint when I was a small child,) instead I can drive without glasses, mark my register and see my reading at the beginning of each class. I now only use glasses for reading small print, and, for the first time in my life, I am spectacles and contact lens free. I count my blessings regularly!

We held a yoga festival at the end of the summer. The therapists did well, and Gemma's workshop was well subscribed, but it was a poor turn-out for the shopkeepers. I had been too poorly to rally the troops. The Yoga Show was a bit of an ordeal that year, too; I felt quite disoriented on the train and Underground. One of my lovely graduated teachers, Tania, offered to come and support me, while Gem was teaching. I remember all the small kindnesses, especially our grandson, Ben, who was only three. He would wait for me and hold my hand to go down the path, when it was dark.

At this juncture, I became aware for the first time that I was not invincible! I had lived my life on will-power, pushing through boundaries to achieve my aims. I have always had very high expectations of myself, and an iron determination. I encourage my students to work with their bodies, and to listen to their own awareness, but often I do not heed my own advice. I had been blessed with good health, an abundance of energy and a strong desire to serve, but I was learning that I must respect these blessings, and not exploit them. As my Danish friend, Inge, said: "If you keep giving and giving, the end result is that you are running on empty. You have nothing left to

275

give. You must learn to replenish, so that you are not giving an inferior gift, or finishing up with nothing to give at all." A delightful student, called Danielle, came to give me a hot rock massage at about this time, and when she massaged my abdomen, she also read my character. She said: "You take things on readily, process them for a long time, and then let them go very slowly." How true this is. Being such a willing volunteer puts me in the position of being exploited, too, and after this episode in my life, I began to watch my patterns, and those of others, more closely.

# Chapter 19

M ercury opposes Saturn: *You have an open mind and rarely come into conflict with your friends. Quick-fire sudden jokes and one liners make a favourite component part of your breezy sense of humour.*

My sixtieth birthday was approaching, and we all needed a distraction and a celebration. I decided on a Bollywood Party. We booked Lovedean Village Hall where I teach on a Friday. Gemma had discovered some Bollywood Dancers, and we hired them along with the local curry restaurant in Petersfield to provide the food. We invited seventy-five friends and family, and everyone turned up in Indian clothes and bindis. We had gone up to Southall for our outfits, and it was like taking the grandchildren to India! It was absolutely brilliant, and Ben was my personal shopper. My sister-in-law, Meg, wore a sari which I had brought back from India; Tim looked amazing as a Tamil Tiger; Gem, Lizzie and Amy looked like Indian princesses; and Mike, Simon and Bryan sported Kurta pyjamas. All my friends glittered in their outfits and bangles. It was such a special evening; we put a lot of thought into the seating plan, and researched Indian elephant napkins; we even had a moving photograph beside the queue for the curry, showing pictures of our last trip to India. It was a loud occasion, the music blaring, and it was an opportunity for Tim to catch up with old mates and to introduce his partner, Bethan. It was our friend, Andy, who is now training to be a yoga teacher in Gemma's last Teacher Training Course, who stood up on the stage, said a few words about my birthday, and encouraged everyone to come up and dance. It was noisy, and I purposely did not invite some of my more gentle, meditative friends, as it would have seriously assaulted their senses.

At the end of the evening, Gem decided we should put on a display. Behind the curtains, she coached us all: Beth, Cate, Lizzie, Amy, Becky, Issie, Sam and Sophie. When she decided we were good enough to be shown to the public, she cued the music and drew back the curtains, ready for the performance. To our huge amusement, everyone had gone home apart from a few who were stacking the chairs and sweeping the floor! Undaunted, we did the routine, anyway!

The evening came to a wonderful climax, with Tim and Beth setting light to lanterns in our front-garden. After the trying fifteen months previously, it was just wonderful to all be together, and to have some fun.

June of that year saw another really important family celebration in the form of Meg and Simon's wedding. I had the great privilege of being the Matron-of-Honour, and I really enjoyed being involved with choosing the bridesmaids dresses, and Meg's stunning wedding dress. We had a wonderful 'girls' day out in London, for the Hen event, with a 'posh' afternoon tea and then a theatre visit to see 'Wicked'. The actual day was just beautiful, but when we came out of the church the bell-ringers were struggling, they were a man down. Mike, resplendent in a morning-suit, was quick to remedy the situation! It is a lovely aspect of bell-ringing that you are always welcome to visit different towers.

It was also the year of our Ruby Wedding, and whilst I resumed my duties as Chairman with fresh vigour, and my day-to-day classes with renewed enthusiasm, Mike set about planning a family holiday for the end of August, to celebrate our anniversary. We all love ferries, and so we decided to take the ferry across to Santander, Spain, and then to stay there in a lovely hotel. Lizzie slept with us in our cabin, Tim and Beth had a cabin to themselves, and Gem and Clive bunked with Amy and Ben. The ship is always enormous fun, with plenty to do for all age groups. We arrived in Santander, feeling very chipper, and the hotel had done us proud. They had placed us in three rooms at the end of a corridor. We split up into groups of two adults to one child; Lizzie was with Tim and Beth, and she felt very grown-up being with the 'hippy contingent'; Amy was with us, and was unpacked and organised in a flash; and Ben, at only four years old, was with his Mum and Dad. We encountered only one problem on this excellent family holiday, and that was that the Spanish eat so much later than we do. We did know this, but did not anticipate how inconvenient it would prove. (We eat earlier even than most English people, since it is imperative to leave at least two hours between eating and drinking and teaching yoga.) Ben and Amy, after an active day on the beach, were starving by five o'clock. Lizzie was later to remark that the beach far exceeded her expectations, but the food did not come up to the mark. We did, however, thoroughly enjoy our time exploring Santander, and we had organised the event so that our actual anniversary was on the return journey on the ferry. We all dressed up, ate in the 'posh' restaurant, and our forty years together was celebrated in real style. We counted our blessings. How lucky were we to have such a wonderful family? How lucky were we to have a family who wanted to spend time with us? We were fortunate indeed to have such special children and grandchildren, and fortunate indeed to have one another.

There was plenty going on in the Yoga Society once the summer was over. We held the A.G.M.s in September, and these took some organising and planning. There were various fixed points in the calendar: the A.G.M; the Yoga Show; the Park Place annual retreat; the Northern Continued Professional Development day (which Kathleen offered each year), and the Kidz Day. I had pledged, as Chairman, to travel around the country, and to try to meet as many members as possible. With this in mind, I taught two workshops in Scotland, hosted by the lovely Fiona, one in Sheffield, hosted by the excellent newsletter Editor, Ann, two in Northants and two in Berkshire, hosted by softly-spoken and huggable Amanda Jayne. It was always a joy to touch base with other FRYOG members, and to share our views and news. My vision of the Society was that it was a family of yogis. Controversy occasionally occurred, but complaints were few and far between. I felt that the organisation would be enriched by encouraging general members to enrol. They join to become part of a yoga family, and are loyal and steadfast. General members are interested in workshops and retreats, and they swell the membership and the coffers. Our Society supports a charity called 'Towards Nirvana', offering well-needed financial help to an Indian Orphanage and school. General workshops give rise to opportunities to fund-raise, and certainly my weekly students loved to be involved. FRYOG is a teaching organisation, and offers an excellent Diploma Course, but I always envisaged each new graduate creating their own yoga family. I offered a discount on class fees for FRYOG members, and strived towards creating a cohesive Society. Yoga is a way of life, and a Yoga Organisation needs to run as a fully functioning, loving family.

We had some very interesting speakers for the A.G.M. afternoons. A dear friend, Jason, talked to us about the Phoenix Prison Trust; Swami Satvikananda Saraswati, who is such a character and is a special yoga friend, gave us a talk and slide show about 'Towards Nirvana'; and Jo enthralled us with a talk on flower remedies. I enjoyed very much interfacing with the members, and catching up with old friends such as Alan, with whom I had served on the committee whilst I was Diploma Board Officer, and he was Treasurer. Mike drilled me in the proper procedure for running a meeting, and I was always grateful for Gemma's support.

The Christmas of 2009 found us in La Gomera. We had been recommended to go by one of my Friday afternoon students, Sheila. We flew to Tenerife and then took the ferry to La Gomera, which is a beautiful island. The hotel where we stayed has created an exquisite World Garden. Christmas Day was spent leisurely reading by the pool, the temperature being twenty five degrees. When the pressure in my eye had shot up, one of my graduated teachers, Jane, researched a gemstone for me. For two years I carried her blue chalcedony, and that Christmas Gem had managed to buy me a beautiful ring from India, featuring this stone. The 'Shiva's eye' ring which Tim and Beth had bought me in Kerala is much beloved, and Mike had purchased an 'Om' ring for me at the Yoga Show. These three rings from my close family are life-long treasures.

For several years we went away at Christmastime, feeling that this removed the conflict for Gem. She was able to spend the holidays with her in-laws without feeling guilty about us, and the previous year we had visited Cape Verde. This particular Christmas, Tim and Beth were away, too. They had gone to Bangladesh to a friend's wedding, and her parents had flown out to join them. Whilst they were there Tim had a frightening adventure. He had been taken out in a boat, and then had been invited to take a swim. Tim is a strong swimmer, and I am proud to say that I taught both of our children to swim.

On this occasion, he was a little way from the boat when crocodiles appeared and decided that he was on the menu! Tim swam as fast as he could, but the current was impeding his progress. Beth and her friend were watching helplessly from the shore, screaming at him to swim for his life, and the boatman was frantically trying to get back to him. Tim described his experience later to us, and said that he reached a moment when he was so exhausted that he simply surrendered. He said that there was a feeling of completely letting go and trusting. I am tempted to believe that his Nana was guarding him that day, but whoever saved him has my undying gratitude.

Our astonishment was immense, after we had all arrived home, to receive a call from Tim saying that he and Bethan were on a trial separation. I would have staked my life on the fact that they were mated for ever. They had always seemed such a loving couple, and Beth truly was a member of the family. They were very sensible, Tim moved into a flat with a friend, and they attended counselling. It was about six months later that Tim phoned to say: "Mum, I've pulled the plug on it. We're flogging a dead horse." We received a very sweet and poignant e-mail from Beth, saying goodbye, and we have never seen or heard from her again. She and Tim have stayed friends, but we grieved her absence. They had been together for ten years, and we had been very fond of her. Tim eventually got custody of the beautiful cats. The children missed their 'Aunt', who had been such fun. Nothing happens for no reason, and I know that Tim will attract a truly special life-companion. We did observe parts of Tim re-emerging, once this relationship had concluded, parts that had been buried. He said that both he and Beth felt that they had been asleep for years. They needed to wake up.

One of our friends, Donna, mentioned that she intended to walk the South Downs Way. This was something I had always planned to do, and now, with no pets and no fixed routine, it seemed like a perfect time. The South Downs Way is one hundred miles long, and we accomplished it in nine separate days, fitting it in on days when I was not teaching. The winds were cruel in the March, and I borrowed Clive's balaclava to protect my poorly eye. It was a most interesting venture for Mike and me, exploring as it did Mike's organisation skills and orientation, and my stamina and endurance. We both enjoyed it immensely, and were very proud of one another when we accomplished the task.

This is an excerpt from a piece that was published in the summer of 2010: *'Mike and I have been walking the South Downs Way. This wonderful trail leads from the historic city of Winchester to the sea-side resort of Eastbourne. We did it in 'legs', fitting it into our time-table where possible and it took us nine days. It is said to be 100 miles long, but we reckon we did 112, the extra miles connecting us to public transport. It is a logistics exercise arriving at the starting point of each walk and returning home at the end. Fortunately, Mike is a planner, so he enjoyed this aspect of our adventure. We walked through all kinds of weather and battled a bleak northerly wind from Amberley to Eastbourne. I am eternally grateful to my*

*Indian water-bottle carrier (thank you, Ravi!), my sun-hat (thank you, Stuart), and the balaclava, (thank you, Clive).*

*We stayed over just once at a delightful B & B in Bishopstone. This night broke up our last two days. On the Saturday, we walked from Ditchling Beacon to Southease (12 miles) and on the Sunday, from Southease to Eastbourne (19 miles, and now add 2 to get to the station! Very sore knees!!!) This last day was a true test of endurance as we climbed the Seven Sisters and then Beachy head.*

*The views all along the South Downs way are amazing. Britain is so beautiful and the scenery we saw was awe-inspiring. What struck us was the respect all users of this trail demonstrated – AHIMSA, non-violence. There was no litter left and all the gates were closed. We met other walkers, dog-owners, folk on mountain-bikes and groups of young people practising their orienteering skills. All manifested SANTOSHA, contentment. Everyone passed with a cheery 'hello' or stopped for a few words. Much of the time, though, we walked without seeing another person and then we enjoyed the birds (skylarks, swallows,) the sheep and the beautiful lambs, the cows (all so serene and tranquil), and the horses.*

*Sometimes we walked in companionable silence, sometimes we had deep, philosophical discussions and sometimes we shared silly jokes. Such idiocies as: "Oh good, another hill" or "only 10 miles to go" could set us off into silly giggles. As Donna says: "Walking is very meditative". This whole project was a meditation for us –*

*DHYANA. And there was a moment on each of these days when I experienced surrender. This moment was often preceded by thoughts such as: "Why are we doing this?" or "Do I really want to play this game?" and then all resistance would dissolve and I would simply walk – one foot in front of the other, nothing else. When all resistance leaves, there is SAMADHI, bliss.*

*We both found mantra invaluable. Mike used 'OM NAMAH SHIVAYA' and I turned to my favourite Tibetan mantra 'OM MANI PADME HUM'. I used it climbing the steps into the forests and Mike while ascending the Seven Sisters. Gun-shots in the distance would press my buttons. I accept that creatures have KARMA, too, but every pheasant is grieved, sent away with love and with a request to BRAHMAN to 'please free his spirit'. Lambs temporarily separated from their mothers fill me with concern and with KARUNA, compassion. I was always aware of my heart chakra, ANAHATA.*

*Yoga is a journey of self-discovery and so was our walk along the South Downs Way. It feels so spiritual treading a path that so many have trodden before, through the ages, and so many more will travel in the future. I learned a lot about myself and we learned a lot about one another (even after almost 41 years of marriage!) I have had 21 months of eye problems and it was important for me to pit myself against a challenge. This certainly was a momentous challenge and how special to arrive at Eastbourne and to open a beautiful card from our daughter and her family, congratulating us on our achievement. Sometimes practising yoga is walking the South Downs Way. Sometimes we need to walk, and sometimes we need to stay still: "The mighty oak was once a little nut that stood its ground." Anodea Judith.*

We met a great number of dog-walkers on our journeys. We had now been without a pet for three years and I was beginning to yearn. As my wise friend in Kentucky, Connie, said: "Having animals is not a choice for you, it is who you are." Add to this the fact that the grandchildren were longing for a dog, and Daddy was saying 'no', and you had a dog-shaped hole. We offered to take care of a friend's dog, as she was keen to have one but worked full-time. We began to research dog rescue centres for her, actually, and discovered a tri-colour collie who needed a home. She was three years old and was called Bonnie. Since our beautiful horse had been called Bonnie, it seemed as though the Universe was guiding us. Tania then decided to go for a puppy, and not a rescue dog, and chose a collie-cocker cross, who was adorable and very lively. She named him Colin. Mike showed a big interest in the collie, and seeing a chink in his armour, I pushed it through and we brought Bonnie home. I felt that a three year old dog would be able to handle the puppy, and fondly imagined that we would all live 'happily ever after'. Unfortunately, Bonnie turned out to be unpredictable. She was a biter; she bit Mike, me and a soldier in Queen Elizabeth Park. It was clear that we could not keep her. Our grandchildren are in and out all the time, and it was utterly essential that we had a trustworthy dog. We only had Bonnie for five days, but already had settled into the dog- owner's role once more, and I cried when she left.

Lizzie researched a number of Dog Rescue Centres on the Internet for us, and we spent several days touring them, but always came home disappointed. None of the dogs we selected could be trusted with children. Eventually, despairing of us ever resolving this issue, Gemma stepped in. She settled down at the computer and said: "Okay, Mum, it's clear that we will have to have a puppy. Now, give me some breeds." I've always been attracted to the wolf types, and I remembered a Keeshond from my childhood. I was eighteen months old when I let go of the pushchair handle and ran to a dog who was sitting outside a shop. I threw my arms around his neck, and gave him the biggest hug. Mum said that her heart was in her mouth, but the dear dog took it all in his stride. So, I suggested a Keeshond puppy. As luck would have it, there was a litter in Crawley, Sussex. One pup was left, he had been chosen but then the folk had taken on a rescue dog instead. We had been looking for a bitch, until a friend said that she much preferred dogs as they were less bossy. Pip had certainly been bossy! Off we went to meet the dog-breeder, who was the most delightful lady, and who interviewed us for an hour and a half. She insisted that we meet all the adults first; we met his father, Dylan; his mother, Bramble; and his grandmother, Ruby; and then we were allowed to see our little boy. I could fully understand why we were not allowed to see the pups first. They were so absolutely adorable that no-one could have refused them! Our little boy had a hare-lip. Gem was to remark to someone, in my hearing, "the last puppy in the litter to be claimed, and having a hare-lip, he was right up Mum's street!" (I wonder sometimes about time-lines and premonitions. Did I, at eighteen months, recognise a dear pet who would feature strongly in my future life?)

We went home jubilant, and began choosing names. I had the fond expectation that Colin and our puppy would grow up to be 'brothers', and would be bonded for life. Everyone had some input into the choice of name, but since the Keeshond is a Dutch Barge Dog we settled on Rudi, which is a Dutch name. They are known as the canine baby-sitters, so ideal for our family.

We were determined to complete the South Downs Way before embarking on our next project, Rudi. We also wanted to get Lizzie up to the Globe in London to see a Shakespearian production. We took her for her thirteenth birthday treat, and had a marvellous day. Lizzie, like me, loves Shakespeare. We introduced her first of all at the age of nine. We took her to Chichester Festival Theatre to see 'Twelfth Night'. She sat mesmerised, and during the interval, whilst we were queuing for ice-cream, I said: "What do you make of it, Lizzie?" She replied: "At first I could not understand what they were saying, and then I realised that you listen underneath the words." Amazing! Another Shakespeare fan was born.

The day that Rudi came home was a huge time of celebration. That was the longest time in my life that I had been without a pet. Gem and the children came around to meet him, and were all immediately enslaved. He was the cutest puppy ever. Ben was so taken with him that he proclaimed: "Now I have a brother!" Keeshonds are bred to be companion dogs. They say that if you want to do a five mile walk they are happy to do that with you, or if you want to walk around the block to the local pub that is fine, too. Rudi is easy in all respects. He is sociable, loving, biddable and fun. He only has one 'vice', he loves shoes and slippers. His biggest joy is to steal my slipper and make off with it, little tail wagging like mad! The children come in and hang up their shoes! Unfortunately, the two puppies had very different natures. They are both beautiful little souls, and we loved them both, but when Colin had bowled Rudi down the concrete steps for the umpteenth time one day (he was just playing, in his mind,) Mike lost patience, and declared that we had an untenable situation. We saw through our commitment  though, I spent Wednesday afternoons with Colin at his home, Mike was there on a Thursday afternoon, and Gemma covered Friday. We did this until Colin was bigger, and then Tania moved. At least we had been able to facilitate her having her dog, and she is delighted with him. Meanwhile, Rudi's best- friend now is Meg and Simon's dog, Murphy. He is a Vizla cross, and he and Rudi have great fun together.

I had hoped that with us having Rudi, Gem's urge for a pet would be satisfied. This proved not to be the case. Indeed it made it worse for her. She mounted a steady campaign as, up to that point, Clive was adamantly opposed to keeping animals. When they first met, she had said that "Clive has only one fault – he does not like pets." Anyway, persistence prevailed and that Christmas they rescued two kittens, Lottie and Spike. Their house became a home immediately.

Mike was beginning to recognise that my total time and attention was devoted to the Yoga Society, and he stated his view, with conviction, that it was time for me to step down. I understood his point of view, but I was not ready to relinquish the post until all my work was done. I believed that this was my pathway, my mission. Certainly being Chairman was the pinnacle of my yoga career, everything that I had done so far in my life had brought me to this point. I had a vision and a very genuine desire to create a working democracy, a family of yogis, and a society that was based on the yogic philosophies of love, peace and harmony. It had astonished me when I had witnessed anger, dominance and hidden agendas at A.G.M.s and Executive Committee meetings in the past, but of course opinions run high, and it is essential that everyone is heard. I felt that if I could not lead with love, as Chairman, then I could not lead at all. One of my beliefs is that yoga is for all ages. We had created a Junior Membership, and I would have liked to have created a Senior Membership, too. (I thought the title 'wiseFRY had a nice ring to it!) Our insurer, Nigel, had once said to me: "FRYOG does not treat its Senior Teachers very well." I had inherited apathy in the organisation, when I took over, and I really wanted to breathe life, energy and commitment into the fabric of the society. A suggestion from one of my graduated teachers, Lucy, was to create a wall-hanging comprised of patches made by the members. I liked to respond positively to suggestions, wherever possible, and this one we embraced with enthusiasm. We did receive criticism for it, some believing that it portrayed a Mother's Meeting or Women's Institute attitude, but it demonstrated community, a 'coming together'. It was beautifully completed by Deirdre and Lynne, and hangs in pride of place in Kate's lovely yoga studio. It was excellent to find a permanent home for it, after proudly displaying it at The Yoga Show, the A.G.M., Park Place and our chanting workshops. It is an expression of our yoga community and, now that Kate is a Tutor, student teachers are seeing the hanging on a regular basis. Later, Fran, who is a beautiful soul and friend, created a Poetry book. This embraced the same 'coming together', and the profits went to the Indian charity 'Towards Nirvana'.

My last year as Chairman was busy. I was determined to hand over a professional package to the next Chairman. We created an e-mail Tutors package to assist new tutors, and aided Andrea, (The Diploma Board Officer,) to update the Diploma Pack. I encouraged more Continued Professional Development Days to be offered, and created new posts. We quadrupled the number of Tutors. I continued to perform a task each day for FRYOG and felt an enormous sense of love and loyalty towards the Society and all its members. I relinquished the post in September 2011 at the A.G.M., delighted that my friend, Chris, was continuing as Secretary. I was utterly intent on getting the 'business' side of the handover correct, and so was bowled over when the committee presented me with a beautiful plaque, and a huge bouquet of flowers. I had not expected such a gesture of appreciation, (my contribution, after all, was my way of 'giving back' to the yoga community), and it really made me tearful. Gemma also stood down as Junior Membership Officer. She had done a wonderful job for five years and it was time for someone else to step up to the mark. I wrote this poem at the time, which is entitled: 'RETIRING CHAIRMAN':

*Here's to the ones who went before,*

*With vision and ideas galore.*

*Here's to the ones you see today,*

*Who fly the flag and light the way.*

*Here's to the ones who loyal and true,*

*Supported my journey and loved me through.*

*Here's to the ones who, truth to tell,*

*Tried my patience, but taught me as well.*

*Here's to the Society, FRYOG by name,*

*Whose progress we serve, and support we claim.*

*And cheers to the ones who understand,*

*The circle of love and that which has been planned.*

The role of retired Chairman was not, it turned out, the cosy 'Grandma Elder' position that I expected, and I realised that I was being asked, by the Universe, to 'let go' again. I stuck around for a year, just in case there were any queries, and to give support. I was determined that our new Chairman would not be alone. Then I realised that it was time to take a huge step backwards and to slip, happily, into obscurity. I had served my purpose, and I had served the members. Being a passive member, after being an active member for fifteen years, is a new experience and I wish Amanda and the team the very best of luck.

Immediately after my last A.G.M. as Chairman, we took Amy to Paris. She had been ten in the July, and it was her turn to choose a European city to visit. Amy is very decisive and chose Paris with no hesitation. We were delighted as we could travel on the Eurostar, a mode of transport we had not experienced, and one which would be kinder to my eye. I postponed making the transition from vegetarian to vegan until our return, fearing that it would be difficult to find vegan food in France. I need not have been concerned. Paris is now wonderfully cosmopolitan, and attitudes to vegetarianism have undergone an enormous shift since our last visit.

We had a lovely hotel, and the desk staff were absolutely sweet to Amy. She slept on the temporary bed for the first night, and then swapped with me for the second. It was delightful to have her to ourselves, and she thrived on the undiluted attention. It is not always easy being a middle child! Amy fell in love with Paris, and proved herself to be an intrepid traveller. We loved rediscovering Paris through her eyes, and her enthusiasm for the Eiffel Tower was contagious. She presented us with a miniature model of the Tower as a thank you for taking her away. It stands in pride of place on the shelves in our hall, and reminds me of our lovely trip. Mike and I particularly enjoyed going to the top of the Arc de Triomphe and enjoying the wonderful view, something we had not done before. Gem had bought Amy a dear little black beret, and with her pink duffle coat she looked like a French model. She was bubbling over with enthusiasm when we reunited her with her family, and so was Rudi at our return. Gem, Lizzie and Ben had moved into Fyfield to take care of him, and he had lots of fun, but still celebrated and pirouetted at our home-coming.

Christmas would include all the family that year, and was perfect for Rudi. We booked two villas at Center Parcs, Longleat, and the weather obliged by providing us with deep snow. Tim joined Mike, Rudi and me in our villa, whilst Gem, Clive and the children had their own. We had the most perfect Christmas. Everyone booked into an activity of their choice. Ben did fencing, Amy entered a climbing challenge, and Lizzie and I booked to meet the huskies. Christmas lunch was in our villa, Christmas tea in Gem's, and we had the most wonderful Jazz Brunch on Boxing Day. It was a Christmas which healed past disappointments, and united us as a family. I felt, in some strange way, that it ticked all the boxes. I had experienced the perfect Christmas; no-one could ever take that away from me, so future Christmases contained no pressure or expectation.

My writing had become very important to me, and took up a great deal of my time. It is really rather curious writing about your life! It is as though you are living two time-lines at the same moment. It can be very disorienting and it is emotional, as well. Rudi is a great companion, happily sleeping beside my desk as I write, and rejoicing when I remove the pen-stick from the drawer to back up my work! Mike and I had long shared a dream of taking on a log-cabin in the woods, for three months. I would have a desk by the window, with a magnificent view, and would happily tap away on the key-board all day. He would do the shopping, cook the meals and walk the dog. It was a lovely dream, for some time in the future. Then, we were invited to friends for dinner, and Rudi came too. Jill and John had also invited Gaye, who loves dogs. She was entranced with our furry boy, and mentioned that she had a static caravan in Swanage, Dorset, which we would be welcome to borrow. She said that the dog walks were exceptional there. We were very keen to take her up on her kind offer and booked the caravan for three days in the Easter holidays. We were about to find our 'log-cabin' and life was giving us a wonderful opportunity.

Mike had always loved camping. We had taken the children on camping holidays in Britain and France, when they were little, and then had bought a camper van when Mike retired. This was a large six-berth motor-caravan, and we had a lot of fun taking Lizzie and Amy away. Then we grew practical and swapped our two vehicles for a two-berth motor-caravan called a Fifer. It was wonderfully well designed, but once Rudi became a family member we began to realise that the lack of space was becoming a problem. Staying in Gaye's caravan, on the beautiful island of Purbeck, convinced us that this was the way forward.

We realised immediately that Gaye and her husband had researched this site thoroughly. It sits in the hills, is small enough to be friendly, but big enough to have all the necessary facilities. We viewed the caravans that were for sale and chose 'Lazy Days'. We believe that it has the best position on the site, surrounded by the views of Nine Barrows hill, and Ballard Down, and looking down over the touring field. There is always plenty to watch and enjoy. We moved into 'Lazy Days' at the end of May, and spent fifty eight nights there in the first year. It is bliss not to have to worry about Airports anymore, to always know where you are going on holiday, and to be able to arrive whenever, without having to book in or pick up keys. We keep a second set of everything there, so packing is minimal. We just love it!

The first time we took the children there was a special occasion, and one that is imprinted on my memory. They were thrilled. After eating dinner, we all went up the steep hill. The children beat us by a mile, and, as it was becoming dusk, I will never forget their silhouettes on the hill: Lizzie, Amy, Rudi and then Ben. It was magical! We have the perfect holiday venue, and it is an area that Gem and Clive already love. They had spent many a happy time there with Gem's mentor from school, Judith. Crossing the little ferry is always exciting, Clive loves the steam train and Gemma loves Corfe Castle. Amy has taken to the caravan like a duck to water, packing her bag and coming with Mike and me whenever she can. She has produced a Powerpoint presentation on 'Why we love Swanage', and is quick to select her favourite walks from our repertoire.

Luckily, the Inn on the site caters for vegans, and Rudi is welcome there. Swanage is incredibly dog-friendly, and often shopkeepers will say: "You are most welcome to bring your dog in." We have made friends and have had beautiful occasions.

Mike was so taken with Dorset that he began studying the Estate Agents windows, while we were there for a month in the summer. At first I looked on tolerantly, until I realised that he was actually serious. We had a long talk, and I put forward my views that the charm of having a static caravan in Swanage was the fact that we were 'getting away'. It is a little 'hide-away' to which we can escape. If we bought a house in the area, it would become work. It is a beautiful place to live, but so is Petersfield. We talked at length, having what we call our 'park-bench' moments. (We have made a lot of our important decisions whilst sitting on park-benches, and certainly two of our very best decisions were buying Rudi and 'Lazy Days', as our caravan is called.)

Eventually we agreed that there was one last move left in us, but it would have to be in Petersfield, and, preferably, in the village of Stroud. Gem and the children still need us to be close. Langrish School is a short walk away, where Amy and Ben were very happy, and The Petersfield School bus passes our house, the bus-stop being at the end of the lane. Lizzie was doing exceedingly well at Senior School, and it was great for us to be able to wave to her as she passed in the morning, and afternoon, and to welcome her home for tea on a Friday. At this time, we had lived in Fyfield for almost nineteen years, and we knew every corner of the village. We discussed the properties that might interest us and what we would wish for in a new dwelling. We both agreed that we would down-size providing the house offered us all our requirements, one of which was a downstairs study, so that Rudi could sleep beside me whilst I write. Now, there is a charming little back-water just across the road from us, which contains four bungalows. We agreed that we would be very interested if any of them came on to the market. (A rather interesting feature of life in our village is that people rarely move. Our next-door neighbour has been here for thirty-five years, her next door neighbours, our dear friends Rosemary and Martin, have been here for thirty. There is something very special and spiritual about this area. The Krishnamurti Centre is just ten minutes to the east of us, The White Eagle Lodge is to the north, and Chithurst, the Buddhist Monastery, is to the East.)

Imagine our delight when, on returning to 'Fyfield' after a month in Dorset, we perused the local paper and discovered that one of the bungalows opposite was indeed newly on the market! We went to see it, loved it immediately, and put our house on the market, too. We knew the couple who lived in the bungalow, delightful people, and when I happened to mention that we have a Keeshond, they produced a beautiful ornament. They had had a Keeshond, called Kaiser! Now, this breed is so unusual that it seemed like an omen. I am always looking for coincidences and messages from the Universe and, later, I had a vision of Rudi sitting on the door-step waiting for me to return from yoga. It all felt right.

Our Estate Agents appeared to be very helpful, but we soon discovered that they spoke with 'forked-tongues!' At best moving is hell, and we were out of the habit. We showed a number of folk around, and they all loved the house, but not the fact that it sits next to the A272. After two months, we decided to give up, and to spend the £25,000 that it would have cost us to move on improvements to 'Fyfield' instead. We embarked upon a major project, which took seven months to complete, and we were discover why the move had not taken place. The vendor died before Christmas, and his wife just three weeks later. They were the most delightful people, and we were very sad to hear the news. It would have been a nightmare, though, had we been in the midst of the legal process. The Universe was protecting us again; just as when we had made plans to go to Thailand, and would most certainly have been involved in the Tsunami, had Gemma not requested that we cancelled our plans. We never can see the full picture of this life-time as we are living it. But in hindsight, it is possible to trace the huge number of times when the Universe steps in. We are guided, and sometimes we must 'get out of our own way' and simply trust.

So, 'Fyfield' received a face-lift. We had a new boundary wall built on the front-garden, new 'silent' windows (which have eliminated the sound of passing traffic), two new bathrooms and a vanity unit in Lizzie's bedroom. We redecorated, re-organised and de-cluttered. Ben was our personal shopper when we went to look for carpet for the hall, stairs and landing, and the children loved playing 'spot the difference' every time they came to tea. Mike put in a new oven, and is delighted with the television and Freesat box. We parted with our very solid and well-loved dining-room suite – (that table which had witnessed so many family dinners, executive committee meetings, and fascinating spiritual discussions with my student teachers!) – replacing it with a light, round table in cream, and six chairs. We brought my beautiful desk downstairs to the dining-room and created my longed for downstairs study. Mike replaced all the doors upstairs, which now looks light and bright. We are thrilled with all our changes, and completed in time for a family get-together at the end of May to celebrate Tim's fortieth birthday.

I have reached the conclusion that the only permanent thing about life is its impermanence. Having a long-established home, though, gives me the roots that I crave. It is now twenty years since we moved to 'Fyfield' and that is the longest that I have lived anywhere in my life. Our previous house, 'Yoellands', was our eighth house in fifteen years! We are so settled in this area, we love the Hampshire countryside and the market town of Petersfield. We can take the train to London to see Tim, very easily, and yet it is no distance to the sea. I feel embraced by the gentle hills of both Dorset and Hampshire, and whilst it is wonderful to visit places like Scotland, Wales and Cornwall, they are not places where I feel at home.

Why am I here at this time of my life? I am learning 'what it is too late for, what it is just right for, and what it is too early for'. I am still learning to 'let-go'. I am learning the enormous pleasure of spending time with real friends, and beautiful family. I am learning the power of writing and expression, and I am focussing on my own Sadhana, (spiritual practice). The yogis believe that for the first twenty-five years of our lives we are students, for the next twenty-five we are householders, the following twenty-five we are teachers, and for the last twenty-five we are recluses or hermits. I am still in my teacher phase. I used to believe that at sixty I would be ready, to teach 'gentle yoga' and meditation courses, but at sixty-three I am nowhere near that yet. I love my classes and my students, and still feel profoundly humble at the privilege of being a yoga teacher. I have consolidated my groups into six classes a week, teaching three blocks of two classes. This works really well for me, and gives me time to sit at my big desk to write. I have time to walk twice a day with Rudi and Mike, which I dearly love. We are 'hands on' grandparents, putting in more time now that Gemma is full-time teaching. We deliver Ben to school each morning and pick him up two afternoons a week. We are on call for picking up the girls, and for covering illness where necessary. We love being involved with the children, and realise how fortunate we are that they live so close. I read some beautiful words recently at the therapy room of a wonderful healer: 'May you be gracious and fulfilled at the end of the day." I aspire to that. I am endlessly learning to trust in the Universe, love, my guardian angels and spiritual guides.

# Chapter 20

Jupiter sextiles Sun: *You like to live according to a high moral code.*

The weather in March 2012 was glorious, sunny and warm with the promise of a good summer. Unfortunately that promise did not come to fruition, and it was the wettest summer ever. Wise words state that 'there is no bad weather, just wrong clothes', and we are well-equipped. Being such a long-haired dog, Rudi gets water-logged so he has two very smart coats. We also have a 'cool-coat' for him for hot days! His preference, of course, is for the bright crisp and frosty days. When the other dogs are shivering, he is in his element. He sleeps against the cold window-pane of the French-doors, and on the cold bricks of the fireplace if he is really hot. Basically, the British climate suits him quite well. Instead of a Dutch Barge dog he has become a British Caravan dog! Everyone who meets Rudi says: "Gosh, I bet he takes a lot of grooming!" Actually, as I reassure them immediately, I brush him just once a week. I save his fur and a friend from the village, Angela, spun the first batch for me. She mixed it with sheep's wool, and I knitted lovely scarves for the three grandchildren. Angela would not allow me to pay her, so I have now found a lady in Midhurst who spins it for me and charges a fee. She uses just Rudi's fur, and it turns out so soft and fine. Although Rudi is white, grey and black, the wool comes out in shades of beige. I knitted a scarf for Meg's birthday with the first skeins, she looks stunning in it and wears it all the time. Now I am looking forward to making scarves for Gem and for me. It is really special having something from Rudi, and Keeshond's do not smell when wet (this is a query we often receive.) There are many interesting facts about the breed, one being that their coats are called 'fur' whereas other dogs' coats are called 'hair'. My next project will be to learn to spin so that I am self-sufficient.

There is a real resurgence in home-made projects, probably because of the recession. Mike fondly jokes about forming a cottage industry with me knitting garments made from Rudi's fur, and Meg baking her delicious vegan chocolate cakes! Creative projects are an expression of who you are, and I really enjoy knitting in the love. It answers another need in me, too. It is essential for my well-being to be busy, and to be serving others. If I sit to watch a movie, and my hands are busy with my knitting, then I feel productive. I am being useful. While I thoroughly admire people like Mike and my mother (both Leos and able to stretch out and totally embrace relaxation, just like lions!) I have a driving need to be productive. It is this characteristic which will keep me teaching yoga for as long as I am useful to the community. I spoke to one special soul in the North of England, not too long ago, and she said: "I keep thinking that I will retire from teaching yoga when my students stop enrolling. But they haven't stopped yet." She was eighty-nine, and died a short while later, still teaching. I tell my students that one day they will look up at the end of their meditation and see that my mat is empty. I will have moved quietly on to Spirit World. A dear friend, Barbara, went on teaching her five classes a week until she had a very short illness and died. She was seventy-five, and her daughter, Angela, finished her yoga teacher training literally at the exact moment to take over her mum's classes. Barbara came to Mike in a dream when we were in Valle de Vida, Spain. She was to have been on the Retreat with us, but died the day we left. She said: "Hello, Mike, they keep telling me that I'm dead, but I can't be because I'm here". She was wearing her FRYOG fleece jacket, and Mike could see her vividly.

Dreams are amazingly instructive. Recently I dreamt that I wanted to write down some ideas for my book. In the dream, I went into my Dad's study; it was the one in 'Yeolands', where we used to live in Somerset, and was known as the Morning Room. I found a piece of A3 paper covered in figures and notes, and began to jot down thoughts. Dad walked in with Beth, and I apologised for using his paper. Any journey that you make, and any exploration of your life, will be supported by loved-ones past and present. I find this invisible support hugely comforting. The Spiritual Healer, who I visited recently, spoke of my 'aloneness'. He said that I embark on a disclosure and then think: "What's the point? They may not care, or understand, anyway." I love people, but there is certainly a part of me which remains locked away. Like a fish, I find hidden and colourful pools to explore, on my own. Then, refreshed by my time in the deep, reflective pool, I re-emerge to face the world again.

I received a Christmas card yesterday from the Prison Phoenix Trust, they do such wonderful work taking yoga and meditation into prisons. Inside the card it says: "The most valuable possession you can own is an open heart. The most powerful weapon you can be is an instrument of peace." What a wonderful message this is at Christmastime. I am so fortunate to have had many moments to remember which open my heart. We went to see His Holiness the Dalai Lama this summer in Aldershot. He is such a wonderful ambassador of peace, and it was a huge privilege to be in his vicinity, even though we shared his presence with five thousand others, and needed binoculars! Remembering his wonderful face always opens my heart. Similarly, I hold the memory of being embraced by the 'Hugging Guru, Amma', and I have many sayings and readings which perform the same purpose. I have met two angels in my life, who have influenced me. One was in Cornwall when we were staying with friends. She manifested as a gypsy, selling lace, and she spoke so reassuringly about the difficulties that I was facing at that time. It was as though she recharged my inner strength. When we parted, I glanced back and she had vanished. The other one I met in Petersfield at a time when I was sad and emotionally low. We walked together, and she gave me a completely different perspective to work with. She, too, instantly disappeared, but I felt blessed and wrapped in love. The memory of the angels opens my heart. Many times my mother has visited me from Spirit World. She reminds me that even death has not separated us, and my heart breaks open.

The yogis in the world bring well-needed peace, and I do feel that we are supported by guardian angels and spirit guides. One of my missions was to train up a body of good yoga teachers for this purpose, and I felt very strongly that we should keep the cost of yoga training accessible to all. I love to think of the eighty teachers that I have trained spreading the word, and spreading peace. It is also why I felt so strongly about teaching children the message of yoga. It is their generation that will change the world. They are faced with the energy crisis, the credit crunch, war and famine. They need the good tools and techniques that yoga will give them.

My life has been a life in yoga. I have been blessed with a purpose and a mission. I have done my best to step up to the mark. I have seen so many changes in the yoga world during my career of thirty-seven years, and I have seen miracles happen in the yoga classes. Yoga works on all levels, and its healing power is extra-ordinary. When yoga becomes your life, it is both a blessing and a responsibility. It is your destiny to nurture an open heart, and to offer yourself as an instrument of peace.

The journey continues, and I know that I am still here to learn lessons. If you are alive you are still receiving lessons! I work with gratitude, compassion, love and I endlessly inquire. I am like a little detective about all aspects of my life, and life in general. My blessings are many, but my trials have been, too. Mike and I have been married for forty-three years, and it is not easy living with any one person for that long! We are companions, and he is still the nicest man I have ever met. We share a lively sense of fun, and a deep enjoyment of life. We also share a huge pride in our children, and admire them both for their achievements. Tim is an accomplished poet and broadcaster. He has his own web-site where he shares short stories and poetry. He is a controller of the couriers who transport blood and blood samples around the country. Gemma is a Teaching Assistant at a prestigious school where she has put yoga on the curriculum. She is a Tutor and has trained thirty-four yoga teachers. We have a huge pride in our grandchildren, and are confident that they will go on to change the world. Lizzie is hoping to apply to Oxford or Cambridge University, and manages to combine beauty with brains. She looks utterly stunning in her Prom dress, bought ready for June. Amy is planning on being a teacher like her Mum, and she will be superb. She is organised and amusing, and is an excellent communicator. Ben has a mathematical brain like his father, can pick up concepts readily, and yet is outstanding at sports. He would make a successful Sports Scientist, but no doubt he will surprise us all. We have statues in the garden which represent our family members. Tim is a boy reading a book, (you never see him without one!) Gem is a sleeping angel; Lizzie is a fairy, blowing a kiss; and Amy is a little girl gathering flowers. When Ben was born, I was astonished to see how closely he resembles a Capo di Monte ornament which stands on our mantle-piece. It was the last gift I received from my parents before they parted. (Is it possible that my mother saw that beautiful boy and knew that, one day, she would have a great-grandson who looked like that?) What will the future hold, for us as a family, for the yoga community, and for the world in general? We all need to read the signs, and to seek out the coincidences which direct us on our pathway. In a moment of clarity I wrote:

LOVE IS THE LIFE FORCE

*Must I seek and strive to find the real me?*

*No. Stop trying so hard and just be.*

*Must I wander and search to find my place?*

*No. Stay really still and fill this space.*

*Must I talk, shout and debate to be heard?*

*No. Be silent now. Love needs not one word.*


*There is no need to journey, you are already here.*

*There is no need to struggle, your purpose is quite clear.*

*There is no need to rush, just love the ones you hold dear.*

*Love is always the answer to our questions and doubts.*

*Love is always the answer, that's what our life is about.*

*We are here to learn, to unite and to find truth.*

*Love is who you are, where you are and love is the proof.*

*Love is the life-force, the prana.*

*Love is the glue, the cement.*

*Peace will be found and established,*

*When love fills your every moment.*

Walking Rudi at Queen Elizabeth Park a fortnight ago, I was stopped by two people who asked the direction to the South Downs Way. They were accompanied by a blind, black Labrador. Shortly afterwards, I met a lady who had lost her two Jack Russells. Rudi and I joined in with the search, and later I began to examine the coincidence of meeting these different seekers. The fact that the Labrador bitch was blind had made a big impression on me, my heart had opened. We are all blindly searching, I suppose, and sometimes, like the small terriers, we go off after a scent which leads us astray. I began to wonder if our lives are concerned with looking for lost pieces of our souls. Perhaps the last part of our life's journey is to revisit experiences that have moulded us, and shaped our progress, and to reclaim scraps of our spirits. If a three year old child realises that she is here for a reason, and that this life is one of a series of lives, surely that is a strong case for re-incarnation. Like picking up shells on the beach, perhaps we pick up pieces of the jig-saw as we

311

progress through each life. How beautiful the finished picture will be!

At sixty-three I sit cross-legged, my hands neatly folded in my lap. My long, brown ringlets have given way to short, white hair. My almond-shaped eyes now contain plastic lens implants. My heart is no longer bouncy and innocent, like a puppy, but is bruised and mended and a little frayed around the edges! But my soul is intact and is keeping a careful tally of karmic progress. Surrounded by my home, the memories of my family, my friends and my beloved animals, I ask myself: "Why am I here this time?"

**OM SHANTI SHANTI SHANTI**

# *In Conclusion*

Interview with a FRYOG Member (published in Autumn 2012.)

## 1. What is your name?

My name is Carole (with an 'e', please), Kerton (with a 'k', please.) My friend and colleague, Kathleen, pointed out that 'carol' is a song that we sing at Christmastime, and 'kirtan' is the chanting which we do in Bhakti Yoga.

## 2. Do you practise yoga and how long have you been practising yoga?

I feel that I have been practising yoga all my life. I have been teaching yoga for thirty seven years, and I am still just as excited to get on my mat.

## 3. What or whom influenced you to start practising yoga?

When I was three years old, I sat in meditation posture and asked my mother: 'Why am I here this time?' (This is the title of the book, that I am busy writing at the

313

moment.) And when I was fifteen, I bought a book on Pranayama. This immediately helped with my asthma, and the realisation was there that yoga is therapeutic. In my early twenties, I booked into Adult Education classes with my friend, Eunice. Our yoga teacher was Lilla Bek, and from the first moment I knew that I had 'come home'. I believe that I was a yogi in a previous life, or many lives. My inner Guru influenced me to start (or continue) practising yoga.

## 4. Do you teach yoga and what made you decide to start teaching yoga?

Yes, I teach yoga. The changes that I witnessed in myself after joining Lilla's classes were SO exciting that immediately I felt enthused to spread the word to others. I became evangelical very quickly, and remain so to this day. Lilla lived her yoga, as I do. The difference between a good yoga teacher and a great yoga teacher is whether they 'live the teachings', and realise that yoga is a way of life. Lilla Bek inspired me by example, she took me under her wing and shared her insights and wisdom with me. Then I found FRYOG. I felt that my energy 'fitted' with the Friends of Yoga Society, and I found Pauline Mainland to be loving, encouraging and supportive. She embodied an attribute which I completely admire – someone who is unafraid to be herself, and to say what needs saying. There is a wisdom going around on Facebook at the moment: 'Be yourself and say what you mean. Those who matter don't mind, and those who mind don't matter.'

## 5. With whom did you train?

I trained with Lilla Beksinska, and then Pauline Mainland of FRYOG. All those years ago, the Diploma was a correspondence course. I was living in Kentucky, U.S.A. I became a member of the Cincinnati Yoga Association, where I met some very interesting and well-known teachers. I was required to attend a weekly class, and the one I chose was in the University of Kentucky. Shelley was the teacher here, and she had studied at Ashrams in India. She was very much into chanting. When it came to my Practical exam, FRYOG required me to do two. This was because I lived remotely, and could not be observed by a FRYOG Assessor. One of my classes was marked by Jill Mc'Connell. She was a remarkable Iyengar teacher, who 'wrote' her own yoga university course. She presented the course outline to the board in the University of Kentucky, and they agreed to allow her to attend the University and to study for her own Diploma. She was ahead of her time!

The second teacher who agreed to assess my class also gave me a Distinction, and all the students of that class wrote charming comments, to send back to Pauline in England. I am very proud of my FRYOG Diploma, which is still up on my dining-room wall, but I have never actually stopped training. As I frequently told my trainee-teachers, you learn more from your students than you do from your teachers! Life is a yoga course, and every day, and every workshop, is an opportunity for growth.

## 6. How long have you been teaching yoga?

I have been teaching yoga for thirty-seven years. Recently at the Park Place Retreat, my friend Perminder asked: 'How do you do it, Carole? How do you get all your family interested in yoga? Mine resist.' I am very fortunate, but I am also very committed and enthusiastic. We had three generations at the Retreat this year. Our daughter, Gemma, was the other teacher there on the stage, and our granddaughter, Lizzie, played Arjuna in the production of the Bhagavad Gita. My husband, Mike, has been practising yoga for eighteen years, and organised the group trips to India, Spain and now the ten Retreats at Park Place. Our son, Tim, has attended our Indian and Spanish yoga adventures, and our two youngest grandchildren, Amy and Ben, are keen smallFRY members. They have been enthusiastic members of the 'Kidz classes' at the Yoga Show each year.

## 7. What kind of classes do you teach and how many per week do you teach?

I teach classical yoga classes, based on the teaching of Patanjali. Each of my classes contains a philosophical aspect, a Pranayama technique, a meditation and a long relaxation. I used to think that by sixty years old, I would be offering gentle classes and meditation courses. This has proved not to be the case. I still love performing the asanas, and watching my students travel the path of self-discovery. It is the light and shade of yoga that I teach: the flowing movement of Surya Namaskar (salutation to the sun), balanced by silent meditation. The best of who I am sits on the mat. Through my own yoga practice, I have been led to give up caffeine, eating anything from an animal, and alcohol. I am comfortable in my skin being a vegan and a teetotaller. I am comfortable that I am not hurting any other being by my behaviour. The first of the Yamas, Ahimsa, non-violence is the golden rule for me. I am humbled by the responsibility of being a yoga teacher. There is so much to learn, and so much to share. I so want the message of yoga to come out of my mouth undiluted, not made cosmetic or adjusted for the sake of popularity. The second of the Yamas, Satya, non-lying, is a golden rule, too! As a people-pleaser, it is sometimes a challenge to say what needs saying. As I become older, I am realising that I am an instrument for other people's growth. We are all here to serve, and sometimes we serve by opening them to their own lessons. If someone hurts us we have an opportunity to examine why. Others bring into sharp focus our own patterns. One of my favourite sayings is: 'If you always do what you always did, you will always get what you always got!'

At one time I was teaching thirteen classes a week, and teacher training courses three week-ends out of four. I am now teaching six classes a week, having just cancelled my Thursday morning group to release more time for writing.

## 8. What does yoga mean to you?

Yoga is my life. Yoga is my community. Yoga is in every breath that I take. I was once out with a young friend in a card shop. She picked up an 'OM' card, and I asked her if she was going to buy it. She said 'no, none of my friends

317

would know what it was.' I was astonished and I realised that ALL of my friends and, indeed, ALL of my family would know what it is!

## 9. Do you feel you have made a difference, either to the people you teach, the community you live in or to your family for example?

This is my 'raison d'etre'.As James Taylor sings;' That's why I'm here.' We have all come to serve. If by a smile, or a hug, or by a kind word we can make a difference to someone's day, then that has made the world a better place. Yoga is all about balance, and yoga teachers are here to bring a balance to our Earth and its inhabitants. Some yoga practices can bring incredible revelations and realisations. If I can serve as a 'channel' for the messages from Spirit World, then I have earned my place in the yoga community that day. The biggest difference we can make is by 'living' our yoga.

## 10. Where do you see your yoga taking you?

What an exciting question!! Right now, my journey is through writing my 'memoirs' – a sort of 'Autobiography of a Yogini.' (My friend and graduated teacher, Victoria Lovatt, has read the first seven chapters, and has given me constructive ideas and lots of encouragement to continue.) I plan a second book after this one, exploring my research into the effects of yoga. A third book may look at the effects of yoga on older folk... I would dearly like to experience an aging yoga community. Mike and I have often talked of setting up an 'Old People's Home' specifically for yogis.

Eventually, my yoga will take me to Spirit World, home to Brahman, promotion!

## 11. What advice would you give to new FRYOG teachers?

When you put your hands in prayer position at the heart (Anjali Mudra) at the beginning of your class, remember what Namaste means. 'The light within me welcomes the light within you.' Taken a step deeper it says that: 'When I am in that place deep within me, wherein is my light, and you are in that place deep within you, wherein is your light, we are together.' I believe that really understanding those words teaches us the humility and responsibility of being a yoga teacher. Yoga means union. You are a messenger. Keep faith with your yoga. Don't 'dilute' the yoga teachings, or become a 'cosmetic' teacher. Recently, a student teacher attended a couple of my classes. After each one she made the same comment:' You are the only teacher I know who actually teaches the teachings'.!!! So, my advice to a new FRYOG teacher would be: TEACH THE TEACHINGS. The way for you to progress along your yoga path, is to teach the teachings to your students.

But also – have fun! Enlightenment does not have to be serious. You'll be amazed at how a tricky message can be softened by laughter! Enjoy your yoga life, enjoy your yoga teaching. I have!

## 12. What changes have you seen in the yoga community during your career?

When Pauline Mainland encouraged me to become a Tutor (Teacher Trainer), I asked her how I should go about setting up my first course. She told me to do it any way that I saw fit. I began with a group who met in my house every fortnight on a Tuesday evening. They dropped a fiver into a bowl when they came, and this money I used to buy more books. It was a rolling course, so new folk could join at any time. Each one worked through the Questionnaire, starting at Q.1 and finishing at Q.15.I marked their essays, and when they had completed them, we set up their Theory and Practical Assessments. WHAT CHANGES WE HAVE MADE SINCE THEN! (And yet, some of the teachers who trained with me in this rather casual and informal way, have turned out to be amazing!) I always believed that the Course should be affordable and taught from the heart. Now our Diploma Course is second to none. It is professional, structured and academic. I taught many of my groups at Highbury College in Portsmouth, adhering to the College's strict criteria as well as FRYOG'S. I trained eighty teachers in all.

I had the privilege of serving on the committee for nine years, first as Diploma Board Officer and then five years as Chairman. During that time, we made enormous strides as an organisation. We have found our own niche in the yoga community, and have gained respect and status. Change will continue, as it should, but we should stay true to our roots. FRYOG is a heart-centred society. It is a family of yogis. As retired Chairman, I am still an Area Officer, and an Assessor.

One change which I have witnessed in the yoga community is offering yoga classes to children. I have taught children for thirty seven years, and wrote and taught the Post-Graduate course 'How to Teach Yoga to Children'. I once said, many years ago, that I would like to see a yoga teacher in every school before I die. We need to offer the structure and values of the yoga teachings to the next generation. They are the ones who will change the world. I was delighted to introduce the Junior Membership to FRYOG, which I called smallFRY. If all children grew up with the Yamas and Niyamas, they would have good values for life.

Hosting the Olympics in London has demonstrated how people can come together and unite. Even the sceptical have been turned around by the commitment, the enthusiasm and the focus of the competitors. During my career, I have seen yoga move from virtually unheard of to mainstream. I have seen Colleges, schools, doctors and all religions embrace its benefits. I have seen many other activities come and go, but yoga, which has been around for five thousand years, has grown in strength and availability. Often my students attend a Physiotherapist and tell me that the exercises they have been asked to do at home are yoga moves. All exercise is based on yoga asanas, just as all language is based on Sanskrit.

I have seen enormous changes in the yoga community during my career, and I expect to see many, many more before I move to Spirit World and join the FRYOG community up there. In Mahatma Gandhi's words: 'You must be the change you wish to see in the world'.